The Praise of Glory

Reminiscences of
Sister Elizabeth of the Trinity
A Carmelite Nun of Dijon 1901-1906

Nihil Obstat.
Dom Edmundus Kendal, D.D., O.S.B.

Imprimatur.
Dom Aidanus Gasquet, O.S.B.,
Cong. Angeliae Abbas Praeses

This authorized translation from the 5th French Edition was made by the Benedictines of Stanbrook.

Imprimatur: E. Morrogh Bernard
Vicarius Generalis
Westmonasterii: Die 3a Maii 1962

Declaration
According to the decree of Urban VIII, we declare that if we have made use of any terms of veneration in this book, they are meant solely in the sense authorized by Holy Church, to whose judgment we submit with filial affection.

First English Edition 1913
Second Edition 1962
This Edition 2007
Published by:

Loreto Publications
P. O. Box 603
Fitzwilliam, N.H. 03447
Phone: 603-239-6671   www.LoretoPubs.org
ISBN: 193027851-9

Printed and bound in United States of America

The Praise of Glory

Reminiscences of
Sister Elizabeth of the Trinity
A Carmelite Nun of Dijon 1901-1906

With a Prefatory Letter by
Fr. Anastasius of the Holy Rosary
General O. D. C.

And the Inroduction to the First Edition by
Fr. Benedict Zimmerman, O. D. C.

Loreto Publications
Fitzwilliam, N. H. 03447
A. D. 2007

Table of Contents

Table of Contents v
Prefatory Letter vi
Introduction xi
Author's Introduction xv
Chapter One: Childhood 1
Chapter Two: The Divine Call 11
Chapter Three: The Mission of 1899 23
Chapter Four: Supernatural Virtues 33
Chapter Five: Farewell to the World 45
Chapter Six: The Postulant 59
Chapter Seven: The Novitiate 69
Chapter Eight: Laudem Gloriæ 83
Chapter Nine: The Inner Life 97
Chapter Ten: Sister Elizabeth and Her Family Circle 107
Chapter Eleven: "Sola Soli" 121
Chapter Twelve: God Calls Laudem Gloriæ
    to Himself 131
Chapter Thirteen: Transformed into Jesus Christ 145
Chapter Fourteen: Close to the Sanctuary 157
Chapter Fifteen: Joy in Sacrifice 169
Chapter Sixteen: Last Consolations 179
Chapter Seventeen: From Calvary to Heaven 193
Appendix 209

Prefatory Letter

To Mother Prioress of Dijon
from
The Very Rev. Father General, O.D.C.

Dear Reverend Mother Prioress,

Sister Elizabeth of the Trinity, venerated daughter of your Carmel, is one of the most privileged members of our order raised up by God in this century. Suffice it to say that many of our religious are proud of the fact that they owe their vocations and deeper understanding of the life of Carmel to the providential influence of this humble Carmelite of Dijon.

It is an undeniable fact that Sister Elizabeth had a profound understanding of and lived to the full the spiritual ideal of our order. In fact, it would be difficult to study her typically contemporary spirituality other than in the light of her characteristically Carmelite ideal. Her doctrine and her spiritual life were nourished by the pure doctrine of Carmel. Her spiritual attitude is one of openness to God in her search for Him. The dominant disposition of her interior life is this quest for her Spouse dwelling within her own soul. This manner of seeking God, this receptive orientation towards Him and Him alone, constitutes the essential attitude of our Carmelite spirituality.

From the very outset, supernatural grace prepared Sister Elizabeth in her search for God by placing her in that atmosphere of solitude which forms an integral part of the Carmelite vocation. At the very threshold of Carmel, she herself affirmed that what attracted her most was silence. To use her own expression, she "thirsted" for silence, because of its fathomless richness in being replete with the presence of God. Her youthful heart expanded in silence and she was ravished with joy at the thought that her whole lifetime was to be passed in silence. "My life is so beautiful", she wrote. "In Carmel all is silence and adoration." "The life of a Carmelite is silence." "Carmel is a real foretaste of Heaven; in silence and in solitude, one lives there alone with God alone."

It is in this silence and solitude that she meets our Lord in prayer and her intimate heart-to-heart conversation with Him becomes deeper and deeper until it gradually pervades her entire life. The ease with which Sister Elizabeth of the Trinity gives herself to prayer is measured by her thirst for silence and retirement. Prayer and silence go hand in hand in framing her in the entire Carmelite ideal which she lived with such heroic perfection. It was in this light that Sister Elizabeth desired, understood, loved, and lived her Carmelite vocation, and it is in the same light that we are to understand her expressions: "My occupations at Carmel . . . a Carmelite has only one occupation: to love and pray." "The life of a Carmelite is a communion with God from dawn to dusk and from night till morning. If He did not fill our cells and our cloisters, what empty places they would be! But all things reveal Him to us, because He dwells within us and our life is an anticipated paradise."

Sister Elizabeth's desire to live in a state of continual prayer explains her unflinching fidelity in corresponding with the least movement of the Holy Ghost. Hers was a prayer of faith (so typically Carmelite) founded on sacred scripture and above all, on the writings of her "dear Saint Paul", wherein she discovered the priceless treasures of God's intimate life and lost herself in "hallowed darkness".

Her desire to penetrate ever more deeply God's mysteries

Prefatory Letter

meant acute suffering, long and painful purification, and passing through the dark night of faith, in order to arrive at immersing herself completely in intimate union with her beloved "Three".

The spirituality of Sister Elizabeth is characterized by her success in making her whole spiritual life converge toward her unique ideal, namely, the "Praise of Glory". We can truly say that this was her specific and precise vocation, in the same way that we affirm that the glory of God is the noble ambition and basic preoccupation of Carmelite spirituality.

Sister Elizabeth of the Trinity received a vital and efficacious grace to dedicate her whole life to the glory of God, not by the splendor of external deeds and achievements, but by leading souls to seek God within themselves and teaching them to abandon themselves to the intimate working of His grace within their own hearts. She herself has described her exalted mission: "To lead souls to recollection, to help them to go out of themselves in order to adhere to God by a very simple, wholly loving movement; to keep them in this great inner silence, which allows God to imprint Himself on them and to transform them into Himself." It is not difficult to see how this ideal of hers to lead souls to deep interior recollection, so that by adhering to God in complete abandonment, they may become the praise of glory of His goodness, is in complete harmony with the apostolic zeal of our holy Father Saint Elias and our holy Mother Saint Teresa.

During the few years of her earthly sojourn, Sister Elizabeth gave constant proof of her absolute abandonment to the workings of grace in her soul: she was always faithful, docile, prompt, and entirely given over to the action of the Holy Ghost. It was an attitude she had learned in prayer from the example of our Immaculate Mother Mary, "the faithful Virgin . . . the creature who knew the gift of God and did not lose a particle of it."

The Carmelite ideal as lived by Sister Elizabeth of the Trinity would not be complete if we omitted referring to her loving contemplation of our Blessed Lady and her intimate union with the Immaculate Mother of God. Herein we have one of the most characteristic features of her spirituality. The humble Carmelite of Dijon continually admired in our Blessed Lady the purest and most attractive example for all who, amidst joys and sorrows, abandon themselves with complete confidence in our Lord and never allow themselves to lose sight of Him, but by continual loving contemplation adhere to His every gift.

To sum up, we may say that what constitutes the object of our admiration and love for Sister Elizabeth of the Trinity—namely, her life of interior silence, her habitual fidelity to God present within her soul, her loving colloquy with Him, her thirst for His glory, and her apostolic zeal for the salvation of souls, all this wealth of interior life she learned from our Lady and lived it beneath the splendor of her maternal eye, Mary, "the model of interior souls, of those whom God has called to live within themselves in the depths of the unfathomable abyss!"

May this daughter of our revered Dijon Carmel draw down God's blessings on her own community and on our entire Teresian family, so that we may all live ever more perfectly our Carmelite ideal, by our loving intimacy with the Master in prayer and by our silence, so that He may be glorified in us! Finally, we hope and pray that very soon we, the brothers and sisters of Sister Elizabeth of the Trinity, may be able to look on her as a model, officially proposed to us by Holy Church for our imitation.

Father Anastatsius of the Holy Rosary,
General, O.D.C.

Introduction

Elizabeth Catez, the daughter of an officer in the French Army, was born July 10, 1880. The family settled at Dijon and, after the premature death of the father, the mother devoted herself entirely to her two daughters, who, in return, were passionately fond of her and of each other. It was an ideal household: pious (but not narrow-minded), cheerful, and evidently in comfortable circumstances. At the time of her First Communion, Elizabeth learned to overcome her temper; she also made up her mind to become a nun—indeed, the thought was not new even then. The wise mother did not oppose the child, but her education had to be completed first. An attractive proposal of marriage was but half-heartedly entertained by the mother, and not at all by the daughter. Instead of this, the love of our Lord grew steadily in the child's heart until it reigned supreme, and at length, exclusively. The mother foresaw the ultimate issue, but demurred until the daughter had come of age, and then she hastened the sacrifice which must have been greater for her than for her child. The latter entered the Carmelite convent at Dijon, August 2, 1901; took the habit on the Feast of the Immaculate Conception; made her profession January 11, 1903; received the veil on the 21st; and died, after an illness of eight months, on November 9, 1906.

It was a short and happy, if uneventful, life. There is a custom in many convents of sending out a circular after the death of a nun, giving a short account of the life and virtues of the deceased. In this case the superiors and sisters were able to

The Praise of Glory

say much of the interior life of Sister Elizabeth of the Trinity. Many of the recipients thought that where there was so much to say there might be more and, with the help of notes left by the deceased, the reminiscences of friends, and letters written both before and after her entrance into religion, a "Life" was published in 1909. It found so many readers that reprints followed each other in rapid succession. The present volume is a translation of this "Life".

The reader will instinctively turn to another "Life" of a French Carmelite nun, Thérèse of the Holy Child Jesus and of the Holy Face, known as the Little Flower of Jesus, who was the senior of Elizabeth by six, and predeceased her by nine, years. They were, therefore, not exactly contemporaries. They had much in common, but there is also a difference which appears in their photographs: the "Little Flower" looks merry, Elizabeth, happy. A large tree is covered with thousands of leaves, all similar, but no two alike. Happiness is the dominant note in the life of Elizabeth. It was the result of her exquisitely tender love of our Lord—a sound, wholesome love, not in the least hysterical; a love that made her yearn for humiliation, mortification, and even suffering in imitation of Jesus. "Do not deceive yourself," said a friend. "God takes such souls as yours at their word. . . . By entering Carmel you are plunging into an abyss of suffering. . . ."

Elizabeth replied: "I am ready to take the plunge. I hope to suffer severely; that is my reason for entering Carmel. If the good God were to deprive me of suffering for a single day, I should fear He had forgotten me." Accordingly, she had much to suffer, but her suffering was ever tempered with an overwhelming sense of happiness. It would seem, however, that she was spared—as was also the "Little Flower"—the keenest trials, such as a sense of dereliction and interior

Introduction

darkness; perhaps these are reserved for maturer years. As an example of the kind of suffering that fell to her lot, there may be mentioned the pathetic story—though belonging to the earlier part of her life—of the conversion of Monsieur N—, so passionately prayed for during a mission at Dijon. Hope, desire, all but the accomplishment of her most ardent wishes, disappointment, fear, and despair succeeded each other; she was already a nun when news reached her of the apparently impenitent death of Monsieur N—.

Many are the saints and saintly persons of whose consuming love of our Lord thrilling accounts have been given. Human language is poor in describing the deepest emotions. In this life we hear much that we have heard before, but rarely have words carried conviction more forcibly: Elizabeth died of love.

The Little Flower of Jesus has taken the world by storm. There is every indication that Elizabeth of the Trinity will prove the peer of her saintly sister in religion.

Benedict Zimmerman, O.D.C.
Saint Luke's, Wincanton.
Feast of All Saints, 1912.

Author's Introduction

On November 9, 1906, Sister Elizabeth of the Trinity, a professed nun of our Carmel, aged twenty-six, was called by God to the eternal "Vision of Peace". The death-notice which it is the custom to send to our convents gave them reason to believe that the history of this soul must have been one of a rare fidelity, and several communities expressed the wish of knowing it. We hesitated for some time. How could we give further entrance into this secret sanctuary and let others admire the wonders which humility and silence had veiled?

Her short existence had included but four years spent within the cloister in the retirement of the novitiate, and all in her had looked so simple and so divine that the details seemed beyond analysis. Yet the reception given by our houses to the first account of what appeared to all so luminous a career, and their earnest request that "no ray of this little star should be kept hidden", filled our hearts with joy.

One letter sums up the feelings spontaneously expressed with sisterly cordiality; it reveals the impression produced by the death-notice of Sister Elizabeth of the Trinity. Coming to us as it does from a Carmel which personifies the great traditions of the order, *of which it was the cradle in France*, the following opinion justifies the esteem felt by her community for the humble young nun whom we are about to describe:

"Thank you for having given us in your notice so intimate a knowledge of this beautiful soul. It is indeed the life of a Carmelite who has fully entered into the meaning of her

The Praise of Glory

vocation and who went straight to God with all the fervor of her love. A real impression of grace is felt, and our hearts have been edified, touched, and affected to the very depths while reading it.

"All in this life is what it should be. The graces your holy daughter promised to pray for after her death are thoroughly in accordance with the spirit of our vocation: serious, religious, and, at the same time, exalted. Thank God for giving such treasures of grace to Carmel!

"I think you have not told us all. It is right and necessary to study brevity in a death-notice, but may I venture to ask you for some further details concerning this life of prayer?"

The same religious wrote to us later on, referring to these details and discussing our hesitation as to publishing a longer account: "Do not be prevented on account of the little there would be to say about this short life, hidden in God; that is the case with many of these lives which give forth a heavenly fragrance, although containing few events. The simplicity and silence of Sister Elizabeth of the Trinity will be a valuable example for Carmel and for many souls. There is but one opinion about it here: you must write an account of it."

Some devout indiscretion regarding our notice, which occurred providentially, spread rumours of her saintly life outside the cloister, and such pressing entreaties reached us from all quarters, that we felt bound to submit to "the voice of God" and to think seriously of publishing our *Reminiscences* ("Souvenirs").

Such is the title we chose for these pages, which are necessarily incomplete in every respect, and which we only consented to edit in order to make the sketch as life-like as possible and to preserve the fragrance of the religious life proper to this flower of Carmel.

Author's Introduction

Thanks to God, Who doubtless intended that His "praise of glory" should be known, all of Sister Elizabeth's letters have been carefully kept. They echo forth her soul and paint her as she was, without the need of being arranged in the order in which she wrote them. Our only documents are a few reminiscences sent by her friends, added to our own, and some notes on spiritual matters which will be printed in their proper place. We have added some poems by Sister Elizabeth, which further reveal her character.

But first let us speak for a moment of this "vessel of election". The opinion of a religious* who, as we shall see later on, providentially interposed in the life of our dear little daughter, will throw great light upon this second "Histoire d'une Ame", as our *Reminiscences* have been called:

"There are human beings who die knowing nothing of human ways and affairs, but they are like a splendid crystal through which the light passes unbroken; when the divine impression is stamped on them the seal remains.

"Elizabeth was pre-eminently of their number. From infancy she was simple, yet instinctively profound. Radically candid, frank, and simple, she was wholly taken up by the things of God, which filled her soul and shone in the purity of her gaze.

"She felt a continual thirst for God and knew how to listen. Her large eyes drank in the light which she received fully and deeply, her whole soul watching for it, yet immersed in the peace of God and safeguarded against such enthusiasms as are often produced by over-excitability of the nerves and which soon work themselves out exteriorly. Her gifts developed in the cloister; what had been but an awakening and a presentiment became a reality.

"Her prayer was for a long time founded upon the Passion; later on it was influenced by her devotion to the Blessed

The Praise of Glory

Trinity and her longing to realize the 'Society' of the Father, the Son, and the Holy Ghost. Her spirituality was enlightened and determined by her study of Saint Paul's writings.

"Silence is a necessity for such a life. Sister Elizabeth returned to it by instinct without an effort, and was evidently led to it by the action of the Holy Spirit. She seemed to be kept in contact with God by the intuitions of the gift of knowledge, animated by the light she received. She also recognized the adorable 'wherefore' of these divine communications—the strange and infinite passion of love with which He pursues souls that He may introduce them into His mysterious treasure-house and, as it were, fix them immovably in Himself. She felt herself strongly drawn into the depths of things and, above all, into the depths of her own soul, by a sort of overflowing sweetness which penetrated her being: this was the gift of wisdom.

"Then, in her last stage, she was stamped with the cross. She knew the joy of it, the joy she willed to feel, borne with a wonderful, a superhuman heroism, more from fortitude than from joy. The Holy Ghost visibly bestowed this gift upon her. I found her in this state of suffering when I visited her for the last time three weeks before she died.

"The light of God which dwelt upon her seemed to make her transparent. Her mind had never wavered, her soul was still further simplified, she rested at the feet of her Master in loving contemplation, realizing that a divine work was being accomplished in her. There was nothing human in such a state.

"Sister Elizabeth of the Trinity fathomed the charity of God; she was in touch with the Giver of all. In this source of love she found the overflowing grace which made her, so to speak, die in God by a progress that was genuine and continuous."

Author's Introduction

What a faithful sketch is this of a life more angelic than human, the details of which we would fain give with the same skill!

Recollection may perhaps be considered as the special characteristic of this soul or, at least, we like to dwell upon this trait; for if prayer, humility, love of suffering, and fortitude in trial lead us to admire the divine work in her, these great gifts fructified in our little sister because she was "the garden enclosed", which the heavenly Spouse alone might cultivate.

"You will never be heroic," she was told, "until the time when you are completely recollected within yourself." These words, engraved in her heart, increased her passion for silence and developed the spirit of solitude which she valued so much as an assured means of attaining sanctity that, before she died, she often said to us: "I think my mission in heaven will be to draw souls to interior recollection by helping them to go out from themselves; to adhere to God by a simple and loving movement; to keep them in that deep interior silence which allows God to impress His likeness on them and to transform them into Himself."

It was not without deep emotion that, in the *journal spirituel* of a privileged soul, we recently came upon these words believed to have been spoken by the Divine Master Himself: "If France would rise to life again, the nation must cultivate recollection. Many are those whom I call to enter into their own heart, yet who listen not to My appeal."* We were struck by the providential character of the work which had evidently devolved upon our angelic sister.

In fact, although several of the numerous favors attributed to her intercession are of a temporal kind, Divine Providence seems to wish to render testimony to the mission which the humble little nun, now so powerful with heaven, had foreseen

The Praise of Glory

would be hers: that of leading souls to become recollected, of drawing them to enter the life-giving mystery of the indwelling of the Blessed Trinity within them.

This accounts for the wonderful circulation of a book which seemed suited but for the few. Several French editions have been called for since 1909, and the "praise of glory", Sister Elizabeth of the Trinity, will soon be able to repeat afresh her song of love in seven other languages and, by revealing her inner life, will teach a far larger number of souls how to find "heaven in this world".

Convent of Saint Joseph

Sous La Protection du Coeur Agonisant de Jésus, et du Coeur Transpercé de Marie Immaculée.

Feast of the Patronage of our Lady,
October 27, 1912

Chapter One
Childhood

Elizabeth's birth, family, and education — She overcomes her natural defects of character — Death of her father — Her conversion — Her musical talent — Her First Communion — The "House of God" — Visits to Carcassonne.

God, Who "gives His angels charge over us, to keep us in all our ways",[1] lovingly prepared the ways of Elizabeth when He formed the home to which to entrust this predestined soul.

Her father, François Joseph Catez, belonged to one of those families of northern France in which religious and high principles are transmitted as the glory of their race. During his military career he always won the confidence of his superior officers, the love of his fellows, and the affection of all by his uprightness and noble qualities.[2]

Divine Providence bestowed upon him such a wife as he deserved. She was a member of the Rolland family, a race of southern origin, whose name, renowned in the army, was also characterized by devotion to religion, to honor, and to its native country.

Marie Rolland possessed the simple yet steadfast faith of her mother, a native of Lorraine, and was fitted by special refinement of soul for the mission reserved for her. She was an enthusiastic admirer of Saint Teresa, the great Carmelite reformer, and delighted in copying out the finest passages of her works, little suspecting that these quotations would one

---

[1] Ps 90:11.
[2] From a speech relating to Captain Catez, delivered over his grave by Commandant de C—, printed in the *Sémaine Réligieuse de Dijon*.

The Praise of Glory

day bring the soul of her child into communication with that of the seraphic mother, thus "nourishing" her early childhood "with this heavenly doctrine".[3]

Divine Providence watched from the first hour over the precious life which these pages are to describe.

Her parents awaited, with unmixed joy, the little one who was to complete their happiness. But joy was turned into the deepest anxiety: the mother's life was in jeopardy and the child's despaired of. Captain Catez, actuated by vivid faith, hastened to the chaplain of Avor and asked him to say Mass that the dreaded catastrophe might be averted. The priest went to the altar and the Holy Sacrifice, offered before the throne of God, won the desired grace. Hope rekindled, and towards the end of the last gospel, little Elizabeth began her life on July 18, 1880. The day was Sunday—a coincidence which she afterwards considered the first call to her special vocation, or what was, at least, the chief characteristic of her religious life—to be a "praise of glory" to the Blessed Trinity.

Her baptism, on the Feast of Saint Mary Magdalen, July 22, may also be regarded as chosen by Providence, which often conceals a divine plan beneath apparently accidental circumstances. The child, regenerated under the auspices of the great penitent, early showed a special devotion to the saint whom, innocent as her girlhood was, she resembled in more ways than one.[4] Wounded by the same

[3] Collect for the Feast of St. Teresa.

[4] Elizabeth liked to link together the feast of the saint with the commemoration of her own baptism. In 1905 she wrote: "Tomorrow is the Feast of Saint Mary Magdalen, of whom the Truth declared, 'She loved much.' It is a feast of my soul also, for I shall keep the anniversary of my baptism; and since you are the priest of love, I beg you to consecrate me to Him at Holy Mass. Baptize me in the Blood of the Lamb, so that, being a stranger to all love but His, I may love Him alone with a passion ever deepening until it attains that blessed union destined for us by God in His eternal and unchangeable will."

Childhood

love, she understood the eager search, the silence at the feet of the Savior, the longing to follow Him even to Calvary, to the perfect union He grants to privileged souls.

Yet the first years of her life gave no presage of her future. Elizabeth, naturally very lively, was, until she was seven years old, subject to bursts of temper, contrasting strangely with the extreme gentleness of her sister Marguerite, two years her junior. She seemed to think that all must give way before her. Fortunately, her mother was firm as well as tender, for her affection rested upon a supernatural basis only too rare even in Christian homes. Madame Catez felt no diffidence about undertaking her daughter's education, especially as in the undisciplined little character she recognized unusual qualities of heart and energy to which she appealed. The most severe punishment for the child, and one which conquered all her stubbornness, was to forfeit her mother's kiss before going to sleep at night. The day would come when Elizabeth would bless her mother for having taught her self-conquest by love—a valuable lesson, to become the law of her soul, and to lead her by repeated efforts up the steep summit to perfection.

The Catez family moved from Bourges into Burgundy: first to Auxonne, and then to Dijon, where a severe trial awaited Elizabeth. Almost immediately after her arrival God called to Himself her grandfather on her mother's side. Monsieur Rolland, a highly distinguished man, was, above all, a good Christian. Skilled in *l'art d'être grand-père*, he knew how to place himself on a level with his little granddaughters, and to delight them with tales that both fascinated and formed their young minds. Elizabeth grieved deeply over his loss. Eight months after, her father also was torn most suddenly from his loving family. Yet the twofold

The Praise of Glory

sorrow does not seem to have had the decisive influence over her life which brought about what she styled her "conversion". God reserved it to Himself. On the occasion of her first confession, this first look into her soul made a deep impression on the child, awakening in her the spirit of religion. Henceforth she firmly resolved to struggle against her besetting fault, which, however, did not dampen her high spirits and natural gaiety.

Elizabeth greatly enjoyed the few weeks spent during her holidays at the camp of Châlons, with its stirring military life and sham fights at the time of the *manoeuvres*. Her soul, full of harmony, delighted in the musical talent which already rendered her attractive. Some children's concerts were organized at Dijon to promote competition among the young performers; Elizabeth's brilliant and expressive style was particularly admired, although, being but eight years old, she could hardly reach the pedals. She took her audience by surprise by her execution of Steibelt's *L'Orage*. People were astonished at the precision of her execution; her little fingers seemed to be scattering pearls.

Such a brilliant success at so early an age might have been dangerous to the little girl, but her mother's vigilance, seconding the work of grace, knew how to preserve in her all the candour and humility which distinguished her through life. When, after being warmly congratulated, the child asked her mother: "How did I play my piece?" Madame Catez, dreading the slightest feeling of vanity, answered: "Pretty well."

"I shall take more pains next time," answered Elizabeth, and never recurred to the praise she had received. Her heart, already enamoured with the divine ideal, was preoccupied with the one thought of her first meeting with Him of Whose love she already felt the presage.

Childhood

At this time she was deeply interested in the catechetical instructions in preparation for her First Communion. The struggle with her impulsive nature was bearing fruit; the nearer the great day approached, the more numerous were her victories over a will that had already begun to master itself. How longingly she sighed for April 19, 1891! At last the day broke on which her soul was to be filled with the light of heaven.

She had opened her heart on the previous evening to the devout chaplain of the camp at Avor, who had baptized her, and who had come to assist at her First Communion. The good priest, deeply affected by what he had learned, wondered what would be the destiny of the child over whom he seemed to see the hand of God.

Elizabeth wept silently during the touching ceremony. "When we left the church," relates the friend who made her First Communion at the same time, "she said, 'I am not hungry; Jesus has fed me.'" How often have we ourselves heard her say, after being absorbed in prayer: "Oh, how He has fed me with Himself!"

In the evening she met at the Carmelite convent the nun who, as prioress, would eight years later console her. "She made an indelible impression on me," writes the reverend mother. "I told her that, according to the meaning of her name, she was the happy little 'House of God'. She was greatly struck by the idea. I wrote it out for her on the back of a picture, little thinking that the mystery of the divine indwelling in her soul would become the watchword of her spiritual life."[5]

[5] The simple little picture, carefully preserved, is inscribed with these lines:
Ton nom béni cache un mystère
Qui s'accomplit en ce grand jour.
Enfant, ton cœur est sur la terre,
Maison de Dieu (Elizabeth) du Dieu d'amour.

The Praise of Glory

This mystery was no longer hidden from her, for the Divine Guest had revealed Himself to her that very morning. Elizabeth did not tell the hidden secret of this first meeting, but others divined that it had been profound and decisive. Nothing proved it so conclusively as the visible change that took place in her from that auspicious day. Henceforth the sweet child became perfectly gentle; no movement of impatience was ever noticed in her, only at times a tear glistening beneath her eyelashes revealed her inward struggle. The priest in whom she confided could not sufficiently admire her energy in controlling the fiery temper and strong affections that characterized her.

The enemy of all good, envious of the peace of so pure and faithful a soul, strove to disturb her. In order to try the child He loved so tenderly, God allowed her to pass through a period of scruples and distress; but the patience and kindness of her confessor, which induced her to confide in him, made her realize the goodness of God Himself, and thus restored her to perfect peace.

At 13 years of age she composed a *memorare* to her holy patroness, of which the childish wording contrasts with the depth of sentiment. The feeling of exile, the thirst for perfection, for the infinite, which made our little angel live less in this world than in heaven, are already noticeable.

Remember, O Saint Elizabeth, my patroness and my heavenly guardian, that I am thy little charge; help me in this desert land, and uphold me in my weakness. Give me thy virtues, thy gentle humility, thy sublime charity. Ask God to change my faults into virtues, as He changed the bread thou heldest into roses. Grant me the wings of hope that I may mount to heaven, and receive me thyself at the gate of paradise when God calls me to Him. Amen.

Elizabeth Catez.

Childhood

Unfortunately, we can discover in her diary no trace of her daily efforts and struggles before attaining the transformation at which she ceaselessly aimed. Her longing to escape notice made her destroy[6] the pages that would have rendered it easy to reconstruct her whole life, as a child and as a Carmelite, with all the charm that characterizes her letters. Gracious and high-minded as she was, as a religious said, on leaving her after an interview in the Carmelite parlor: "She really has charming qualities." Indeed she was charming in every way, and all the more so because she never seemed to suspect it. "If you could see the beauty of a soul in a state of grace," said our Lord to Saint Catharine of Siena, "you would die of love for it." "Such was the first impression made on me," said a priest charged with the care of Elizabeth's soul a few years later, "when, as its director, this pure soul displayed itself before me in all its candour and innocence, as limpid as the pure crystal of translucid water. A restrained enthusiasm gave ardor to a piety that was simple, orderly, and perfectly natural in its supernatural character; there was no exaggeration or craving for what was unusual. The self that is so detestable never seemed to have been born in her." Let us rather say that it was kept in check by a longing for suffering very rare at an age when nature thirsts for every pleasure. Her heart, given up to divine love, found no rest save in pain. Though still a child, she craved for immolation; each leaf of her diary echoes with generous aspirations of which she never wearies; and in what words does she express them![7] She

---

[6] With the exception of a manuscript book from which we shall make some extracts.

[7] We find other traces belonging to this period showing her craving for the cross. No doubt our little sister's first attempts at poetry are very faulty, yet how touching are the verses she wrote on Good Friday, inspired by the sufferings of our Savior!

The Praise of Glory

did more. She gave herself as a sacrifice as far as her life admitted of it, and sacrifice, constantly offered, softened her and formed her as an imitation of her Divine Model Whose sweetness and humility she would soon exemplify until, raised to heroism, she would receive from Him the imprints of the Cross.

Before going further we give the reminiscences of a venerable canon of Carcassonne, with whom the Catez family often stayed for a short time. The worthy priest knew Elizabeth well, as from her earliest days she had made him the confidant of her secret feelings.

"What can I say of her who chose me for her friend but that she was a saint? A saint, indeed, in the widest acceptation of the word. So firmly was I convinced of it that I wrote one day to her mother: 'I burn all the letters I receive except Elizabeth's, which I preserve carefully, and will leave to your grandchildren. Who knows whether they may not be wanted some day for her beatification or canonization?'

"Hymn to Suffering

"Strike me, beloved Suffering, strike with crushing blow!
Strike, strike, O Pain, that I desire to bear;
Thou who didst not e'en the Redeemer spare,
Be thou my hope whilst dwelling here below!
Strike! For I cannot live apart from thee!
Strike! That my Jesus may behold in me
One nailed in anguish on the Cross with Him,
Whose lips drink from the chalice' bitter brim.
Strike! For in sacrifice and trial a joy
Dilates my heart with bliss without alloy,
Since I dare hope my anguish may impart
Some solace to my Savior's grieving heart!"

Childhood

"God is wonderful in His saints, and His grace, skilled in its work, began its labors early in this predestined soul.

"Elizabeth was saintly from her earliest years. I affirm that she never flagged. Ask her mother, who will tell you that in our conversation and correspondence we never styled her by any other name than 'our little saint'. I believe that she died in her baptismal innocence.

"She was the more praiseworthy because she was naturally lively, ardent, and passionate. The child and descendant of soldiers felt their warm and generous blood course through her veins. She might easily have been hot-headed, wilful, and hasty. Fortunately, her vivacity was balanced by her two-fold affection—for God and for her mother. For her mother, to whom she was absolutely devoted; and for Him Whom she always named in fervent accents 'Him'. She fixed her large, beautiful eyes—with their heavenly expression that you know so well, Reverend Mother—on God and on her mother, and her constant question was: 'What must I do?'

"She was very fond of playing with her little friends, and no one knew better than she how to make the games amusing. I can see her now on our excursions among the mountains, woods, and fields, crossing the rivers, always at the head of the band. A single look or word from her mother would stop her in the midst of her most giddy flight.

"What a contrast to her little sister Marguerite, who was just as good and charming! The one active, exuberant; the other so calm and serious that we nick-named her 'Justice'.

"When Elizabeth left the world her only regret was for her mother.

"I shall never forget her last visit. We were feeling sad at the prospect of a parting that we knew would be final. Her mother was weeping, but the child, forcing back her tears,

The Praise of Glory

leant towards me, and murmured two words which I alone could hear: 'Thank you . . . Mamma!' I never saw her again. May her prayers win me the grace to meet her in heaven!

"Why did she thank me before recommending her mother to me? Because she had always thought that I favored her vocation. I do not deny it; indeed, I had the courage to say to her mother: 'She belongs to God rather than to you!'

"One evening the little girls, tired of playing, were talking together in their childish way. Elizabeth, by an artful little trick, managed to draw near me, and even to clamber on my knee. Bending toward me, she whispered, 'Canon, I am going to be a nun! I will be a nun!' I believe she was only seven years old . . . I shall always remember the angelic way in which she said it . . . as also her mother's rather irritated manner as she asked: 'What is the foolish little creature saying?'

"Madame Catez well knows the cloister where she sought me next day. She asked me anxiously whether I believed the vocation to be genuine, and I stabbed her to the heart by answering: 'I do!'

"The holy woman has climbed her Calvary; she has borne her share in her daughter's immolation. Tearful but faithful to her post, like the Mother of Jesus, she has offered the sacrifice. God will reward her as she deserves. Meanwhile she has the glory and consolation of having given a great saint to heaven.

"Others, more fortunate than myself in having witnessed it, can describe how Elizabeth prepared for the great day of her First Communion. I can only say that from that time I never saw her pray or heard her confession or gave her holy communion without saying to myself, 'The child is an angel!'"

Chapter Two
The Divine Call

She resolves to give herself wholly to God — Her vow of virginity — Her home — Her vocation is tested — Her sister pleads for her — Elizabeth's diary.

"I shall be a nun! I will be a nun!" the child of seven had said. She could not understand how people could give themselves to God by halves. Her conversion started her on the way of perfection.

"I was naturally very gay and fond of pleasure", she said, when recalling her childhood. "Yet even at that age I was afraid of worldly amusements lest they should win my heart. However, my resolution of giving myself wholly to God preserved me from being drawn away by enjoyment. . . . When I was invited to children's parties, before starting I used to shut myself in my room and pray for some little time, for, knowing the eagerness of my nature, I watched myself carefully."

Her determination to belong wholly to God had at first but a vague tendency towards perfection.

"I cannot remember when Elizabeth first confided to me her desire of consecrating herself to our Lord," states an intimate friend, "but while still very young her favorite amusement was playing at being a nun: that was her one idea, and I never knew her to swerve from it. She told me one evening that she wanted to join the Trappists, for the Carmelites did not seem austere enough. . . ."

She made her choice later on. "She was hardly 14," says Madame, "when I found her one day looking sad and thoughtful, her lovely eyes fixed on heaven, as if in prayer. I went to her

The Praise of Glory

and asked why she looked so mournful, while she had everything in life to make her happy. 'Madame, I am thinking how joyful I shall be when I enter Carmel; and the time seems to me to pass very slowly, for I should like to be already given to God's service.' I laughed at her premature decision, explaining to her that she could love and serve God in the world while showing care and affection for her devoted mother. She waited until I had finished and answered: 'God wants me for Himself. Mamma will understand my wish. She will be glad at my leaving her, since it will make me happy. Besides, I shall love her just as well.'"

Elizabeth tells why she decided upon entering Carmel. She writes:

"I had a great love for prayer, and such love for the good God that, even before my First Communion, I could not understand giving one's heart to another; henceforth I resolved to keep my love and life for Him alone."

"When I was 14, one day, during my thanksgiving after holy communion, I felt irresistibly urged to choose Him for my Bridegroom, and I bound myself to Him by a vow of virginity. We did not speak to one another," she said, "but gave ourselves to each other with such fervent love that my resolution of being wholly His was stronger than ever. Once after holy communion I heard the word Carmel pronounced within my soul, and henceforth my one desire was to be hidden behind its grille."

Six years passed before her wish was fulfilled. Long and weary years of waiting for her, but passing rapidly and fraught with blessing for her mother and her sister, Marguerite. What reverence she showed her mother! After hearing a sermon on the education of children, she wrote: "I thanked God from the bottom of my heart for having given me such a mother, gentle but strict, who has known how to overcome my most evil character."

The Divine Call

She played her part of elder sister charmingly. "She taught as much by her good example as by her sterling advice and good judgment", declares Marguerite. She continues: "One day, when Elizabeth was 12 or 13 years old, she said to me on leaving some service at our parish church: 'I heard the good God tell me not to use two chairs in church; it is not right to be so comfortable.' I laughed, and told her that it did not matter to the good God whether she had one or two chairs. Later on I understood how my angelic sister lived in dependence on divine grace, and the secret of her rapid progress in perfection stood revealed. Even before that age her conduct proved that her heart was already filled with divine love. One day, when quite a little child, she exclaimed on passing a theater: 'Oh, how I should like to be an actress!'

"'What, Elizabeth! You wish to be an actress?' someone exclaimed in surprise.

"'Yes,' she said, 'because then there would be at least one person there who loved God!' Her one aim in life was to love God and to make Him loved. She watched over me lest my soul should offer some obstacle to His action within it, and tried to correct me of shyness, as being a want of simplicity caused by self-love."

Self-denial had become so habitual to her as apparently to require no constraint; indeed, she showed a pleasure never evinced save by the thought that she could make a fresh sacrifice, a fresh act of love, or give some joy to others.

Her friends bear the same testimony to her goodness. "I never heard her speak ill of anyone," writes one of them, "nor did she give praise that was undeserved. She knew how to discover good in everybody, without denying any weak points. Her tact equalled her charity, and her indulgence never prevented her from showing firmness when occasion required."

The Praise of Glory

Elizabeth wished to die young.[1] She cared for nothing in this world, yet dreaded the particular judgment, and never went to sleep at night without preparing herself for death as if she were to die before morning. Her fear was soon to be succeeded by the most glowing love.

"A tender devotion for Saint Catharine of Siena", we are told by another correspondent, "led her to imitate the Dominican's continual retirement within the little cell of her heart, where she delighted in keeping beside her Divine Master, offering Him the flowers of her sacrifices. I often witnessed her efforts to hide some pain, or to repress impatience or a sharp word", continues the same narrator.

A note by Elizabeth reveals the secret of her victories. "When a remark that seems unjust is made to me, nature so rebels against it that the blood seems to boil in my veins. . . . Today I have had the joy of offering my Jesus several sacrifices connected with my besetting fault. How dear they cost me! It proves how weak I am, yet Jesus was with me; I heard His voice in the depths of my heart, and I was ready to bear anything for love of Him."

Jesus indeed lived and reigned in her virgin heart; His presence was evident to those around her. "Something I cannot describe seemed to emanate from her," declares another friend, "it was so pure, so ardent—yet so gentle, sweet, and simple as the perfume of virtue itself."

These few accounts suffice to sketch the character of the child, who was really wholly possessed by God, as was evident from her candid, serious expression; her modest, recollected mien. The soul of the "little saint" was revealed in all her being and actions, even to the very music she performed, into

---

[1] When she was 14 she asked one of her little friends to accompany her to the sanctuary of Notre Dame d'Etang in Burgundy to obtain this favor.

The Divine Call

which she put a feeling that was more and more remarkable. "No one can interpret the great masters as she does," people said, "she has the soul for it." And they felt that her soul was alien to this world.

Whence did she obtain this genius for interpretation? She reveals her secret in a letter she writes about a child who was afraid to play at a musical performance: "I shall pray that God may penetrate Madeleine, even to the tips of her tiny fingers; then I defy anyone to rival her. Do not let her feel nervous; I will tell her my secret: to forget those who are listening, and to imagine herself alone with the Divine Master, then the instrument will give forth full and strong, yet sweet, notes. Oh, how I used to love speaking thus to Him!"

Such a soul was indeed not made for this world, and no wonder she used to exclaim, when speaking of this epoch of her life: "The world frightened me!" We have seen how, while very young, when she was going to a children's party, she "watched carefully over her heart". We know how vigilantly, and with what jealous care and delicacy, the faithful, fervent girl kept guard over herself until she entered Carmel.

"The struggle was over by the time I was eighteen", she said. "When I went into society the thought of the presence of the Divine Master and of holy communion next day so absorbed my thoughts that I was oblivious of all around me."

Madame X— relates that once, in the midst of the gayest of parties, she was so struck by the girl's expression that she could not resist saying to her: "Elizabeth, your mind is centered on God." The young girl only smiled in reply. Madame Catez, whose attention had been attracted by her daughter's face in the midst of the gaiety round her, realized that her child's heart was elsewhere. Besides, Elizabeth's longings were not hidden from her. How could she forget the lines she

The Praise of Glory

had read in her diary: "O Carmel! When will your doors open to me?" Henceforth the mother's conviction of the sacrifice demanded of her never left her mind.

In 1897, the Abbé S— changed his residence and, before leaving, spoke to her seriously of Elizabeth's vocation, pleading her cause, and striving to avert the delay likely to occur. Although Madame Catez submitted to the will of God, she wished first to test the vocation and to let it develop.

One of the most severe trials the poor girl had to undergo was her privation of the intercourse with Carmel which would have consoled and strengthened her while she waited. She accepted it in her usual spirit of obedience and calmly aquiesced in all the wishes of her mother, in whom she felt absolute confidence.

She went next summer with her mother and sister into Lorraine, where for three weeks there was a succession of continual gaiety. Elizabeth's dress, faultless in its elegant simplicity and absence of all that was studied or pretentious, gave evidence of her perfect taste. Her sweet and gracious manners led no one to suspect that she was about to enter the cloister.

On leaving Lorraine she went to the camp of Châlons, where she excited the same admiration in military circles; but though many hopes were raised by her charms, she never forsook her higher ideal.

Her mother silently esteemed her exceptional goodness, yet still nourished faint hopes. However, she decided on leaving the decision as regards the future to the judgment of a priest in whom she felt full confidence.[2]

Madame Catez learned one day, while discussing her doubts with her second daughter, that Elizabeth was more

---
[2] Explanation: The Chanoine G— was Elizabeth's director until she entered Carmel. He soon recognized her divine vocation and when, at the moment of separation, the poor mother begged for another year's delay, he persuaded her to complete the sacrifice at once.

The Divine Call

desirous than ever to become a nun, and was, at that very time, making a novena to our Lady to obtain the longed-for permission. Marguerite generously pleaded the cause, which was a sore trial to her own heart, to her mother, who, overcome by her persuasion, sent for her elder daughter. The touching scene that followed is described by Elizabeth:

"Sunday, May 26, 1899—O Mary, thou hast heard my prayers; continue to protect me!

"Marguerite has again touched upon the subject of my vocation. Mamma answered that I was to think no more about it, and that she would not be the first to mention it. However, after lunch my poor mother questioned me. When she saw that I had not changed my mind she cried bitterly and told me that she would not prevent my quitting her when I was twenty-one; that I had only two years to wait, and that I could not conscientiously leave my sister before then.

"How I admire her resignation! Mary must have gained this grace for me, for my mother has never spoken so before. When I saw them both crying, I, too, shed tears. O my Jesus! were it not Thou who callest and dost succor me; did I not see Thee above those I love so well holding out Thine arms to me; my heart must break. There is nothing I would not do to spare them a single tear . . . yet it is I who cause them such bitter sorrow! O my Master! I feel that Thou dost call me and give me strength and courage, for in the midst of all my pain I feel an infinite peace. Yes, I will answer Thy summons soon; during these two years I will strive more keenly to become a bride less unworthy of Thee, O my Beloved!

"I seem to be dreaming! It is too much to believe that Thou keepest such happiness in store for such a wicked, miserable creature! Mayest Thou be forever blessed for it! And now, O Thou Who canst compensate my heart for all the rest, burn and

The Praise of Glory

uproot all that displeases Thee in me! I thank thee, Mary. Continue the work thou hast begun; uphold my mother in her noble courage; reward my dearest little sister, whose only thought is for my happiness. Give them strength and fortitude; make them understand that, in spite of all my love for them, I am ready to leave them for my Jesus. Let them recognize that it is He Who calls me, that it is for Him I sacrifice them. . . . O my Beloved! uphold them and her who is dying with love for Thee and who can find no fitting words to thank Thee!"

Her prayer was heard, and the two generous souls made rapid progress in the ways of God. Meanwhile Elizabeth's only thought was how best to profit by the delay her ardent longings found so wearisome. "Since Jesus does not want me yet," she wrote, "may His will be done! Let me sanctify myself in the world, and let it not keep me from Him; nor may any earthly vanities amuse or hinder me. I am the bride of Jesus! We are closely bound to one another; nothing can sunder us. May I be ever worthy of my heavenly Bridegroom and not squander His graces, but enjoy the happiness of proving to Him how I love Him!"

Her journal reveals her constant faithfulness, and shows how seriously she applied herself to the work of her sanctification.

In this account-book of her conscience her efforts are consigned as deposits and her deficits humbly noted. Things are set down just as they come, with simplicity and with deepest love. She longs to please Him Who has won her affections and chosen her for Himself, and to console the Divine Heart for the outrages over which she mourns with Him. Knowing that the Christian virtues alone can prove that love is genuine, she strives zealously and perseveringly to acquire the perfection of which she is to make definite profession at Carmel.

Elizabeth destroyed these private papers on the eve of her entering the cloister, thinking that they would be of no interest

The Divine Call

to any one. Besides, she wished to disappear completely, buried behind the grating, leaving the mother and sister she loved so tenderly nothing but the assurance of an affection that was to endure throughout eternity.

One manuscript book alone escaped the flames. She had not noticed it, as it principally contained notes upon her reading and instructions; it continues, in another form, the history of her private life:

"I am reading Saint Teresa's *Way of Perfection*, and am delighted with the book, which is doing me great good. The saint speaks so well about interior mortification—the mortification which, by the help of God, I mean to master. I cannot, for the present, inflict great sufferings upon myself; but I can sacrifice my will each minute."

Again: "My director spoke to me today about interior mortification. God led him to do so when I needed it. . . . I have been working so hard at it since my retreat. I am to understand that the bodily suffering for which I long is but a means, excellent in itself for attaining interior mortification and complete detachment from self. Jesus, my Love, my Life, help me! It is absolutely necessary for me to attain to the crossing of my will in all things. O my good Master! I immolate this will to Thee; make it one with Thine. I promise Thee I will make every effort to be faithful to my resolution of renouncing self in all things. I do not always find it easy, but with Thee, O my Strength and my Life, is not victory certain?[3]

[3] Elizabeth regularly attended the retreats given by the Jesuit fathers. She prepared herself most fervently, and eagerly assimilated the lucid teaching of the Exercises, which enlightened and strengthened her in her struggle for perfection. Her resolutions that year were inspired by the *agendo contra*, which roused her generous soul to enthusiasm. She took Saint Ignatius' terse maxim for her motto: "Renounce and oppose self-will in all things"—a plan of courageous abnegation by which her heart continued to rise to higher degrees.

The Praise of Glory

"I cannot express what good this book of Saint Teresa's does me. How well she speaks to her daughters of Carmel concerning friendship! What true and perfect friendship it is when a person in the world, or a nun, strives for the spiritual progress of her neighbor! Such a friendship is a thousand times more precious than the worldly one shown by affectionate speeches, which are a great deal too common," the saint declares.

"O my Jesus! I see that I have loved creatures too well; I have given myself up to them too much and wished inordinately for their affection; or rather, I have not understood what Christian love is. But now I realize that I owe it to Thee alone, and, above all, I desire the love of none but Thee, Thou Beloved of my heart!"

"I went to confession yesterday and told my confessor of my resolutions and the graces which God has showered upon me during these last few days. He advised me to accuse myself in each confession of my failures in keeping my resolutions, which, he declared, would help me to make progress; and I desire to make great progress, O my Jesus, that Thou mayest love me more! For I am envious of Thy love, and I love Thee so dearly that sometimes I think I am dying of it."

The following lines testify to Elizabeth's strong filial affection. In her zeal for perfection she had made a plan of which her mother disapproved, upon which she at once yielded without demur. "Mamma does not like it," she said, "so I shall say no more about it."

In another place she writes: "I should have liked to go to holy communion again today, which would have been four days running, but it was too much happiness. . . . As I saw that it annoyed Mamma, I made the great sacrifice and offered it to Jesus.

The Divine Call

"I thought of Mamma when the preacher said: 'Poor mothers, from whom God asks your sons or daughters, come and draw strength and courage from Him.'" She said after a sermon: "I beg Thee, my Jesus, to support her; it is painful to see her sorrow."

In 1899 Madame Catez had a dangerous illness. In her anxiety Elizabeth rose during the night to listen whether her mother still breathed, wishing to know the truth, however painful it might be. Prayer was her chief resource, and God granted her petition. "At last Mamma is well again", she cried delightedly.

"What a trial didst Thou send me, O good Master, and yet I thank Thee for it, for it was Thy means of detaching me from earthly things and attaching me entirely to Thee—to Thee alone for Whom I long to suffer and to die!"

Elizabeth's affection for her mother was to undergo a trial of another kind, of which her diary gives the history: "O Jesus, keep my heart, for it is Thine!

"I gave it Thee, and it is mine no longer. Mamma came home very late this morning in a state of great excitement. She had been spoken to about a marriage for me—a splendid match, such a chance as I should never have again. She went to consult my confessor about it, and he advised her to tell me about the proposal and its advantages, saying that it would test me and that I ought to consider the matter; that he would give no opinion about it, but that no interview ought to be arranged without my consent. My heart is no longer free—I have given it to the King of kings, and it is mine to dispose of no more. I hear in my heart the voice of my Beloved: 'My bride, you refuse all earthly honor to follow Me; like Me, you shall meet with sorrow and the cross; you will have much to suffer, and you could not bear it were I not

The Praise of Glory

beside you to support you. Even the spiritual consolations so dear to the soul will be withdrawn from you. What trials those have to bear who follow Me! Yet what sweetness and joy I will make you taste in your tribulations! The part I have chosen for you is by far the better one, nor should I have kept it for you had I not loved you dearly. Do you feel that you love your Jesus well enough to accept these sufferings for Him? Will you console Me? I am so abandoned, daughter; do not forsake Me! I covet your heart, I love it, and have chosen it for My own! I long for the day when you will be wholly Mine! Guard well your heart for Me!'

"Yes, my Love, my Life, Bridegroom whom I adore! Yes, I am ready to follow Thee upon the path of sacrifice. Thou foretellest the troubles I shall meet with, Jesus. We will walk together! I shall be strong if I follow in Thy footsteps. I thank Thee for having chosen a poor little creature like myself to console Thee; Thou didst know that I would not forsake Thee, for I should be more guilty than the wretched men who crucified Thee 20 centuries ago. O supreme Love! I am wholly Thine; but uphold me, for without Thee I am capable of any crime or baseness. My mother is wonderfully good; it is a miracle worked by Mary, for she does not even try to shake my resolution. When she asked me to reflect, I told her that my answer would be the same a week later as today, but, if she wished it, I would consent to her deferring the answer. She understands me at last! 'It would have been a comfort to me,' she replied, 'but God wills that it should be otherwise. May His will be done!'"

Chapter Three
The Mission of 1899

Apostolic zeal — Correspondence with grace — Sorrow for sin — A general confession — Fervent gratitude — The end of the mission.

In 1899, Elizabeth was deeply interested in an important mission that was to be held. She writes:

"We are to have a grand mission during Lent, and I am already praying for its success. How I long to bring souls back to my Jesus! I would give my life to help ransom one of those He so dearly loves! I long to make Him known and loved throughout the whole world! I am so delighted to belong to Him, and I wish that all men would place themselves under His easy yoke, and bear His light burden. How I long to bring back Monsieur N— to Jesus! He is an excellent man, as charitable as it is possible to be, but he is estranged from God. I have offered several communions for this intention, and I depend upon the mission's carrying out this splendid work. It would be too great a boon for me to have some small part in it. What would I not do to help it!

"Saturday, March 4—I have just returned from the cathedral. The opening ceremony was most impressive. The bishop spoke from the pulpit of the mission, which was intended to awaken souls from their torpor. After the sermon there was a grand procession in which all the dignitaries took part. The pure, sweet voices of the choir rose to the vaulted roof of the ancient basilica, and the chant was fine and affecting."

Elizabeth was engrossed by her longing for the salvation of souls, for which her heart, inflamed with divine love, offered fervent prayers.

The Praise of Glory

"Sunday, March 5—I offer Thee, O my God, the sacrifice of my life for the success of this mission; let me suffer, only hear my prayer! Look upon my tears and sighs, and have mercy, Almighty God, in the Name of Jesus, my beloved Spouse!

"Art Thou not, O Father, moved to pity? What more dost Thou require? I must win souls, O my God, let them cost me what they may! My whole life shall be their expiation, and I stand ready for any suffering if Thou wilt but have mercy on the world, in the Name of Jesus, my Divine Bridegroom, Whom I long to console!

"Monsieur N— came to the mission, and I thanked God fervently.

"Sunday, March 12—There was a very fine sermon at Vespers. I think I liked it best of all. When I heard of the fervent zeal we ought to have, my eyes filled with tears. O good Jesus! Though I have so long been careless about the salvation of others, and have myself offended Thee, now, at least, I long to bring back souls to Thee; my heart burns for this work of redemption. I crave to console Thee, my Divine Spouse, to make Thee forget the pain that sinners cause Thee! Christ wrought His work of Redemption by suffering, and He calls us to follow Him on the path of sacrifice, the certain means of saving souls.

"O Jesus! behold I implore Thee to send me suffering! There is nothing that I would not welcome, only give me souls! Give me the special soul for which I pray. I hoped that all I wished for would be realized when I saw that sinful man at the mission, and now he comes no more! . . .

"Tuesday, March 14—We had a splendid sermon on eternity. The Redemptorists speak of God with such wonderful love. How I love them for preaching such a gospel! Ah! They

The Mission of 1899

have been able to follow their vocation, and they are happy, for they bring back many souls to God. Let them rejoice in such blessedness! When, O Jesus! shall I follow my call, and give myself to Thee? I thirst for sacrifices and bless all I meet with in my daily life. My ardor has redoubled during this mission, and my heart burns to convert souls; the desire pursues me even in my sleep, and leaves me no moment of repose. My God, look Thou upon the vehement longing of my heart, and send me sufferings, which alone can make my life endurable! O heavenly Father, let me suffer or die!

"Sunday, March 19—Today my two novenas to Saint Joseph and our Lady of Perpetual Succor end. I am very grieved, although I still feel confident. I expect a miracle—yes, I really do expect one! When Jesus entered my heart this morning I told Him that with His help I would try every means in my power to win back this soul. I cannot sleep at night on this account. O heavenly Father, wilt Thou not let my appeal move Thy pity? I am ready to do anything to convert Monsieur N——. Give him to me, and let me endure all the torments he has deserved. I will bear them for my Jesus, with my Jesus! Let not this poor sinner lose this time of special mercy; let him profit by this mission to return to Thee. My heart is breaking, O my God! Hear Thou my prayer! Whenever I feel any pain I rejoice, and say to myself: 'Mary has heard my prayer! Yes, she must do so; I expect a miracle!'

"Maundy Thursday, March 30—Pardon, pardon for sinners, for I have wept and prayed so much, O Jesus, that I hope to give Thee this sinner! I redouble my prayers to our Lady, and I feel more confident. How glad I should be if he returned to Thee! I cried for joy this morning when I saw all the men approach the altar to receive Thee, as I thought of how it must delight Thee. Yet it seemed to me that Thou didst

The Praise of Glory

speak to me in the depths of my heart of the absent! Forget them, O my Savior! Remember them only to forgive them. Suffer Thyself to be consoled by those who love Thee. My grief is unbearable when I think that Thy heart is wounded."

On Holy Saturday Elizabeth gave full vent to her sorrow: "Poor Jesus! What a thorn to pierce Thy heart! She whom Thou lovest suffers with Thee, for there is no sacrifice I have refused for this conversion—is there, Jesus?

"The missionary's teaching upon charity has done me great good, for I am not always ready to make excuses for others. I have made firm resolutions about it, and do Thou, Jesus, help me, and remove all unkindness from my heart. . . . How hard it is to bear with people's characters! One of the saints called it 'the flower of charity'. Henceforth, my Jesus, no word against my neighbor shall pass my lips: I will always make excuses for him, and if I am unjustly accused, I will think of Thee, and I shall be able to bear all without complaint."

Elizabeth ends her notes on the sermon on sin with these words: "After a very stirring sermon on sin, the preacher pronounced an act of contrition aloud, which made me cry bitterly.

"O Jesus, grant me pardon! Forgive my offences, my fits of passion in the past, the bad example I give, my pride, and all the faults that I commit so often. I know that there exists no more wretched creature than myself, for Thou hast bestowed so much on me. Nor dost Thou ever weary of bestowing more. Forgive me, O my Master! How dare I, guilty as I am, ask Thee for grace for others? Why hast Thou not turned from me after my many offences, O Lord Jesus? My Bridegroom, my Life, pardon me! . . ."

Two days later she was "deeply moved and disturbed" by an instruction on confession. "For some time I have been

The Mission of 1899

thinking about contrition. I feel that I would rather die than offend Thee wilfully, even by venial sin. But in the past, when I was 10, 11, 12, or 13 years old, had I the same regret? Did I even think of it? I tremble as I remember the time. I have decided to make a general confession. Yet I am frightened at it. How can I remember the number and the different kinds of sins? But God will help me. He will show me my sins in all their malice and their horror.

"Dear Master, if I am to fall again as deeply, rather let me die! How canst Thou bear the sight of me after such offences? Why hast Thou been beforehand with me by granting me so many graces? I thank Thee. . . . Forgive me! How I grieve on remembering what pain I have given Thee, Whom I love so dearly, and whom Thou hast chosen for Thy bride! Forgive, Jesus, forgive me, unworthy as I am! No one else would have shown such ingratitude hadst Thou bestowed on her such gifts. I love Thee and weep for the sins that have wounded Thee so deeply. Pity me, forgetting all but Thine own great mercy!"

"Wednesday morning, March 1—I have been to confession. I met with an exceptionally good confessor, for which I thank the good God. The father found that I had the signs of a genuine vocation; he also believes that Jesus calls me to Carmel, and says that this is the most beautiful of vocations. I made a general confession, reckoning from my first Communion. He assured me that I had not lost my baptismal innocence." Elizabeth makes no comment upon this assurance which we know was a great joy to her, but her thanksgivings are many. She never tires of praising Him Who has done great things in her and Who keeps fresh favours in reserve.

After a sermon on death and judgment she writes: "It is

The Praise of Glory

very extraordinary that I did not feel at all frightened. Why should I tremble at appearing before Thee, Jesus? Couldst Thou condemn her who, in spite of her countless faults, has lived but for Thee? She is, indeed, a most wretched creature, and has deserved to go to hell a thousand times, but, Jesus, Thou canst not deny that she is Thy bride. Then let her follow Thee; let her sing the virgins' song, and be inebriated with the delights of Thy presence! O Death! did I not hope to suffer and to do some little good in this world, how eagerly should I cry to thee to come! If I am ever to commit a mortal offence against the Bridegroom Whom I love above all things, mow me down before such misery is wrought! Let me suffer and endure all things, my Jesus, but never let me cause such pain to Thee! Keep me!—my heart is Thine own! Watch over it, protect it, consume it with the fire of Thy love!"

She was moved to heartfelt gratitude by the discourse upon the world. "I thank Thee, my God," she exclaims, "for having shown me the vanity of this world from my earliest days: I thank Thee for having drawn me to Thee!

"How deep is my gratitude to Thee when I hear the world and its pleasures condemned! Never shall I be able to thank Thee sufficiently for the better part that Thou hast chosen for me. The preacher said this morning that when on the point of Thy return to heaven, Thou didst recommend Thine apostles to God, Thou saidst in praise of them: 'Father, they are not of the world; they live in the world, but they are not of the world.' And I also, good Master, am in the world, but I see nought but Thee; I desire nought but Thee and Thy Cross. This world cannot satisfy me; I pine and suffer, for I seek for Thee. Oh, make me wholly Thine! Thou art powerful to do all things. I beg Thee, Jesus, for a miracle!"

A few days later she writes: "We had a beautiful sermon

The Mission of 1899

this evening on divine love. I wept when I heard of the love God bears for my soul. I wish I could write out the whole sermon, for it was the finest of all. O Jesus! I cannot bear to hear that Thy Heart bleeds with grief at seeing how men withdraw from Thee. It tortures me. Dost Thou suffer—Thou Whom I love so well? Yes, and in Thy bounty Thou dost deign to ask me, wretched worm that I am, to console Thee! Is it possible? My Jesus, it is too good, too consoling to my heart to be true!"

Elizabeth, thus enslaved by divine love, was more watchful than ever respecting the smallest details relating to perfection. She sought the light of which she believed she stood in need, and longed for the strengthening manna of holy doctrine. After hearing further instructions on the Christian life, she writes:

"I intend asking the advice of Pére L— on this subject. . . . I have several other things to say to him, and long to see him.

"What a pity! the mission is nearly over. How quickly it has passed! I feel sad, but Jesus bids me be full of joy at the thought of soon being all His own. I look at the world and all to do with it as a passing show, and do not let my heart go out to it. Every morning, when I forecast the coming day, I promise certain sacrifices to my Divine Bridegroom. When there is one that costs me dear, and I hesitate, Jesus insists so strongly that it is impossible to refuse it.

"O my God, Thou hast overwhelmed me with benefits during this past month, especially during the last few days![1] How happy I am! I cannot comprehend this prodigy of Thy love! When I recall all my weakness, my tepidity, Thy bounty overwhelms me! Soon I shall be all Thine own, employed and living for Thee, conversing with no one else. I know and feel that Thou dost long for the day when Thy loved one will at last be wholly Thine; she, too, awaits it impatiently. I shall have a great

[1] An allusion to the consent to follow her vocation given at the end of Lent.

The Praise of Glory

sacrifice to make by leaving those I love so tenderly, yet there is infinite sweetness in such sacrifice, since it is made for Thee—for Thee Whom I love above all things, Who hast wounded my heart and made it captive by Thy charms, Thou, my Bridegroom, my Mother, my Sister, and my supreme Love, Who canst supply the place of all else in my heart. What a mystery of love! Thou art willing to raise me to Thyself, bestowing on me the highest of all vocations! Let there be an end to all tears and sorrow! O my soul, be thou intoxicated with thy joy! I count the days that separate me from the blissful hour when, by my three vows, I shall be irrevocably Thine. I shall be Thy bride; a poor, lowly Carmelite, crucified like Thee. Sustain me, O my King, in the way of the cross which I have chosen as my part, for without Thee I can do nothing! I shall not be always thus upheld by grace, but shall meet with conflict; be there, my Jesus, to strengthen me! Let me suffer much during these two years to be spent in preparing for the religious life; detach my heart from all things; free it from all that would prevent its seeing Thee; break my will, crush my pride, Thou Who art humble of heart; make it a fit dwelling-place in which Thou mayest love to rest and hold intercourse with me in ideal union. O Divine Heart! Uproot, consume all that displeases Thee, so that my poor heart may be one with Thine! Two years more! What a long time! But my happiness will be so sweet that I feel and taste it already. Tell me, my Beloved, will nothing come between us? No, I feel confident; and, perhaps—who knows—perhaps it may be shorter! Plan as Thou wilt; I trust all to Thee. Take pity, Jesus; enlighten my confessor; strengthen my mother, who is so nobly resigned; reward Marguerite; and as for me, make me suffer; take me, I am all Thine own!"

Easter Day—Easter joy does not cause Elizabeth to forget her sorrow for him for whom she has prayed so fervently.

The Mission of 1899

"Alleluia! Alleluia! Good Jesus, I am weeping on this day of glory and joy. I weep because the mission is over, and, above all, because of the obstinacy of Monsieur N—. I heard Thy voice in the depths of my heart this morning bidding me not despair, for if my prayers seemed unheard, at least all my petitions and sufferings had consoled Thy heart. The thought comforts me; yet can I be happy while Thou, my Spouse, art suffering? But rejoice, O Lord, over all the conversions won during this mission, and I will unite myself to the joy of Thy heart that I may spend this Easter Day less sadly. On this beautiful feast think solely of the lost sheep that have returned to the fold.

"The missioner bade us farewell, recommending those whose prayers have remained unheard not to be discouraged, as he assured them that their petitions must inevitably some day be granted, for God will take account of so many prayers and sacrifices. His words did me good."

Alas! That hardened sinner, follower of Voltaire as he was, justified the fears of the Reverend Père L—. When his death, characterized by every sign of impenitence, was announced at Carmel, Sister Elizabeth of the Trinity, raising her eyes to heaven, drew a deep sigh and adored the justice of God, exclaiming: "Poor man!" We did not know at the time all that his soul had cost her. Wholly given as she was to God, she never seemed to think of her side of the question; her sole grief was on account of the indifference shown to the divine love, as the following lines prove: "I was deeply pained at hearing of the death of Monsieur N—. What love has God shown, and yet men close their hearts against it!"

The burning zeal which so consumed her in her early youth was rooted in a charity "set in order" by the Divine Spouse Who had "brought her into the cellar" of prayer.

"Have you not heard," writes an ancient author, "what the

The Praise of Glory

bride says—that the King 'brought me into the cellar of wine, He set in order charity in me'?"[2] That is what happens to the soul, and God wishes it to come out stamped with His seal—that is, with His own love, with His desire for the salvation of souls, and with His pain at seeing the great offences committed against His Father.[3]

---

[2] Canticle of Canticles 2:4.
[3] Catéchisme de Sainte Térèse, par le Rév. Père Pierre-Thomas de Sainte-Marie, chap. 38; also The Interior Castle, M. v, chap. ii. 11-13.

Chapter Four
Supernatural Virtues

Sister Elizabeth's spirit of prayer — Her degree of prayer — Her influence — *O crux, ave, spes unica!* — Her intercourse with Carmel — Her last retreat while in the world.

It is not to be surprised at that so generous a soul was overwhelmed with graces. "Thy measure will be My measure," said our Lord to Saint Catharine of Siena. Elizabeth's measure must have been full to overflowing.

Her first grace was a spirit of prayer, which led her to spend hours at a time in church. One of her mother's friends asked her what she could be saying to God for so long together. "O, Madame," she replied, "we love one another!" An answer worthy of a daughter of Saint Teresa; for did not the seraphic mother teach that prayer consisted less in thinking much than in loving much?[1] While still very young, Elizabeth instinctively practiced prayer. At 13 years of age the Last Supper was her favorite subject for meditation. How did this privileged soul spend these cherished hours? We can imagine her as resting on the Heart of the Divine Master, like the virgin apostle, reposing peacefully in the confidence that characterized her. Then the mystery that was to absorb her life began to be revealed to her in the secrets of divine love. The Agony in the Garden also attracted her. We mentioned a period of trial which followed her First Communion. Perhaps her own sufferings made her dwell upon those of the Divine Sufferer of Gethsemani. Were they the cause of her long

---

[1] *The Interior Castle*, M. iv., ch. 1. 7.

The Praise of Glory

watches beside the Savior, "sorrowful unto death"? However it may have been, the generous young girl sought to console Him by a compassion the sincerity of which was proved by her offering to share His bitter chalice.

Elizabeth's soul gained in fortitude by her office of angel of consolation. The longing to suffer in her turn, produced by her loving contemplation, upheld her in her difficulties, for, in her case, the movements of grace always bore practical results.

At about this time, feeling that she was called to the mystic nuptials, she forestalled them by a vow of virginity that was followed by a genuine grace of recollection; henceforth nothing distracted her attention from God. Penetrated by the divine presence and overcome by the effects she experienced, she said to herself: "When I see my confessor I shall ask him what is passing in my soul." The prudent confessor endeavored less to enlighten her about her state of contemplation than to teach her to make the necessary efforts to conform her life to the good pleasure of Him Who already took such delight in her soul. God revealed to her His dwelling within her soul; it was there she was to enter into herself like Saint Teresa and the virgin of Siena. "Since I cannot break with the world and live in solitude," she writes, "at least give me solitude of heart, that I may live with Thee in intimate union from which nothing can distract me. . . . Thou knowest well, my Divine Master, that when I mix with the world I find my consolation in retiring into myself to enjoy Thy presence which I realize so clearly within me. No one thinks of Thee amidst such gaieties, and it seems as if Thou wert glad that one heart, even though as miserable as mine, should remember Thee."

Prayer was her delight. Her love for it was insatiable, and she rose before daybreak even in the coldest wintry weather to obtain an extra hour for it. Fear of missing the trysting-place made her wakeful. "How many matches I was obliged to hide," she said, "to avoid inconvenient questions!"

Prayer was for Elizabeth—as for all sincere souls—the school of sanctity. "O Christ, crucified upon the Cross," she wrote, "as I gaze on Thee I realize all the malice of sin! While Thy tormentors pierced Thy feet and hands, while Thou didst endure a thousand torments on the Cross, my countless faults and infidelities were before Thine eyes. Ah! How dear they cost Thee! Yet Thou didst also foresee the love that I should bear Thee, and how, in return for Thy love for me, I should be ready to yield Thee my life a thousand times. O my Jesus! Forgive me all the anguish I have caused Thy Divine Heart! Grant me pardon, and look solely on my love. . . .

"Who can describe how sweet it is when heart speaks to heart; when one no longer seems to belong to this world, but sees and listens to nothing but God? God, Who speaks tenderly to the heart, asking it to suffer for Him, and to console Jesus, Who longs for a little love. How eagerly do I beg Jesus for the cross at such times—that cross which is my stay, my hope; the cross I long to share with the Master Who deigns to choose me as the confidant and consoler of His Heart. I strive by my love, my interest, my sacrifices, and my prayers, to make Him forget His sorrows! I desire to love Him for those who love Him not."

She seems, to a certain extent, to have experienced a higher state of prayer described by Saint. Teresa. "How much I like the way the saint, while speaking of contemplation, speaks of the degree of prayer in which God works more than the soul, uniting it to Himself so intimately that it is no longer we who live, but He Who lives in us . . . which I recognize in the hours of supreme happiness that the Divine Master

The Praise of Glory

deigned to grant me during this retreat (1899), as well as since then. What return can I make Him for His benefits? . . ." After these short ecstasies, during which the soul forgets self, and sees nothing but its God, how hard and painful ordinary prayer appears, how laborious it is to struggle to control all the powers, how much it costs, and how difficult it seems!

The spirit of prayer lit in her heart the living flame of love which was so swiftly to consume her. Already her gentle influence was felt by others. Elizabeth showed the signs of a soul that holds within it heavenly treasures. She began to benefit those around her, for the flowers of this garden gave forth so fragrant and so sweet a perfume that people longed to draw near her.[2]

From very early youth her influence attracted others. One of her friends, who later became a nun, writes: "She was 12 years old when we first became acquainted. Her fervor and generosity attracted me at once, and I foresaw that she would do me much good. While preparing for my First Communion, I loved to talk to her of the great day and its deep joys, for I guessed what her own dispositions must have been."

Another correspondent writes: "I shall never forget how Mademoiselle Catez edified me during a retreat we made together. The touching fervor with which she made the Stations of the Cross so impressed me that my devotion was more roused by watching her than by making them myself. I was irresistibly compelled to remain in my place, uniting my soul to hers, and making her feelings my own, that I might offer them to our Lord.

"I saw her once more, kneeling near the confessional of the Redemptorist Fathers, during the mission of 1899.

[2] "Catechisme de Sainte Térèse", chap. 38.

Supernatural Virtues

During the long delay I had leisure to observe her. She was so deeply recollected that I never saw her move for an hour and a half; she seemed surrounded by a kind of atmosphere that isolated her from all around. Great graces were evidently being reserved for her, and she would, no doubt, give herself with a rare generosity, as the later events of her life proved."

Elizabeth gave a very good example in the parish choir of young girls. She always showed herself ready to help others. Yet so modest was she that, in spite of her talent, she never permitted herself to offer the slightest criticism.

She devoted herself with great fervor to the catechism class which offered her an occasion of proving her love for the Divine Master and of exercising the zeal that consumed her. The undisciplined pupils of the secular schools were subdued by the hidden charm of her goodness, and their love for her made the most rebellious obey her joyfully.

A little girl, aged 14, who had not yet made her First Communion, was confided to her. She devoted herself to the charge and spared neither her prayers nor her sacrifices. "The good God gave me this chosen soul to prepare me for my First Communion and to complete the very rudimentary religious teaching I had received", writes the girl. "Her angelic face won my heart immediately, and my veneration and affection for her increased every time I visited her. Nothing could equal her patience and sweetness. How lovingly she spoke to me of the great sacrament I was about to receive! How she urged me to pray to our Lady, implanting in my heart the germs of a filial devotion to her! Her zeal redoubled during the retreat made in preparation for the great day. I remember particularly her piety as she prayed with and for me; and I was struck by her recollection as we walked to church together. I understand now how deeply she realized that she was the

The Praise of Glory

tabernacle of Jesus. She told me that this was what I was about to become, and that I must be very pure, and carefully prepare my general confession for which she helped me to examine myself. I had but a very short list of sins of which to accuse myself. 'My dear,' said Mademoiselle Catez, 'you are happy enough to have committed few sins; I was not like you, I cannot say how many I could remember', which was her delicate and humble manner of telling me to examine my conscience more carefully."

Elizabeth did not forget that suffering is the sole way of rendering our zeal active and fruitful. She wrote: "My God, in union with Jesus crucified, I offer myself as victim. I desire the cross as my strength and support, and wish to live with it, that it may be my treasure, since Jesus chose it for my sake. I thank Him for this mark of predestination. *'O crux, ave, spes unica!'* Yes, Thou shalt ever be my support, my strength, my hope. Holy cross, supreme treasure that Jesus reserves for those His heart elects, I wish to live with Thee, to die with Thee, like the Bridegroom Whom I love! I wish to live and die on the cross.

"My Savior, I desire to return Thee love for love, blood for blood. Thou didst die for me, therefore I will daily endure fresh sufferings for Thee; every day shall bring me some fresh martyrdom because of my deep love for Thee."

The passion for suffering grew in her as the fitting expression of her love, and the generous girl courageously imposed severe penances upon herself. In her longing to resemble her Master she went so far as to ask Him for the impression of His crown of thorns, and her request was heard. She was continually tortured by unaccustomed and severe headaches, although her expression remained joyful and happy. Her secret, which for long she closely kept, was at last discovered.

Supernatural Virtues

She was told to pray that her trial might be ended; it ceased under the grace of obedience after having lasted two years.

To her great delight she became the possessor of a hair shirt, which she wore at night, as she could not do so during the day. Her health soon became affected, although the reason was unsuspected. She confided in the mother prioress of Carmel, who traced her illness to the imprudent penance, and her health was restored by the sleep required by a girl of 20.

It is evident from this that she was no longer forbidden to visit her longed-for convent. It greatly comforted her, during her last two years of exile, to open her mind to one who sympathized with her and to receive Teresian counsel. Elizabeth joined a small group of young girls connected with Carmel who delighted in helping the out-sisters to decorate the chapel on the eves of festivals, as they had read of their predecessors doing in the old chronicle of the Carmel of Dijon. People still remember Elizabeth's energy as she dusted the choir grating for the ceremony of a clothing, how happy she looked during the short time she spent in the shadow of the convent she loved, and how wistfully she gazed at its closed door.

"It was a real trial to me", she confided to us, "to be taken during the holidays far from my Carmel, from Dijon and its churches, that I loved so well. Fond as I was of my friends, I felt a void while in their company; and though I appeared to live, yet I felt lifeless."

No one suspected anything of the sort; the brave girl knew how to hide her feelings for the sake of those dear to her, so that she was as popular as ever, and as charming in society.

Elizabeth spent the summer of 1899 in travelling, as usual—first in France, and then in Switzerland, which enchanted her by its beauty. Her enthusiasm was easily

The Praise of Glory

aroused by the beauties of nature and she became absorbed in the contemplation of the works of the Creator.

"Enjoy those beautiful landscapes," she writes from her little cell in Carmel. "Nature leads us to the good God. I used to love the mountains which spoke to me of Him." In a letter to her sister, staying in the Pyrenees, she says: "One never gets tired of watching the sea. Do you remember the last time we saw it together at the Rocher de la Vierge at Biarritz? What happy hours I spent there! How lovely it was to see the ground-swell covering the rocks! The sight used to thrill me with its grandeur. Enjoy it thoroughly. As for me, I discover all these vast horizons in God now that I am at Carmel."

The balls commenced again in the winter, and Elizabeth accompanied her young sister to them in order to please her mother.

"Now the parties have begun again; you know how little I care for them. However, I offer them to the good God, and nothing seems able to distract my mind from Him. When all one's actions are done for Him, in His holy presence, beneath the divine gaze which penetrates the soul, one hears Him still in the silence of a heart which longs to be His alone."

Elizabeth's diary ends with her last retreat made in the world.

"Tuesday, January 23—O my God, what graces hast Thou bestowed upon Thy poor little creature since last year's retreat! Thou, Who knowest all things, dost know, at all events, that I love Thee! I wish to become a saint for Thy sake. I have one more tedious year to pass in the world; let it be spent in doing much good! Make me a true Carmelite, for in soul I can and will be one!

"Help me, my God, during this retreat, for I long not only to save my own soul, but to bring others back to Thee; I am consumed by this longing. Thou Who canst read my heart

Supernatural Virtues

knowest that if I desire to suffer and to leave all for Thee, it is not to be freed from Purgatory, but only to console Thee, O my Beloved! Were it Thy will, I should be ready to live in hell, so that the prayer of a heart that loved Thee might ceaselessly rise to Thee from the depths of the infernal regions. I recommend to Thee, my God, all the souls that are about to follow this retreat. If it be Thy will, I renounce for their sake all the consolations that Thou mightest bestow on me. But I am weak; do Thou uphold me! Let me live during this time of blessing in a closer union with Thee; let me remain in that hidden recess of my being where I see and feel Thee so clearly. Alas! I often leave Thee as lonely as Thou wert in the desert! How like me, feeble as I am! Yet I love Thee, and envy the great souls that have loved Thee devotedly!"

After the instruction on death she exclaims: "O my God, may I die with Thee! May I die bearing Thee within my heart! When I appear before Thee, my Jesus, mayest Thou recognize Thy bride who left all for Thee! Let me not give Thee cause to feel ashamed of me, nor let me see Thee look on me with anger. No, I trust in Thee! Then at length, my Beloved, I shall see Thee, I shall possess Thee without fear of losing Thee, and shall be inebriated with Thy love. The thought transports me with happiness. Perhaps, O my Jesus, Thou wilt call me to Thee soon; may Thy will be done! I only wish for what Thou dost will. Thou knowest I have given Thee all, and that I would have no desires but Thine! But, if ever I am to offend Thee mortally, I beg, as I have done so many times before, that Thou wilt take me to Thyself. Take me, I beseech Thee, I conjure Thee, while I am still wholly Thine!"

After the sermon on the last judgment, she writes: "O Master! I know that I have offended Thee deeply, yet I love Thee dearly! I go to Thee in perfect confidence as to a loving

The Praise of Glory

friend. Thou seemest to be pleased by this loving familiarity; therefore I await with perfect self-surrender the moment when I shall forever be united to Thee, and I hope at least that I shall still be able to labor for Thy glory.

"Let me, as long as I remain on earth, do some good; I am Thy little victim; make use of me, do with me what Thou pleasest. I abandon all to Thee—my soul, my body, will, and desires—I yield them all to Thee!"

"I have given myself to the good Master," she cried on the last day, "I have surrendered all to Him, even my dearest wish. I only will what He wills; let Him take me when He chooses!"

"After these days spent in recollection, I cannot say how sad I feel at the thought that I must go back to my ordinary life. 1 offer Thee this suffering, O Master; I am ready for all Thou askest, to follow the path Thou settest me!"

"I have made the same resolutions again this year: humility and self-renunciation, which include all the rest, and I beg Thee, my Jesus, to help me to keep them faithfully. Yes, I promise Thee, my Beloved, to humble and renounce myself whenever occasion offers! . . ."

"I saw the prioress of Carmel at the end of my retreat. How much the long interview with her did for me! On leaving the parlor, I visited the chapel and consecrated myself anew at Mary's altar to my dear Mother; may she keep me pure and preserve my heart, which is wholly yielded to Jesus, free from the slightest stain!"

"O my Divine Master, let my life be one continued prayer; let nothing, nothing, distract me from Thee—neither work, nor pleasures, nor sufferings! Let me be immersed in Thee!

"In five days M— is to leave all for Thee; I yield her to Thee, thanking Thee for having chosen us both for Thy brides.

Supernatural Virtues

I wish that I, too, could respond to Thy call, but the hour has not yet come. May the holy will of God be always mine...."

"Yes, Lord, may Thy will be done! I can belong to Thee even in the world. Then take my whole being; let Elizabeth disappear, and nothing remain but Jesus!..."

Chapter Five
Farewell to the World

Tarbes and Lourdes — The Carmel of Dijon — The hour of grace — Faith and self-renunciation — Letters and souvenirs.

The summer holidays of August 1901, were spent in a series of farewells to her friends and the places Elizabeth would never revisit. While staying at Tarbes she sometimes called upon the reverend mother prioress of the Carmelite convent.

"At the end of quite a long visit," the latter relates, "I was obliged to summon one of the out-sisters to the parlor while Elizabeth was still there. The sister asked me if I knew that she was on her knees. She must have been kneeling beside the grille the whole time. It was easy to see from her conversation that her soul was given to God, so that we were less surprised than delighted at the marvels of grace described in the 'death notice' we received from Dijon."

It was at Tarbes, while visiting a young nun who had just taken the veil, that her mother gave her final consent. When the latter saw the overflowing joy of the new Carmelite and her daughter's tears, she realized that her child's happiness was at stake, and said to her on leaving: "Do not cry; I will not make you wait much longer."

Elizabeth was unspeakably consoled during her two days' sojourn at Lourdes. She had the happiness of receiving holy communion in the Grotto, a place from which she could not tear herself away.

She was specially attracted by the mystery of the purity of the Immaculate Virgin for whom she had a tender and filial

The Praise of Glory

devotion, and had already received many graces and heavenly inspirations when she visited the rocks of Massabieille, in the Pyrenees, with her family during earlier holidays. She came this year for the last time to beg the "Star of the Sea" to guide her safely into port.

Her travels ended with a short stay in Paris. Her mother and sister went there to see the Great Exhibition, but the sanctuaries of Notre-Dame des Victoires and Montmartre were the only spots that interested the future Carmelite. She longed to return to Dijon to her beloved convent, to prepare for her entrance into the holy ark, the chief matter that occupied her during these last few months.

Fortunately, the organization of the chants for our services furnished her with a pretext for numerous visits to the reverend mother prioress. "Dear, poor, little parlor, what delightful moments I spend there! My Jesus, I beg Thee to repay the kind mother for all the good she does me; she understands so well how to bring Thee to my soul!"

On her side, the mother prioress said of her: "What a charming child! She consoles me for everything. . . ." "We used to speak of prayer", she writes in a letter we received today. "Hers was quite simple and uniform. The Divine Master was there within her, fashioning her as He chose. She complained that she did nothing, ravished as she was by Him Who did all."

At Carmel, Elizabeth met a Dominican priest who was destined by Providence to exercise an influence over her inner life. This father had a special grace for speaking of the Blessed Trinity. The august mystery had not yet been revealed in her soul, which was concentrated on love of the Divine Master and a desire of becoming absorbed in the contemplation of His sufferings. Transformation into Jesus

Farewell to the World

crucified was already her ideal of sanctity, so that it cost her something to submit when the mother prioress told her to renounce her name of Elizabeth of Jesus, as she intended to consecrate her to the Three Divine Persons. The young girl soon blamed herself for such a regret, for the name of Elizabeth of the Trinity was for her a vocation—indeed, it was her whole vocation.

Meanwhile, the religious, putting into words what she already felt by intuition, set before her what might be described as boundless views of the exceeding love of God. Her soul was transported by it and her prayer became still deeper. In this light of faith, which was always her guiding beacon, she used to remain in silent adoration of the divine treasures laid open to her.[1]

"It was a real joy", writes the Dominican, "to speak of our Lord and His grace dwelling within us to this soul, so pure, so intuitive, and yet so simple, whose will and intelligence had been given to the Divine Master from the very first."

The fruit of her realization of this truth was a childlike faith which grafted her in a peaceful and loving abandonment

---

[1] "One recreation day, after an intimate conversation with Elizabeth, astonished at the beauty of her soul, I could not refrain from asking her: 'Who has taught you all this?' She answered with a careless gesture peculiar to her: 'I don't know how I learned it, Sister. However, I own to you that Pere Vallée influenced me very strongly. The first time he saw me he spoke to me about the divine charity towards us. I felt overwhelmed. . . . Never have I forgotten the impression made on me by what he said about the infinite love which seeks and pursues each soul.'" "The effect of this first meeting", continues another nun, "was one of the things which most clearly revealed to me the soul of Sister Elizabeth of the Trinity. Others, initiated like herself into the mystery of divine love, are only under the influence of the light they have received at certain times. She never withdrew from it. It was because she was in a fit state to correspond at once with the gifts of grace, like soft wax ready to receive the stamp of the seal, or like the calm and lovely lake spoken of by Saint John of the Cross, in which the heavens can mirror their beauty."

The Praise of Glory

to the care of Him Whose Divine Fatherhood, now that it stood revealed, brought solace to the anguish of her longing.

"I yield myself to Him; I abandon myself, and am at peace. I know in Whom I trust. He is almighty; let Him arrange all things according to His good pleasure. I only will what He wills; I desire what He desires. I ask but one thing of Him— a true, generous, and strong love for Him."

Two months later, our little dove, full of hope and joy, would enter the ark. From her letters and diaries we can follow her till she ends her calm and steady flight, and listen to her last songs in a "strange land".

"May 19, 1901

"Dear Canon A—,

"How good God is! How sweet it is to give ourselves, to yield ourselves utterly to Him. When He wills, He knows how to overcome all obstacles and smooth away every difficulty.

"I entrusted all that concerns me to Him; I asked Him to speak to dear Mamma Himself. He did it so well that I needed to say nothing. Poor Mamma! If you could only see how good she is! She leaves all to the good God and realizes what He wants, so that she will allow me to enter Carmel in two months. I have wished and waited so long for the day that I feel as if I were dreaming now. But do not imagine that I do not feel the sacrifice. I offer it to God whenever I think of the separation. Could I make a greater sacrifice than that of such a mother as mine? Ah! He understands, His heart is so tender, and He knows that it is for His sake; He upholds me and prepares me for the sacrifice!

"You know that this good Master wants me for Himself alone. I knew it, so I felt confident and was sure He would take me. Thank God for your little Elizabeth; He has given

Farewell to the World

her so much, especially graces known to no one but Himself—things which take place in the very depths of the soul. Oh, what love! But He knows well that I love Him, and that seems to me to include everything.

"Is not to live by love—that is to say, to live no longer except with Him, in Him, by Him—to be already partly in Paradise while still on earth? I will tell you a secret. If you only knew how homesick I sometimes feel for heaven, for I wish so intensely to go there to be near Him. I should be glad if He took me even before I entered Carmel, for Carmel in heaven is far better, and I should be a Carmelite just the same in paradise. When I say this to the mother prioress, she tells me I am lazy; still, I only wish what the good God wishes, and if He chooses to leave me on earth for a very long while, I am quite ready to live there for Him.

"You will think me rather heartless. I am ashamed of all the foolish things I say; but you asked me to write freely to you, and I obey; besides, I think you understand me.

"I still beg you for your holy prayers, of which I have special need. Pray above all for my darling mamma; ask God to take my place in her heart and to be all in all to her."

"Friday, June 14, 1901

"For the last ten days I have been suffering with a slight attack of synovitis in my knee. I am glad: it is a favor from my Beloved, Who wishes His little bride to share the pain of His divine knees on the way to Calvary. I am deprived of church and holy communion, but the good God can come to me without any sacrament; I feel that I have Him with me quite as much. It is there, in the very depths of my soul, that I love to find Him, since He never leaves me. God in me and I in Him—oh! That is my life! . . . What a consolation to think

The Praise of Glory

that, except that we do not see Him, we possess Him already as the blessed possess Him in heaven; that we are able to keep ever beside Him, never letting ourselves be distracted from Him. Pray that I may allow Him to make me wholly His, and to take me to Him.

"Did I ever tell you what my name is to be in Carmel?. . . Elizabeth of the Trinity! I think this name points to my special vocation. Is it not beautiful? I delight in the mystery of the Blessed Trinity; I lose myself in its depths.

"Only a month to wait! The last moments are agonizing. Poor Mamma! Pray for her. I give her entirely into the care of the good God. 'Think of Me, and I will think of thee,' our Lord said to Saint Catharine of Siena. It is so sweet to abandon all to Him when we know Him in Whom we confide!

"Good-bye, dear Canon A—. I send you my photograph. I was thinking of Him while it was taken, so it will bring Him to you. Pray for me; I assure you that I need it.

"Elizabeth"

Let us listen again to the reminiscences of one who can speak with authority of her whom we shall soon call "Sister Elizabeth of the Trinity". Her charming account will form a fitting close to the first part of our biography:

"When I first met Elizabeth she was 17. I was captivated by her at our first interview. A year later I made acquaintance with her mother, and Elizabeth, who knew that I had been connected with Carmel, made friends with me. We soon became very intimate, and I could read the secrets of the interior life already taught her by God. They were all comprised in the one word—Love! She was passionately devoted to our Lord, which explains the extraordinary thirst for suffering that prepared her for her sublime vocation.

Farewell to the World

"Love is of two kinds—the love that receives, and the love that gives. Hers was the latter. For her to love was to devote, to sacrifice, to immolate herself—'to love until I die of very love', as she says in her beautiful prayer.[2] She longed to prove her love for God; and as contemplation did not suffice, she gave herself. And this she did once for all and entirely, consecrating her life within the cloister, where, drop by drop, she spent her life's blood, crucifying her body, her heart, her soul . . . until she died. She followed the example of her Master and her Bridegroom to the very end.

"I was specially struck by two things in her sensitive, impulsive soul—her longing for suffering, and her desire for death. When we talked together about her grand and noble vocation, I could not resist saying: 'Do not deceive yourself, Elizabeth. God takes such souls as yours at their word. He will accept your gift of yourself, and you may be sure that by entering Carmel you are plunging into an abyss of suffering. I do not know what sufferings God is keeping for you; perhaps yours will be crosses of every kind, since you wish to be like your Jesus. . . . It is a bottomless abyss. . . .' She answered with her sweet and beaming smile: 'I am ready to take the plunge. I hope to suffer deeply; that is my reason for entering Carmel; and if the good God were to deprive me of it for a single day, I should fear that He had forgotten me.'

"Sometimes, homesick for heaven like all the saints, she longed for death to destroy the obstacle that separated her from the Beatific Vision. She often said to me with glowing eyes, like a child that talks of going home: 'For me death would be like the crumbling of that wall (pointing to the wall of my room). I should fall into the arms of Him I love!'

[2] This prayer is to be found in the Appendix.

The Praise of Glory

Her accents showed how she yearned for it. Then calmly and quietly she added: 'However, I must wait.' She had not long to wait, for she loved 'until she died of very love'. God did not forget her for a single day, for she suffered, as she craved to, until she died of it.

"She often came to see me, and always talked on the same subject. 'When shall I enter Carmel? What a joy it is to love the good God! My soul cannot dilate itself with His love except in the solitude of the cloister. . . . I long to be there, that I may pray and suffer and love!'

"Except when she poured out her heart in confidence, she never appeared different from other people. She was quiet and cheerful, peaceful and smiling; but her smile was serious, and her gaze seemed fixed on something beyond this world. I was struck by it on the point of her entering the convent. While waiting for her in the chapel to say a last good-bye, I heard a slight noise, and, turning round, my glance met hers. . . . I could not describe it. . . . Her expression was rather angelic than human. Her eyes were luminous and transparent—shining with the light of heaven. . . . She made an impression upon me that I shall never forget. . . . It was the last time that I saw her outside the grille."

Another incident concerning Elizabeth before she entered her convent testifies to the generosity of the postulant who constantly endeavored to renounce self and to be resigned to the will of God. The prioress of Dijon was preparing to make a foundation at Paray-le-Monial when she first met Elizabeth, and the idea naturally occurred to her of including, in the little group of nuns to be sent there, one who so fully realized St. Teresa's ideal of a subject for a fresh community and who would be an example and blessing to the novitiate. The reverend mother, therefore, offered Elizabeth the grace of being

Farewell to the World

one of those chosen for the Sacré Cœur. The latter, thinking it more perfect to have no choice in the matter, accepted the proposal with simplicity, without owning her preference for the Carmel of Dijon, upon which she had so long set her heart, and of which she felt herself already a member. On the other hand, the work of making a foundation—a real grace for some religious, on account of its endless opportunities of well-doing—was distasteful to Elizabeth, who needed regular and established observance for her longed-for life of solitude and prayer.

As the time drew nearer the poor girl suffered more and more keenly in the increasing struggle against her preference, for she had "abandoned herself entirely to God, leaving Him to direct all things according to His good pleasure, reserving nothing for herself except a valiant, generous love for Him."

The disappointment felt by her mother and sister increased her sorrow, while making her more careful not to betray her feelings, lest nature should intervene in what ought to be entirely supernatural. She submitted her own will as her love led her to do in all else.

Her postulant's dress had been sent to Paray-le-Monial, and the day of her departure drew near. Madame Catez, overcome at the prospect of so complete a separation from her daughter, regretted that the mother prioress was about to make the foundation; yet her conscience was too delicate to allow her to withdraw her promise of letting Elizabeth enter her house. She confided in a friend, who advised her to consult some competent authority. Madame Catez did so, and was encouraged in her wish of keeping her daughter near her. She told the mother prioress. The reply, given by one whose sole thought was to follow the Divine will, regardless of the sacrifices which for many months that will had demanded of her,

The Praise of Glory

was addressed to Elizabeth:

"No doubt you are aware that your mother and Marguerite have asked me to leave you at Dijon, which it seems is also your wish. I recognize in it the will of the good God, which we ought to love and obey without demur. Give yourself to our Lord in the place where He wishes you to be; I would not have brought you here against His will. I will receive you for Dijon, dear child; bring your whole heart and soul with you, with which to love our Lord. I wish I could be there to offer you to Him, but business keeps me here; yet my prayers and my heart will be there to bless you."

"Then, and not till then," says Marguerite, "Elizabeth owned to me that she had felt very sad at the prospect of not entering the Carmel of Dijon; but she had thought that her sacrifice would be more complete if she renounced even the choice of her convent."

As her daughter's health suffered from the trials of her last days in the world, Madame Catez, forgetful of her own feelings, came to us and asked us to fix an earlier date for Elizabeth's entrance into Carmel, and on August 2 the doors were opened to the happy postulant.

There is a touching simplicity about the last hours spent together by those who loved one another so tenderly. On the eve of the first Friday of the month, Elizabeth, faithful to her tryst at Gethsemane, had spent part of the night in prayer, when her poor mother, who could not sleep, came to kneel and weep beside her bed, mingling her tears with those of her devoted daughter, who did not seek to hide her anguish. "Why do you leave me, then?" asked the mother. "Ah! Dearest Mother, can I resist God when He calls me? He holds out His arms to me, and tells me that He is despised, outraged, forsaken! And shall I, too, abandon Him? He wants

Farewell to the World

victims, and I must go. Grieved as I am to leave you and to cause you sorrow, I must follow His call!"

When, at last, the time came for Elizabeth to leave her home forever, she knelt before her father's portrait to ask him for his blessing. Then, calm and brave, she came to Mass at our chapel. Her mother and sister and a few attached friends accompanied her to the altar, and then to the enclosure door which was shut upon her as she turned for a last look at those she loved so fondly.

At daybreak on that great day she had written to Carcassonne: "I want to send you a last farewell before entering Carmel. We are to receive holy communion at eight o'clock, and when He is in our hearts, Mamma will take me to the enclosure door. I love my mother as I never loved her before, and my soul is filled with peace now that I am about to accomplish the sacrifice that will separate me from the two I so fondly cherish. I no longer belong to this world, but feel that I am entirely His, that I keep back nothing, and I cast myself into His arms as though I were a little child."

It was thus, with the self-surrender and simplicity of a child, that she cast herself into the arms of her who was to stand for her henceforth in the place of God.[3]

---

[3] This was the subprioress, as the reverend mother prioress was still at Paray-le-Monial. The former was placed at the head of the community by the next elections.

Part II
At Carmel

The joy of my life consists in my intimacy with the Guest Who resides within my soul.

Sister Elizabeth of the Trinity

Chapter Six
The Postulant

The chief characteristics of a Carmelite vocation — Impetuous joy — Recollection — Echoes from the cloister — Fervent preparation for her clothing — The ceremony.

August 2, 1901, the day on which the doors of Carmel opened to the happy postulant, was the first Friday of the month, a day consecrated to the sufferings of our Savior and to reparation—Elizabeth's two special devotions at the time she entered our convent, which was dedicated to the agonizing heart of Jesus.

There, seconded by the grace of the mystery which had so long inspired her prayer, she was to be, till death, an angel of consolation, fulfilling Saint Teresa's object in making her foundations: "To give our Lord friends whose devotion nothing can affect, now that so many forget and offend Him."

While the Divine Master, exposed upon His Eucharistic throne, was receiving her adoration for the first time within the cloister, we rejoiced at being able to offer a victim of such purity as this innocent girl to the great High Priest.

"Her soul is altogether angelic; there are few like it even among those who enter the cloister", said the Dominican father who had come to consecrate her generous self-oblation. His words fitly describe the beginning of her religious life. She had passed through the world preserving her innocence without a stain, and might have said, like another of heaven's chosen souls: "Touch me not; I am passing by!" She would "pass by" at Carmel "as a bright fire, and frankincense burning

The Praise of Glory

in the fire."[1] Her gifts, both of nature and of grace, were an augury of her future career. She already possessed the spirit of the eremitical life with which Saint Teresa endowed her convents. While in the midst of worldly society she dwelt within the little cell she had constructed in her heart, and now that she was set on the Holy Mountain, she would soon win the graces of solitude.

From the very first she was delighted with a saying of our mothers in the old days, "Live alone with the One", which became the motto of her religious life.

Prayer, which the *seraphic* mother termed the cement that held her convents together, was already familiar to the postulant. We have seen how she was actuated by the spirit of penance and apostolic zeal, so that the chief characteristics of the Carmelite were already to be recognized in her.

Elizabeth of the Trinity set forth joyously on her holy career. She was delighted with everything, above all with her name, which gave the characteristic of her special drawing towards God. In order to correspond to it, she entered into the profound recollection which in the end absorbed her entirely in her "Three".

We were struck by this on seeing her at her first community duty in the refectory. After having finished her meal, she sat with closed eyes, her hands folded beneath her little cape, her whole attitude being that of one in deep prayer rather than of mere recollection. Indeed, to have opened her eyes she would have needed no slight effort.

A young nun who was serving, struck by such religious demeanor and entire oblivion of all around her in a postulant so soon after her entrance, said to herself, "It is too good to last; no one could be so mortified on the very first day!" Yet

[1] Ecclus 1:9.

The Postulant

to the last no one ever saw her raise her eyes needlessly during a conventual duty; she was always retired and absorbed in God. Elizabeth was told that she might, and should, take notice of what was around her. She obeyed, but with a certain amount of constraint which showed that she was not distracted from the thought of her Divine Master. "In the garden, in the cloisters—indeed, everywhere," she said, "He is so truly present that it seems as if we were only separated by a thin veil, and He were on the point of appearing."

She wrote more playfully, but to the same effect, to her family: "As you like details, I will tell you something very interesting. We have washed our clothes. I turned my dress up for the occasion, covered myself entirely with a large apron, and put on a pair of clogs to complete my costume. I went down to the wash-house where every one was rubbing away with all her might, and I tried to do the same. l splashed and soaked myself finely, but never mind—I was delighted with it! Everything at Carmel is delightful! We find the good God at the wash just the same as at prayer; there is nothing but Him everywhere; we breathe Him and see Him. The prospect widens before me every day."

She wrote to the priest who had been the confidant of her great secrets for the last 15 years, and who was now a consolation to her mother:

"I thank you with all my heart for your kindness to dear Mamma; I am not surprised at what she tells me. You know how grateful I am to you; no day passes that I do not pray for you. I feel that all the treasures of the soul of Christ belong to me, so that I am infinitely rich. How overjoyed I am at drawing from this source for those l love and who have helped me!

"How good the good God is! I cannot express my happiness, which I realize better every day. There is nothing here

The Praise of Glory

but Him; He is all; He suffices for all. I like the hour of the great silence best—the time at which I am now writing to you. Picture me to yourself in the little cell of which I am so fond—the tiny sanctuary kept for Him and me alone. You can imagine what happy hours I spend there with Him I love. The Blessed Sacrament is exposed on Sundays in a little small oratory in the house. When I open the door and look at the Divine Prisoner Who has made me His captive in Carmel, I almost feel as though I were opening the door of heaven. There I lay before Jesus all those who dwell in my heart, and I find them again near Him. You see, I often think of you, and I know, too, that each morning, when you offer the Holy Sacrifice, you remember your little Carmelite, who entrusted you with her secret such a long while ago. I do not regret the years I spent in waiting; such great happiness deserves to be bought dearly. Oh! How good the good God is!

"I am glad that I live in the days of persecution. How holy we ought to be! Pray that I may attain to the sanctity for which I long. I want to love as the saints and martyrs loved."

Elizabeth writes to her mother:

"Tomorrow is the Feast of our Lady of the Seven Dolors. I thought that it might be called your feast too, dearest Mamma, so I prayed fervently for you, and put your soul into the soul of the Mother of Sorrows, asking her to console you. I have a great devotion to a statue of the Mater Dolorosa that stands at the end of our cloister; I go there every evening to speak to her of you. I love the tears of our Lady, which I unite to those my poor mother sheds when she thinks of her Elizabeth. If only you could read my soul, you would learn how happy I am at Carmel; my joy increases every day, and is known to God alone. What a wonderful lot He has chosen for His poor little child! If you could but see all this for a single

The Postulant

instant, you would be bound to rejoice, for before I could enter this little corner of heaven your *fiat* was required. I thank you again for having given it so bravely.

"The good God loves you, and your daughter is more fond of you than ever."

She writes to a little friend who would not be consoled for her absence, trying to make her understand the depths of her joy, and reassuring her about her health, which had suffered slightly from the trials of her last days at home.

"If you only knew how happy I am, you could not possibly cry any more, but would thank God for me. You will wonder, perhaps, how I can be so happy after having left all those I love to enter the solitude that delights me. I possess everything in God, and find those I left again with Him. We are not separated; there will never be any grille between our hearts, and mine will always be the same. It dilates in Carmel, and knows how to love better than ever.

"The good God has restored my health without powders or quinine: I am stronger every day, and have a ravenous appetite. They take great care of me here; you need not feel anxious. I sleep more soundly on the straw mattress than I ever slept before. I did not feel very safe on the first night, but expected to roll out on one side or the other before morning, but nothing of the sort happened, and now that I am used to it, the bed is delightfully comfortable. I like everything at Carmel; the time flies, and I feel as if I had always lived in the convent."

Elizabeth was as gentle and obedient here as she had been in the world, and from the very first showed a tender charity that revealed Who was the Guest Who dwelt in her little "house".

The nun in the next cell suffered from violent headaches, and could not bear the least noise. For five years Sister

The Praise of Glory

Elizabeth was careful of her slightest movements, never seeming to suffer from the extreme constraint, for unselfishness had become her second nature. She had practiced virtue for so long that she seemed to require no effort to conquer self, and had we not known of her extreme sensitiveness, we should have thought her indifferent to the inevitable friction of opposite characters.[2]

As a postulant, she gave evidence of a spiritual life laid on solid foundations. The following letter describes her intimacy with God:

"Life for the Carmelite is communion with God from morning till night, and from night till morning. How empty our cells and cloisters would be did He not fill them! But we see

---

[2] Perhaps those among our readers who are making a study of her soul may be interested in reading the list of questions answered by our little sister at recreation in the noviceship a week after she entered Carmel.

"What do you consider the ideal of sanctity?"—"To live by love."

"What is the quickest way to attain to it?"—"To become little, and to surrender self once for all."

"Which saint do you prefer?"—"The beloved disciple who rested on his Master's heart."

"Which woman saint do you prefer?"—"Our holy mother, Saint Teresa, because she died of love."

"What is your chief characteristic?" "Sensitiveness."

"What is your favorite virtue?"—"Purity 'Blessed are the pure in heart, for they shall see God.'"

"What fault do you most dislike?"—"Any kind of selfishness."

"Give a definition of prayer."—"The union of one who is not with the One Who is."

"What book do you like best?"—"The Soul of Christ," which reveals to me all the secrets of the Father Who is in heaven."

"Do you long greatly for heaven?"—"Sometimes I feel homesick for it; but excepting the vision of it, I possess it in the depths of my soul."

"What kind of martyrdom would you prefer?"—"I love them all, especially the martyrdom of love."

"What name would you like to have in heaven?"—"The will of God."

"What is your motto?"—"God in me and I in Him."

The Postulant

Him in everything, for we bear Him within us, and our life is heaven anticipated. Prayer is rest and repose; we come quite simply to Him we love, we keep close to Him like a babe in its mother's arms, and let our heart go out to Him."

It was evident that her whole time was spent in the perpetual communion with God of which she speaks. The silence of Carmel was a joy to her, for she could fix her thoughts on heaven. "You ask me what I am doing", she wrote to a friend. "I might answer that a Carmelite only does one thing: love and pray. But as she is still on earth, though living in heaven, she must, while devoting herself to love, do some work in order to accomplish the will of Him Who first submitted to labor as an example to us. We begin our day with an hour's prayer; then we say the Divine Office, and assist at Mass. Vespers are at two o'clock; mental prayer from five to six; Compline at a quarter to eight; we pray from then until Matins at nine o'clock, and leave the choir at a little before 11 to go to rest. We have two hours' recreation during the day, and keep silence at other times. When I am not employed elsewhere, I work in our cell. A straw mattress and a small chair are its only furniture, but it is full of God, and I pass many happy hours there with my Bridegroom. There is something sacred about the cell; it is a private sanctuary for Him and His little bride. We are so happy there together! I am silent, listening to Him and loving Him, while sewing the dear serge that I have so longed to wear."

The months passed by, and our dear little sister was looking forward to wearing the holy habit of the Immaculate Virgin—"Queen and Glory of Carmel". She was particularly fond of our mantle, the symbol of purity. When would she approach the altar, wrapped in its white folds? She pondered over it—indeed, she did more: she questioned Saint Teresa

The Praise of Glory

herself, and put her cause into the holy mother's hands.

During the octave of the great feast of October 15, Elizabeth spent the hour between Compline and Matins in prayer before the relic exposed in the saint's hermitage. One evening, while praying more fervently than ever for the "double spirit" of Carmel and the mantle, which was to be for her also the sign of special blessing, she was informed, interiorly, that it would be given her on the approaching Feast of the Immaculate Conception.

On the next day she told the mother prioress, who, to humble her, replied that before thinking of wearing the habit of an order, its spirit and virtues must be acquired. Sister Elizabeth accepted the little trial with her usual calm, and went away as sweet and peaceful as she was before.

A month later Chapter met, and considered the question of her clothing. The mother prioress told her that she would have to make her petition on that very day, and bade her pray a great deal, adding: "I do not know what the decision of the good God and the community will be, but you must prepare yourself to receive the answer peacefully, whatever it may be. You have still much to work at, so perhaps you will be put off." "Yes, Mother", she replied, "I am very imperfect; but I think the good God will grant me this grace, and how can my sisters refuse it me? They must love me, for I am so fond of them!" Every voice and heart was in favor of the young sister for whom the nuns already felt such warm affection.

Sister Elizabeth of the Trinity, overwhelmed with gratitude, had recourse for her preparation to Him Who she knew loved her deeply. The Divine Master responded to her appeal, operating such great things within her soul that she sometimes seemed quite faint. "I can no longer bear the burden of these graces", she said. Her longing for heaven became more ardent.

The Postulant

Like the bride in the Canticles, she languished while waiting for the Vision, the eternal union; her holy languor alone could check her constant presentiment of a speedy end to her time of waiting and her hopes of suffering greatly for God.

We need only look into the *Spiritual Canticle* of our father, Saint John of the Cross, to find the history of Elizabeth's soul: "The wise man saith that the soul that seeketh Him as a treasure shall find Him. God grants a certain spiritual presence of Himself to the fervent prayers of the loving soul which seeks Him more earnestly than treasure, seeing that it has abandoned all things, even itself, for His sake. In that presence He shows certain profound glimpses of His Divinity and beauty, whereby He still increases the soul's anxious desire to behold Him. For as men throw water on the coals of the forge to cause intenser heat, so our Lord in His dealings with certain souls, in the intermission of their love, makes some revelations of His Majesty, to quicken their fervor, and to prepare them more and more for those graces which He will give them afterwards. Thus the soul, in that obscure presence of God, beholding and feeling the supreme good and beauty hidden there, is dying of desire of the vision."[3] Thus God Himself prepared Sister Elizabeth of the Trinity for the interior transformation of which her clothing was but the symbol.

When the date of the ceremony was discussed, her obedience and self-surrender prevented her expressing the desire she still cherished that it might be on the day for which she secretly hoped. The wishes of her family and the preacher's engagements both seemed to oppose the fulfilment of Saint Teresa's promise, and the clothing was fixed for December 27, the Feast of Saint John the Evangelist. However, circumstances made it necessary to choose an

---

[3] *A Spiritual Canticle,* by St. John of the Cross, stanza x., note. Lewis. Baker, 1909.

The Praise of Glory

earlier day, and Sister Elizabeth wrote to Carcassonne: "Mary will clothe me with the habit of Carmel on the Feast of the Immaculate Conception; I am to prepare for my betrothals by a retreat of three days. When I think about it, I feel as if I were no longer in this world. Pray hard that your little Carmelite may give and surrender herself completely, and may gladden the heart of her Divine Master!"

Her ardent longings were gratified on December 8, 1901. The day was Sunday! Elizabeth, whose devotion to the Mystery of the Blessed Trinity was daily becoming deeper, was delighted at the coincidence; the Immaculate Virgin presented her as a sacrifice of praise to the glory of the Three Divine Persons. The young girl's joy was so great that she was unconscious of what she was doing and what was going on around her. The prioress noticed it on meeting her at the enclosure door, and wondered how the ceremony would pass off. The Divine Master rewarded the generous novice for the gift of her heart by filling it with an overwhelming love.

The first stage of her religious life ends here. Sister Elizabeth of the Trinity had tasted the sweetness and joys of Thabor, but she was not to stay there. Like the apostles and saints, she was called to follow our Savior in the anguish of His Agony, in the sufferings of Calvary. Her love knew no limits, and God desired that there should be no limit to the favors He had begun to bestow on her. The soul, fainting beneath "the burden of His grace", must be dilated; a deeper bed must be made for the flood of grace which was already overflowing. This divine work was to be wrought by suffering.

Chapter Seven
The Novitiate

"The dark night" — The reward of trial — The secret of happiness — The profession retreat — The bride of Christ — Sanctity — Heaven within the soul.

After the brightness of her life as a postulant, Elizabeth was plunged into a dark gloom, to which were soon added anxieties, spiritual distress, and strange fancies of the imagination, such as those described by Saint John of the Cross in the fifteenth stanza of his *Spiritual Canticle*: "The devil, beholding this prosperity of the soul, and in his great malice envying all the good he sees in it, now uses all his power, and has recourse to all his devices, in order to thwart it, if possible, even in the smallest degree. He thinks it of more consequence to keep back the soul, even for an instant, from this abundance, bliss, and delight, than to make others fall into many and mortal sins."

The sufferings of the poor child, who had been established until now in a peace that seemed as if it could never fail, cannot be described. In her candor and simplicity she spoke of feelings which were the more humiliating because it seemed as if a word ought to have gotten rid of them, and the more painful on account of their contrast, not only with her life of prayer, but with anything she had ever known before.

The faith and blind obedience which led her to open her mind to her prioress also brought her strength and peace, while at the same time seconding the divine work that God was doing in her soul by these trials.

The Praise of Glory

After having suffered in this way for six months, the poor novice hoped to obtain relief in a retreat to be given in October by the Reverend Father V— then in exile at some distance from Dijon. However, her sufferings only increased, for she found it impossible to take any pleasure in what had formerly delighted her, but which now seemed only to thicken the darkness of her night, so that the eight days were a real torture to her. Her soul in its desolation drank deeply of the bitter cup of suffering and humiliation without exhausting it. Three months more were to pass before the work of love would be done.

Although Elizabeth was well suited to our life, and had fully entered into it, we do not claim that she was already perfect. Not only had she to advance, but to undergo the transformation which we saw take place in her during the year of trial. She was already thoroughly Christian, but had to become such a Carmelite as our seraphic mother wished her daughters to be.

It was well for her, humble and modest as she was, to realize by experience the weaknesses of humanity. Nature had rebelled at times in the past; there were other revolts of which she knew nothing. Having conquered all her difficulties by the efforts of her will and the graces of prayer, she was astonished at discovering sometimes that there were other states less free from temptation, and she might, unknowingly, have felt some secret self-complacency, or have judged others harshly. She had, indeed, been warned against such subtle self-love, but "What doth he know that hath not been tried?"[1]

Schooled by trial, Sister Elizabeth would learn more quickly that kind of self-knowledge which is both the foundation and the summit of humility. God made use of

[1] Ecclus 34: 9.

The Novitiate

temptation to show her the abyss of her own nothingness, and to insure that glory would be ascribed to Him alone for the graces which He intended to bestow upon her soul. Thus, at times, by His permission, the devil has recourse to the sensual appetites . . . ; stirs up many movements in the sensitive part of the soul; and causes other vexations, spiritual as well as sensual, from which the soul is unable to deliver itself until our Lord shall send His angel, as it is written: "The angel of the Lord shall encamp round about them that fear Him and shall deliver them."[2]

Indeed, the divine messenger brought some relief from this painful state, "establishing peace, both in the spiritual and sensitive parts of the soul",[3] for the time of prayer generally brought the poor novice a truce from struggle, although she received no consolations. However, her simple form of prayer, which the increase of her faith had rendered higher than before, kept her like a little child at rest within the arms of Him Whom she loved without feeling His presence, in Whom she believed blindly, and in Whose love she trusted, though she felt nothing but the rigor of His Divine jealousy.

Her efforts to keep recollected during the day in spite of the tumult of her imagination and feelings helped her in her troubles, and kept the same aims and objects before her so that no one around her suspected what she was suffering. Her letters of that time show that she rested on the same foundation, enlightened by faith, developed by the darkness of her soul.

During August she celebrated with gratitude the anniversary of her admission into Carmel. "How quickly the time passes in Him! A year ago He brought me into the sacred ark,

---

[2] *Spiritual Canticle* of St. John of the Cross, stanza xv., note.
[3] *Ibid.*

The Praise of Glory

and now, as my father, Saint John of the Cross, says in his *Canticle*: '. . .the turtle dove hath found its longed-for mate upon the verdant river banks.'

"Yes! I have found Him Whom my soul loves, 'the one thing necessary', which no one can take from me! Oh! How good, how beautiful He is! I want to live in perfect silence and adoration so that I may penetrate deeper and deeper into Him; to be so filled with Him that I can give Him, through prayer, to poor souls ignorant of the gift of God.

"I know that you pray for me every day at Holy Mass. Put me into the chalice, so that my soul, bathed in the blood of my Christ for which I thirst, may become so pure and transparent, that the Blessed Trinity may be reflected in it as in a crystal. The Three Persons delight to contemplate Their own beauty within a soul: it attracts Them to bestow still more on it, to fill it more completely, to complete the great mystery of love and unity. Ask God to make me live my Carmelite life in all its fulness as the betrothed of Christ, which means so close a union. Why has He loved me so much? I feel how petty and full of misery I am, yet I love Him, and I do nothing else. I love Him with His own love; it is a double current between 'He Who is and she who is not!'"

"The double current", or rather, the "two abysses", as Saint Catharine of Siena calls them, had been revealed to Sister Elizabeth of the Trinity in her year of severe probation, so that she seemed firmly rooted in humility. Her faith and will had both been strengthened by the trial, and, being perfected by suffering, served as counterpoise to a tenderness which might have become over-sensitiveness. Her advice later on to a person undergoing interior trials shows us what had been her own conduct during this painful period.

The Novitiate

"I think that the secret of peace and happiness lies in forgetfulness and disregard of self, which does not mean that we do not feel our miseries of body and mind. Since you allow me to speak to you as a sister, I tell you frankly that I think the good God asks of you perfect abandonment and trust. When you suffer from the feeling of a terrible void, believe that He is preparing for His indwelling in your soul fresh capacities which are to be, to a certain extent, infinite like Himself. Try to be joyful, as far as depends on you, under the hand that crucifies you, or rather, look upon each suffering as a proof of love straight from the good God, in order to unite you to Him. Do not be discouraged when your soul is oppressed and wearied by the burden of your body, but have recourse by faith and love to Him Who said: 'Come unto Me . . . and I will refresh you.'[4] Never let yourself be depressed by the thought of your wretchedness. The great Saint Paul said: 'Where sin abounded, grace did more abound.'[5] So it seems to me that the weakest, even the most sinful, person has the greatest right to hope. By forgetting self and casting herself into the arms of God, she glorifies Him more than by any self-examination and self-reproach, which keep her attention fixed on her own defects though she possesses a Savior within her Who is always willing to purify her.

"Do you remember those beautiful words of Jesus to His Father: 'Thou hast given Him power over all flesh that He may give eternal life to all whom Thou hast given Him?'[6] That is what He wants to do in us. He wishes you to go out of self, to give up all that preoccupies you, in order to retire into the solitude He has chosen as His dwelling-place in the depths

[4] St. Matt. 11:28.
[5] Rom. 5:20.
[6] St. John 17:2.

The Praise of Glory

of your heart. He is always there, although you do not realize it. He is waiting for you, and wishes to establish with you a wonderful intercourse, *admirabile commercium* as the liturgy terms it, the intercourse of bride and Bridegroom. By His continual contact with you He will free you from your weaknesses and your faults and from all that troubles you. Nothing ought to prevent our going to Him.

"Never mind whether you are fervent or discouraged: we pass from one state to the other during our earthly exile. You must believe that He never changes; that in His care for you He is always bent towards you, longing to bear you away and establish you within Himself. If, in spite of all your efforts, you are overcome with sadness, unite your agony to that of the Divine Master in the Garden of Olives, when He said to His Father: 'If it be possible, let this chalice pass from Me.'[7] Perhaps you will think it difficult to forget self. Do not be anxious about that; it is extremely simple. I will tell you my secret: think of God Who dwells within you, Whose temple you are. St. Paul tells us so—and we can believe him. By degrees the soul becomes accustomed to live in His blessed company, realizing that it bears within it a little heaven in which the God of love has made His home. Henceforth the spirit breathes a divine atmosphere—indeed, the body alone seems on earth, the soul being behind the veil with Him Who is unchangeable.

"Do not tell me that such a thing is not for you, that you are too miserable a creature, for that is all the more reason why you should go to your Savior. We shall never be purified by looking at our own misery, but by gazing on Him Who is purity and holiness itself.

"When you feel very unhappy, think to yourself that the Divine Sculptor is using the chisel to beautify His work, and

---
[7] St. Matt 26:39.

The Novitiate

remain peacefully under the hand that shapes you. After Saint Paul had been ravished to the third heaven, he felt his own infirmity and complained to God, Who answered: 'My grace is sufficient for thee: for power is made perfect in infirmity.'[8] Is not that consoling? Then take courage! I entrust you to the care of a little Carmelite nun of Lisieux, who died at the age of 24 in the odor of sanctity; her name is Thérèse of the Infant Jesus.[9] Her special grace is to dilate souls, to inspire them with love, confidence, and self-surrender. She says that she found happiness when she began to forget self. Will you join me in praying to her every day for the wisdom that makes men saints, and brings the soul full peace and happiness?"

The moral strength gained by the novice had a favorable effect on her health. Her constitution, which had suffered slightly at first, was re-established by her peace of mind, and adapted itself better every day to the observance of our austere Rule. Her soul influenced her body and, as this seemed likely to be permanent, our little sister was admitted by the Chapter to holy profession. She was overwhelmed with joy at the prospect of the final consecration to the Spouse of virgins.

On the evening of December 25, 1902, she wrote: "The Infant God has bestowed a great joy on me: on this happy Feast of His Nativity He has told me that He is about to become my Bridegroom. On the Feast of the Epiphany He will make me His queen . . . uniting me to Himself by my profession."

In a letter to Canon A— she says: "The Spouse has called me, and on January 11, a feast full of illumination and praise, I shall pronounce the vows which will unite me to our Lord forever.

[8] 2 Cor. 12:9.
[9] In consequence of the wishes of those who have read "l'Histoire d'une Ame", and of the signal favors obtained by her intercession, the cause of beatification of this nun has been brought before the Church. She was canonized in 1925.]

The Praise of Glory

"You who have known me from childhood, and who have been my confidant from the first, will understand what joy fills my soul. I asked the prayers of my dear community tonight at recreation, and shall begin my ten days' retreat to-morrow. The whole thing seems to me a dream; I have longed for it so intensely. Will you give me a special intention every morning at Holy Mass for my preparation? I feel encompassed by the mystery of divine charity and, on looking back I see how my soul has been pursued by it. Oh! What love! I feel overwhelmed by it, and adore in silence!

"On that morning of the Octave of the Epiphany, the supreme day of my life—although the good Master has bestowed on me days so divine that they were a paradise—on that day, when all my desires will be fulfilled and I shall become 'the bride of Christ', will you, dear Canon, offer the Holy Sacrifice for your Carmelite and then give her to God, so that she may be entirely possessed by Him and may be able to say with Saint Paul: 'I live, now not I; but Christ liveth in me'.[10]

"Need I tell you what favor I shall ask for you? You know my heart! I leave you to enter perfect silence with the Bridegroom."

Though this retreat began with joy, yet her former torments recurred so persistently that the poor novice was overcome with anguish when the eve of the great day arrived; however, during the afternoon she was comforted by an interview with a prudent and enlightened religious.

Next morning, while she mounted the stairs leading to the chapter-room, her mind was filled with the thought of immolation described in the *Capitulum* for the Vespers of the day: "I beseech you therefore, brethren, by the mercy of God, that you present your bodies a living sacrifice, holy, pleasing unto

[10] Gal 2:20.

The Novitiate

God, your reasonable service."[11] It was thus that she pronounced the holy vows of poverty, chastity, and obedience, which made her the consecrated bride of Christ.

What feast could have been more suitable to the mystic nuptials of this young girl, on whom the "glory of the Lord" had shone? Beckoned by divine light, she, too, in spite of the momentary eclipse of the star, had persevered bravely in her search for our Lord. She had opened her treasures and offered Him the gold of a pure heart, the incense of a life devoted to prayer, and the myrrh of the sacrifice of all things, including herself.

Holy Church also celebrated, on that Sunday of the Epiphany Octave, the manifestation of the Blessed Trinity at the Baptism of Christ. Sister Elizabeth, whose profession united her by a special bond to the Three Divine Persons, had come to Carmel in order to listen to Him in Whom the Father finds all His pleasure. And we read in the Gradual: "Blessed be the Lord, the God of Israel, Who alone hath done great wonders from the beginning. Let the mountains receive peace for thy people. Alleluia! Alleluia! . . ." The King of Peace responded to the unstinted gift of the generous girl, and ended her long period of trial, so that she overflowed with gratitude.

"How can I describe my joy," she wrote a few days later, "when, as 1 looked at the crucifix given me after my profession and placed by our reverend mother prioress as a seal upon my heart, I could say to myself: 'Now He is all mine and I am His, all His; He is my all!' Now there is only one thing I want: to love Him—to love Him every moment; 'to be jealous of His honor, like a true bride'; to offer Him a home, a shelter in my heart, there to make Him forget, by my love, all the abominable sins committed by the wicked."

[11] Rom 12:1.

The Praise of Glory

In another letter she says: "My joy is deep and divine, a joy that cannot be expressed. Thank God for me; my lot is so sublime—to pass my whole life in silence, adoration, heart to heart with my Divine Bridegroom! Beg Him to make me faithful, to fulfil all His designs for my soul, to accomplish all His will."

She took the veil on January 21, a day sacred to the virgin Agnes and her glorious immolation, the twin attractions of a soul which combined the two virtues characteristic of Christianity: innocence and penance.

During evening recreation Sister Elizabeth gave vent to her joy and gratitude in a poem beginning with the lines:

Henceforth in secrecy profound I dwell;
In life, in death, buried within my Lord.
Grant me to sink into Thine endless peace!
I live but in Thy love, O Word adored!

The verses, like the following lines addressed to the reverend mother prioress of Paray-le-Monial, contain the characteristics of her short, but well-filled religious life:

"My dear Mother, offer a few of your prayers for the little 'House of God', that it may be completely filled by 'the Three'. I have entered into the soul of my Christ, where I am about to spend my Lent. Ask Him to grant that I may live no more, but that He may live in me; that my union with Him may be closer every day, that I may fix my gaze upon the great Vision. I think that is the secret of sanctity, and it is so simple. Only to think that we have our heaven within us, the heaven for which I sometimes feel so homesick! What joy when the veil is drawn aside at last and we are face to face with Him Whom alone we love! Meanwhile I live in love, I plunge into it, and lose myself; it is infinite, the infinity for which my soul is thirsting."

The Novitiate

Sister Elizabeth was faithful to her resolutions and rapidly attained the perfection to which the Divine Master called her, for she had discovered the secret of sanctity. The excess of the charity of God had manifested itself to her, and she dwelt in this light which would never again be darkened.

"My life can be summed up in one word," she said, "it might be inscribed upon every moment of my time. It was Saint Paul's life, too: 'for His exceeding charity'.[12] Whatever happens to me is a message or an assurance of the exceeding love of God; I cannot live my life apart from that.

"I believe that to reach the ideal life of the soul we must live in the supernatural, must realize that God dwells within the depths of our soul, and do all things with Him; then nothing can be trivial, however commonplace in itself, for we do not live in, but above, such things. A supernatural soul does not deal with secondary causes, but solely with God.

"How this simplifies our view of life! It resembles the existence of the blessed spirits, and the soul is freed from self and from all else. All things are comprised in the one, and in the one thing necessary of which the Divine Master spoke to Magdalen. We become really great and free, for our will 'is enclosed in the will of God', as a mystic writer says."

Elizabeth surrendered herself entirely. She made this "ideal life" her own, and we saw her daily given to it more completely until she passed from the darkness of faith to the regions of peace, of light, and of love, where God is seen face to face for all eternity.

She was able to declare in one of her letters : "I am beginning my heaven already, though sometimes I should like to be in the other world, that I might see and love Him, and lose myself forever in His infinitude. Your heart is passionately

---

[12] "God for His exceeding charity wherewith He loved us" (Eph. 2:4).

The Praise of Glory

affectionate. Can you not understand what it is to love One Who has so deeply loved us?"

During the summer of 1903, she wrote to the confidant of her childhood:

"How many things have happened since my last letter! Holy Church has said to me her *Veni, Sponsa Christi*. She has consecrated me, and now all is over, or rather, has begun, for profession is only daybreak, and my life as a bride seems to me more beautiful, resplendent, and full of peace and love every day.

"During the night preceding the great day, while watching in the church for the coming of the Bridegroom, I realized that heaven was beginning for me on earth already—a heaven in my faith, my suffering, my immolation for Him I love. . . . I want to love Him deeply, like my seraphic mother, to love Him even unto death. My one ambition is to be Love's victim. . . . A life of love is so easy in Carmel. The Rule tells us every instant, from morning till night, what is the will of the good God. How I love the Rule which shows me the way in which He wishes me to become a saint! I do not know whether I shall have the joy of giving my Spouse the testimony of blood, but if I follow the Carmelite observance fully, I shall at least have the satisfaction of spending myself for Him, and for Him alone. Then what does it matter how He wishes me to employ myself; since He is always with me? Prayer and our interchange of love never cease. I feel so distinctly that He dwells in my soul. I have only to recollect myself to find Him within, which is the source of all my happiness. He has put into my heart a thirst for what is infinite, and a longing to love which He alone can satisfy. I go to Him like a little child to its mother, that He may give me what I long for, and take possession of me. I think we ought to behave with great simplicity towards the good God.

The Novitiate

"Will you come some day and give your blessing to your little Carmelite, and join her here in thanking Him for His 'exceeding love'? I can no longer describe my joy. Listen to the hymn of my heart for God and for you. Wash me in the Blood of the Spouse at Holy Mass, for is not He the purity of the bride?—and she is thirsting for it."

Chapter Eight
Laudem Gloriæ

A life of faith — The teaching of Saint Paul — *Laudem Gloriæ* — The spirit of praise perfects the virtues — Second portress —The guardian angel — A penitential spirit — Sister Elizabeth of the Trinity in community life.

Sister Elizabeth had regained her former peace, but interior sweetness was not to be her ordinary state. Now that trials had developed her soul, she was to live by faith. If the Divine Master said to her, as to Magdalen, "Touch Me not!" [1] it was because He meant to introduce her into that hidden school, far removed from the senses, wherein the Word makes Himself heard; that obscurity in which it is made evident to the soul that God gives and unites Himself to it.[2]

It was then that she made acquaintance with the writings of Saint Paul, who henceforth became her spiritual guide. Taught by him, she strove to understand "the breadth and length and height and depth" of the Mystery hidden in God before time began; "the charity of Christ which surpasseth all knowledge", that she might "be filled unto all the fulness of God".[3]

The most beautiful texts of the great apostle confirmed the characteristic tendencies of her contemplative soul. With the penetration belonging to the pure in heart, she discovered their depth of meaning and assimilated their solid teaching which fortified and nourished her continual prayer.[4]

[1] St. John 20:17.
[2] St. Augustine, "Des États d'oraison de Bossuet," chap. 24.
[3] Eph 3:8, 19.

The Praise of Glory

One day, when they were discussing the "new name" of which the Apocalypse speaks as being that of the elect, Sister Elizabeth said that she had found hers in Saint Paul. The apostle writes, she continued, that we have been "predestinated according to the purpose of Him Who worketh all things according to the counsel of His will. That we may be unto the praise of His glory."[5]

"I have found my vocation there", she declared. "I am to be 'the praise of His glory' eternally. I wish to be *laudem gloriæ* here on earth."[6]

A few notes drawn up for her sister show how she intended to deserve the title.

---

[4] Hitherto her daily readings in the New Testament had brought her comparatively little light . . . She made it less from inclination than from obedience; but now the sense of the Holy Scriptures was really given her, as can be seen in the lucid explanations, particularly on Saint Paul, with which her letters teem. Her correspondence, visits to the parlor, poems, confidential chats, are henceforth full of the words of St. Paul, while her own delightful comments on them were the joy and stimulus of her companions in the noviceship.

[5] Eph 1:12.

[6] This name, by which Sister Elizabeth of the Trinity loved to call herself, because she was inwardly inspired to earn a right to do so, needs some explanation, and even some defense. She discovered it in the writings of St. Paul, who twice says in his Epistle to the Ephesians (Eph. 1:6, 12) that we are predestinated unto the adoption of children through Jesus Christ for "the praise of the glory of God— in *laudem gloriæ ipsius* Our life here below and our glory in heaven may be termed "praise of the Divine glory", or, more briefly, "the praise of glory", and as it is lawful for a name common to many to become proper to a soul which has earned such a title by its special zeal and, above all, when earned by a sole or supreme preoccupation, Sister Elizabeth of the Trinity appropriated this name belonging to all the elect as her special device, and as expressing most fully what she wished to be. Such an ambition was worthy of one whose heart was wholly given to God. "However, some apology may be required for the young nun who cared little for the niceties of the Latin tongue. In her impulsive fervor she never noticed that she was expressing herself in bad grammar. She took Saint Paul's term as it stands, using it like a French noun which is not declined, when laudem can only be used in the accusative. Happy the souls who have only faults of grammar to repent of!"—Father —, S.J.

Laudem Gloriæ

"How can we fulfil this great dream of the heart of our God, this immutable desire regarding our souls—in a word, how can we respond to our vocation and become a perfect 'praise of the glory' of the most Blessed Trinity? In heaven, every soul is a praise of the glory of the Father, the Son, and the Holy Ghost, because each soul is grafted unchangeably in pure love and lives no longer its own life but the life of God. Then, as Saint Paul says, it knows Him as it is known by Him.

"The 'praise of glory' is a soul that dwells in God, with the pure, disinterested love which does not seek self in the sweetness of His love; a soul that loves Him above all His gifts, and would have loved Him as much had it received nothing, which wishes well to the object of its tenderness. But how can we wish well to God, except by accomplishing His will, since this will ordains all things for His greater glory? Such a soul should surrender itself fully, blindly, to this will so that it cannot possibly wish anything but what God wishes.

"The 'praise of glory' is a silent soul, a lyre beneath the touch of the Holy Ghost from which He can draw divine harmonies. Knowing that suffering is a chord that emits still more exquisite tones, this soul rejoices at giving it forth, that it may impress the heart of its God more pleasingly.

"The 'praise of glory' is a soul that contemplates God in faith and in simplicity; it reflects His whole being, and is a fathomless abyss into which He can flow and outpour Himself; a crystal through which He can shine and view His own perfections and splendor. A soul which thus permits the Divine Being to satisfy within it His craving, to communicate all He is and has, is truly the 'praise of glory' of all His gifts.

"Finally, the 'praise of glory' is one who is always giving thanks, whose acts, movements, thoughts, aspirations, while more deeply establishing her in love, are like an echo of the

The Praise of Glory

eternal "Sanctus" in the heaven of glory. The blessed rest not day or night, saying, 'Holy, holy, holy, Lord God Almighty . . . and, falling down, adore Him that liveth for ever and ever.[7] The 'praise of glory' begins now, within the heaven of her soul, the task that will be hers for all eternity. Her chant is uninterrupted; she acts beneath the influence of the Holy Ghost, although she may sometimes be unconscious of it, for human weakness prevents souls keeping their attention fixed on God without distractions. She sings and adores perpetually and has, so to speak, gone out from self and become absorbed in praise and love, in her passion for the glory of her God.

"Let us, in the heaven of our soul, be an homage of glory to the Blessed Trinity. One day the veil will be withdrawn and we shall be brought into the eternal courts; there we shall sing in the bosom of infinite Love, and God will give us the 'new name' promised to him that overcometh. What will that name be—*Laudem Gloriæ*!"

Such was the inner life of this chosen soul, in which faith worked by fervent charity. During prayer and the Divine Office she was evidently absorbed in adoration, and seemed already in paradise, joining with the blessed spirits in their praise of the thrice-holy God.

Sister Elizabeth's zeal for the psalmody and ceremonies of the Church did not prevent her making rather frequent mistakes, which we attributed to her mind being absorbed in her devotion. It has been related of several of the saints that when their deep contemplation distracted their attention from all outward things, their guardian angels warned them of their part in the ceremonies going on. This favor was not granted to our little sister, but she must have given glory to God by her

[7] Apoc 4:8, 10.

Laudem Gloriæ

minute attention in preparing herself as well as in the sincere humility she showed in reparation.

The spirit of praise perfected all her virtues by uniting her to the Divine Example, Whom she strove to represent in the sight of the Father.

The first utterance of the Word on His entering the world, "Behold, I come to do Thy will, O God",[8] ought to be as the very pulse of the bride, and this will of Him Who had sent her should be at once her food and the sword that immolates her. This was the opinion of Sister Elizabeth of the Trinity, and from this point of view our customs in the most trivial matters were no less dear to her than the Rule itself and her superior's orders. "I have purchased Thy testimonies for an inheritance forever: because they are the joy of my heart." [9] By her constant fidelity to these exterior or interior "ordinances", the bride will bear witness to the Truth, and can say: "He that sent Me is with Me, and He hath not left Me alone: for I do always the things that please Him."[10]

She never failed to give this testimony fully. Some instances will give an idea of the perfection of her obedience. She had charge of the noviceship, and was told to close the shutters in the evening. One night she forgot to do so, and suddenly remembered it after Matins, just as she was going to sleep. She rose at once, and went down in the dark across the cloister to perform her task. We find such examples in the lives of the saints, such as that of our father, Saint John of the Cross, getting up one night because he remembered to have left in his scapular one more pin than a simple tradition allowed, and putting it outside the door of his cell.

[8] Heb 10:9.
[9] Ps. 118:111.
[10] St. Jn 8:29.

The Praise of Glory

For some special reason Sister Elizabeth was dispensed from sitting on the floor during prayer and allowed to use her stall without leaning on it. She always sat in the way that gave her the least possible comfort. Two years later she again received the same dispensation, on account, now, of her illness.

However, she kept strictly to the same practice, so that a sister who watched her never saw her lean on her stall, however slightly, nor did she ever ask for permission to do so. She always obeyed to the letter without putting any personal interpretation on the order, as the following instance shows:

She was told, for a time, to take a short walk every day, but later on she had a painful complaint in her foot, so that she was dispensed from all duties that required her to walk. The prioress met her one day in the garden, limping along and apparently suffering greatly. "What are you doing here?" the superior asked. "I am taking a walk, Mother, as you told me." We could give many other such instances of the perfect obedience of one who said, a few days before her death: "The will of our mother has been the law of my life; when she had spoken, peace filled my soul."

Her humility was just as admirable. "The inability to pray which cost me so much suffering is a blessing to me now", she said. "It seems to magnify God, and His little 'praise of glory' realizes the truth more clearly, and depends more upon Him."

Her humility made it "really sweet to her to feel her powerlessness before God", as a devout author says, from whom she quoted the words that describe herself: "No one can trouble the humble soul, which has cast itself into an abyss too deep for anyone to follow it." In fact, nothing seemed to disturb her; whatever was said to her, she never excused herself,

Laudem Gloriæ

nor did a shadow cross her face. Yet from childhood she had struggled daily against a sensitiveness which had been the cause of her greatest victories. "In heaven alone will it be known how I have suffered during my life", she said before she died.

She had written at the end of a retreat made in the world:

"I have taken the same resolutions again this year—humility and self-renunciation, which include everything." Now she reaped the reward of her efforts on a point of which she had recognized, while very young, the primary importance.

"If I were asked the secret of happiness," she wrote, "I should say self-forgetfulness and continual self-denial, which effectually destroy pride. The love of God should be strong enough to destroy all love for self."

Our little sister practiced it, and we used to admire the way in which she continually effaced self that others might come forward, although she would often have been justified in taking the lead.

Her patience, the fruit of her humility, was inexhaustible, and never seen to fail. Yet how often it was tried, particularly in her office of help at the turn. Always at the beck and call of the first portress, she was especially anxious to smooth away the difficulties resulting for the out-sisters from our strict enclosure. They frequently had recourse to her ungrudging kindness. One day one of them asked to be forgiven for disturbing her so often. "Oh, don't say anything about it!" answered Sister Elizabeth. "I am so glad to be able to help you. I want you to forget that you cannot come in and fetch what you require."

She was as good-natured and obliging even during the most acute sufferings of her last days, so that we were always

The Praise of Glory

glad to apply to her in our needs. Her smile never vanished, although she was sometimes obliged to interrupt her work when very busy, to give up an hour's extra prayer, or change her little plans. She never seemed to mind so long as her self-denial was sanctioned by obedience.

Naturally of a very loving disposition, Sister Elizabeth's affections for those in the convent, as well as for her own family, were influenced by supernatural motives. The same charity that made her help her sisters in her own charming way led her to pay special attention to those who would probably humiliate her or try her virtue, so that all shared in her kindness.

She was twice given the office of angel![11] A young girl who passed some months in Carmel writes to her former prioress: "I remember my entrance into the convent; my little angel was there, and I guessed at once that she was an angel of charity. How she enjoyed giving some sort of a religious character to my worldly dress! How well she knew how to come to my help, to rectify my mistakes! How sweetly, how humbly, simply, and delicately she found an excuse for my faults! She saw to everything and kept constant watch over her Tobias.

"When she showed me how to keep the noviceship in order, she said: 'You must prize all this sweeping and dusting, for you begin your life as a Carmelite in this room.' Her reverence, inspired by her spirit of faith, as she told me how to do my work, proved that she lived in the presence of God, and looked to Him in her most trivial actions.

"Sometimes I apologized for having made her leave the silence she loved so well, but looking at me affectionately, she answered: 'I am your angel; come to me at once without hesitation; it is my duty to look after you and help you.'

---

[11] This is the name given to the sister who is charged with teaching a postulant the customs of the community.

Laudem Gloriæ

"How joyful she used to be when she could say: 'Our mother will see you today.' If her own turn was put off for mine, she said: 'Your pleasure makes me so happy that I am quite willing to sacrifice my own. You are going to see our mother: profit by it, for it is sacramental.'

"On several occasions, when she found me in tears, she took me in her arms affectionately, and must have gone to tell you, Mother, for you always sent for me on those days to set me right and comfort me. I was struck by her goodness, which always edified me indeed, I had only to imitate her to advance in the love and intimacy of the Divine Master."

Needless to say, such a soul was irresistibly impelled to perform penance, absorbed as it was in the thought of the "exceeding love" of God. As we used to tell her when she was on the point of doing something very imprudent, not only had she no instinct of self-preservation, but she felt such self-contempt that she had to be restrained on that score. Elizabeth was unable to practice such severe macerations as she wished, but her keen insight made her the better appreciate the constant sacrifice demanded by the Carmelite Rule, as well as the trials sent her by Providence, so that she realized the saying of Saint Paul in its appeal to her faith: "I die daily."[12]

It was impossible to guess what she liked or disliked. Dead to self, she bore her weariness, and especially her headaches, with no outward sign. She preferred an extra hour for prayer to the rest that was offered her on their account, saying that was the only time when she felt no pain. She was delighted at honoring the Crown of Thorns, not by her own choice, but by the will of her Divine Master.

---

[12] 1 Cor 15:31.

The Praise of Glory

Sister Elizabeth had often expressed the wish of spending herself in silence. Her apparent good health furthered her desire, and we never dreamed of our mistake until she entered the infirmary, never to leave it. From what she there disclosed, we learned something of the heroism she had practiced.

How bravely she kept to her work, realizing that it was part of our penance, and performing it in that spirit, rather than from natural inclination, for although very skillful with the needle, she found some difficulty in combining her very high form of prayer with the industry prompted by her zeal. She said that wonders, real little miracles, had occurred on this score when, watching against over-eagerness, she found her work advance in proportion with the intensity of her union with God.

With her spirit of order and poverty, Sister Elizabeth rendered invaluable service in the vestiary.[13] She had a wonderful gift of combining the requirements of an office, which was often overwhelmed with work, with the higher call that kept her calm and recollected in the little heaven of her soul.

A sister once spoke to her of her difficulty in getting rid of wandering thoughts during prayer. "To avoid that," answered Sister Elizabeth, "we must be very watchful during the day. On two or three occasions, when I saw the first vestier very over-worked, I hurried over my task and became excited about it, but God does not wish that of His brides." This is a proof of the care she took to keep herself entirely for God.

The opinions of some of the community complete the description of the angelic little nun.

"Our dear little sister excelled in all the virtues. Although so contemplative that one would have expected her to be

---

[13] The room used for work by Carmelite nuns. Those who make the clothes of the community are termed "vestiers".

Laudem Gloriæ

incapable of activity, her zeal was unwearied. She was noticeable for her perfect calmness, the result of her remarkable energy, for it seemed as if her soul were so perfectly possessed by the 'God of peace' that she had no need of further struggle. And how she shed forth this peace around her!

"Although naturally grave, serious, and fond of silence, Sister Elizabeth was always sociable in our little family festivities. She was particularly fond of Saint Martha's Day.[14] We used to arrange our plans beforehand, but she had a charming way of letting others enjoy the success of them. She was especially careful that our recollection should not be disturbed, so we used to imagine we were at Bethany, serving our Lord. She used to think she could invent no treat good enough for the sisters, and was delighted when she pleased them."

During the recreation days[15] the seniors liked to talk with Elizabeth of the Trinity, for she understood the Carmelite vocation in the sense of former times. "I was always delighted with her humility," says one of them. "Though her prayer was very high, and she was far advanced in the spiritual life, she was ever ready to learn, and acted as though she knew nothing. Although divinely instructed in the way of prayer, I used to see her listen with interest, and apply to herself whatever was said, never letting anyone suspect that she was far better informed."

One of her companions in the novitiate says: "Our recreations were delightful! How many times she spoke to me of the consuming Fire and the simple gaze, whose secrets she knew so well. I do not remember her ever being less amiable, sweet, and unselfish for a single day."

[14] On that day the novices take the place in the kitchen of our lay-sisters, to whom we give a holiday.
[15] Days on which the sisters are allowed to visit one another in their cells for conversation.

The Praise of Glory

"Even while she was sweeping the floor, although most active over her task, I used to be struck with admiration at her serious, recollected expression. She seemed never distracted from her incessant praise."

Let us end by quoting the opinion of one of the senior nuns, who cannot be suspected of enthusiasm, and whose rigorous observance of the Rule gives weight to her judgment:

"Having heard that no one had ever been able to discover any imperfection in Sister Elizabeth of the Trinity, I wished to make sure of the fact, as I was by no means predisposed in her favor. To my mind the polished manners of the world and a great facility of expression, joined to a keen intelligence and loving nature, might combine to give the impression of a perfection of virtue which had not yet been tested. Although we saw much of one another, when anyone talked to me about her virtues I spoke with reservation, and would not admit that they were so perfect or so unvarying; indeed, the mother subprioress asked me one day whether I disliked Sister Elizabeth. 'No,' I replied, 'I like her very much; but I shall wait before giving my opinion.' 'Well,' she answered, 'I can only say that I have frequently humiliated her, and have always found her sweet and humble.'

"From that time I studied her still more attentively, and was forced to own that I had never discovered any imperfection in her. Some people may have thought this a rather strong expression to use in the 'death notice', but it is the simple truth.

"Hers was not a perfection of the narrow and provoking kind, but was so humble and hidden as not to exclude certain faults of weakness or inadvertence, although I never saw her give way to any natural impulse; she always appeared to me not only faithful, but, I may say, heroic, especially under some particularly trying circumstances.

Laudem Gloriæ

"My cell was next to hers, and I used to hear her get up every morning directly the first signal sounded. When she reached the choir, or oratory, she at once knelt down, however tired her knees might be, or later on, whatever she might be suffering. One year we made a challenge of silence. She kept it most strictly; the two or three failures she had to note down every week were always caused by her kind-heartedness."

Sister Elizabeth of the Trinity's relations with those in the world bore no less evidence of her inner life. Her angelic disposition, zealous above all things for the glory of God, was combined with a tact, simplicity, and supernatural affection which won the confidence of everyone. She appreciated our severe laws regarding the parlor, and knew how to curtail an interview when she found it difficult to keep the conversation within the bounds she had set herself. If, however, she was in sympathy with her caller, she opened her heart, and her visitors listened spellbound. "It was impossible to come near her without being impressed and penetrated with the presence of God", says a friend. "One could never tire of hearing her speak of the most sublime subjects."

"Our rare interviews did me the greatest good", says another; "they always led me to love our Lord better and to sacrifice and recollect myself more. Grace seemed to pass from her through the grille which separated us."

One day a relation, who came from a long distance to visit her, was so impressed that she exclaimed impulsively: "Elizabeth, I place myself and my children under your protection." She wept at parting, and always begged Elizabeth to pray for her whenever any important matter was concerned.

"I talked with the dear young nun on February 27, 1905", writes a friend of Madame Catez. "I had not seen her since she entered Carmel, and I found she had become perfect. She

The Praise of Glory

was absorbed in the love of God, yet said such tender things to me, and spoke of her mother with such outbursts of affection, that I cried then, as I do now, when I recall the very short time I passed with her."

Such was Sister Elizabeth of the Trinity in the years following her profession; such were the fruits of the long and deep silence in which she listened to the divine word, that "efficacious" word which worked for the "praise of divine glory", the blessed transformation described by her in the following lines:

> "Oh! would that I could say, as did Saint Paul,
> that I for love of Him had lost my all.
> For no desire have I of aught below,
> Save that my love each day may deeper grow!
> To strive to know Him better be my goal—
> My Christ, and the Redeemer of my soul!
> May I so fashioned to His likeness be,
> That men in me my Savior's image see!"

Chapter Nine
The Inner Life

Continual prayer — The retreat of 1904 — Prayer — Devotion to the Holy Trinity and the Blessed Virgin — November 21, 1904 — "The only thing I do is to enter into myself."

No one will ever know how deep was the spirituality of this angelic young nun, who uttered the most sublime speeches with the frankness of a child, as though they were the most natural remarks to make. Absorbed as she was in God, when the time came she could climb her Calvary with the fortitude of a martyr; her heroism then revealed to us how genuine had been her prayer, which no pain, however intense, could henceforth interrupt.

"I cannot reveal what He teaches me in the depth of my soul", she said. "He shows me all things and responds to all my needs."

At other times the divine light was eclipsed, but Elizabeth, unshaken in faith and hope, remained perfectly collected, dwelling on the words of our holy father, which delighted her: "Faith is presence in the darkness, possession in obscurity." "During the night that obscured her soul she clung to Him she loved and for Whom she suffered, following Him by the glimmering of the obscure light."[1]

Those experienced in the states in which faith is purified and simplified will know that our little sister was heroic in keeping assiduously to prayer.

No one who saw her, calm and peaceful before the Eucharistic throne, would have supposed that sometimes on

[1] *Life of the Venerable Margarite of the Blessed Sacrament.*

The Praise of Glory

the Sundays and feast days she passed in the oratory, without sparing a moment from her worship of the Divine Master, she was being "tempted to get up and leave".

"I often spend all these hours in 'the dark night'," she said; "but at my prayer in the evening He compensates for it, and still more so next day. Then I receive the reward of my acts and silence of the day before, so that I would not miss my communion on Monday on any account."

Her first retreat after her profession established her in this state of soul: the way of faith, obscure, yet luminous, because she clearly realized the love of God. He was her light, enlightening her in the darkness of her night, so that she blessed the Lord at all times. God appeared to wish to recompense her generous fidelity during this retreat, for she was overwhelmed with graces too sublime and substantial to be described, so that when Sister Elizabeth of the Trinity gave an account of her dispositions, she raised her lustrous eyes to her prioress, and could only say: "He imparts eternal life to me."

"The kingdom of God must needs bring eternal life with it", says the holy Abbot Moses, "and is entered by the practice of virtue, purity of heart, and spiritual and divine knowledge."[2]

After this retreat, her prayer seemed still simpler. "We must keep our eyes on Him," she said, speaking of the Divine Master, "we must be silent; it is so simple!" This was her one rule. If a novena was to be made, a feast to be prepared for, when she was asked what she was going to do, she always answered: "I am going to be silent, so that He may flow into me."

This invariable answer was generally expected by our young nuns, who used to say to her, rather mischievously: "You will be quiet, won't you? Silence!" And she used to smile.

[2] *Lives of the Fathers of the Desert.*

The Inner Life

Sometimes, however, she felt very doubtful whether she ought to be constantly passive; ought she not to act more during prayer? Her peace, disturbed for the moment, was always restored to her by Him Who wished her to be thus recollected under His direct and continuous action. One day, during the "Forty Hours", Elizabeth, after listening to her companions urging one another to make reparation, felt rather sorry, as she began her prayer, at not being able to act in the same way; but she had hardly prostrated herself to adore our Lord, when He enveloped her with a luminous and peace-giving radiance. It was suddenly revealed to her that the obstacle created by sin against God's diffusing Himself into the souls of men was one of the things which most deeply wounded the Divine Heart, and that to console Him and to make reparation for such an outrage, she must let herself be taken possession of by God, giving full liberty to His grace and love to act within her. Now that her form of prayer was divinely approved, it became more and more her habitual state of soul.

"Do you not delight in listening to Him?" she wrote to a young seminarian. "Sometimes I feel so strongly impelled to be silent that I should like to do nothing but sit at the Savior's feet with the Magdalen, eager to hear everything and to penetrate deeper and deeper still into the mystery of charity that He came to reveal. Have you not found that while we are active and appear to be filling Martha's office the soul can remain buried in contemplation like Magdalen, or like a thirsty man at the fountain? That seems to me the mission of the Carmelite and the priest: both can show forth God and give Him to souls if they are always close to the Divine source. I think we should draw very near the Master, be in communion with His soul, identify ourselves with all His impulses, then go forth, like Him, according to the will of His Father.

The Praise of Glory

"I like the thought, 'the life of the priest (and of the Carmelite) is an advent that prepares souls for the Incarnation'. David says in one of the Psalms: 'A fire shall go before Him.'[3] Is not love that fire? And is it not also our mission to prepare the way of the Savior by our union with Him Whom the apostle calls a consuming fire? By contact with Him, our soul will become a flame of love, spreading throughout all the members of the Body of Christ, which is the Church. Then we shall console our Master's Heart, and He will be able to show us to His Father, saying: 'I am already glorified in them.'"

Sister Elizabeth interpreted the apostolate of Carmel like a genuine daughter of Saint Teresa and Saint John of the Cross. As our holy father says in his *Spiritual Canticle*:

"The soul that enjoys solitary love seems idle, but . . . an instant of pure love is more precious in the eyes of God and the soul, and more profitable to the Church, than all other good works together, though it may seem as if nothing were done. Thus, Mary Magdalen, though her preaching was most edifying, and might have been still more so afterward, out of the great desire she had to please God and edify the Church, hid herself, nevertheless, in the desert 30 years, that she might surrender herself entirely to love; for she considered that she would gain more in that way, because an instant of pure love is so much more profitable and important to the Church. . . . In a word, it is for this love that we were all created."[4]

The following lines show more clearly that Sister Elizabeth of the Trinity fully grasped the truth of this great doctrine:

"Since our Lord dwells in our soul, His prayer is ours, and I desire to partake of it unceasingly, keeping like a little

---

[3] Ps 96:3.
[4] *Spiritual Canticle of St. John of the Cross*, 28., notes 2, 3. Lewis, London, 1909.

The Inner Life

pitcher beside the fountain, so that I may be able to give life to others by letting His inexhaustible streams of charity overflow on them.

"'For them do I sanctify Myself, that they also may be sanctified in the truth.'[5] Let us make these words of our adorable Master our own. Yes! Let us sanctify ourselves for the souls of others, for as we are all members of the same body we can cause the divine life to circulate throughout the great body of the Church in proportion to the share we possess of that life ourselves.

"All sanctity and apostleship seem to me contained in two words: 'union, love'. Pray that I may live beneath their sway by abiding within the Blessed Trinity."

"When I think of my name," she wrote to the same seminarian, with whom the bonds of grace connected her more closely than can any ties of relationship, "my soul is conducted by the great vision of the mystery of mysteries into that Trinity Which even in this world is our cloister, our dwelling place, the infinite Being enclosed in which we can traverse all things. I am just reading the beautiful teaching of our father, Saint. John of the Cross, about the transformation of the soul into the Three Divine Persons. To what sublime glory we are called! I can understand the silence and recollection of the saints who could not withdraw from their contemplation, so that God could lead them to the divine mount where union is made perfect between Him and the soul, which is His mystic bride.

"What an adorable mystery of charity that God should call us by our vocation to live in such a knowledge! . . . I should like to respond to it by passing through this world like our Lady, 'keeping all these things in my heart', retired, as it

[5] Jn 17:19.

The Praise of Glory

were, into the depth of my soul, so as to lose myself; to be transmerged into the Blessed Trinity Who dwells there; then my device, 'my radiant ideal', as you call it, would be realized, and I should really be 'Elizabeth of the Trinity'."

Her special devotion for this august Mystery led her to make every Sunday a feast of the Blessed Trinity. When we recited the Athanasian Creed in the office of the day she used "to feel as if she were in heaven" as she sang it.

She never missed reminding her relations when Trinity Sunday came round and kept it herself with even deeper recollection than usual. It was in the center of her being that she sought it and there adored the Mystery.

"This is my own feast," she wrote to her sister: "there is no other like it for me. It is celebrated in silence and adoration in Carmel. I never before realized the sense of my vocation hidden in my name. Let this great Mystery be our meeting-place, our center, and our abode." Sister Elizabeth's dedication to the Three Divine Persons increased her devotion for our Lady, and formed a closer bond of grace with her whom she termed the great "praise of glory" of the Blessed Trinity. "The movements of Mary's soul are so deep," Sister Elizabeth often said, "that we cannot fathom them; she seems to reproduce on earth the Divine, the simple Being. She is so transparent that we might mistake her for the Light itself, yet she is only the 'Mirror of the Sun of Justice'. It seems to me that she is more easy to imitate than any other saint; it brings me peace whenever I look at her."

Sister Elizabeth of the Trinity loved to think of the hour when the Holy Spirit came upon Mary, the power of the Most High overshadowed her, and the Word became incarnate in her. One day, moved by contemplating this mystery, her heart overflowed in a prayer in which she besought some of

The Inner Life

its ineffable graces.[6] It was written on November 21, 1904, on the Feast of the Presentation of our Lady, dear to her on account of the mysterious bond entered into between the child Virgin and the Three Persons of the Blessed Trinity. Our little sister used to delight in placing herself, in imagination, on the threshold of the temple, where she adored and renewed her vows in the same spirit of oblation.

She was also particularly attracted by the season of Advent. "I need no effort", she said, "to enter into the Mystery of God dwelling within the Blessed Virgin; it seems to resemble my usual attitude of soul and, like her, I adore the hidden God within me. When I read in the Gospel that Mary went in haste to the mountains of Judea on her charitable mission to her cousin Elizabeth, I can see her as she passes, calm, majestic, recollected, holding commune within herself with the Word of God. Her prayer was always the same as His: '*Ecce*, here am I.' Who ? 'The handmaid of the Lord', she, His Mother, the lowliest of all His creatures.

"Her humility was sincere because she was always forgetful of self; unconscious of, freed from self; so that she could sing: 'From henceforth all generations shall call me blessed. Because He that is mighty hath done great things to me.'"[7]

These words of Sister Elizabeth's recall a remark made about her by a religious: "She possesses a soul of an exceptional simplicity which has set her at perfect liberty." She had said to him during a retreat: "It is very dark and painful, yet I think it is as simple to suffer as to enjoy." Her character is in this sentence. In fact, she went straight to God, without devoting herself to the practice of any special virtue. Her Carmelite life, contained in the words of the Divine

---

[6] See Appendix.
[7] St. Luke 1:48, 49.

The Praise of Glory

Master: "I do always the things that please my Father",[8] implicitly includes all the virtues without further thought of them. "Love dwells within us," she used to say, "so all I do is to enter into myself and lose myself in Those within me."

"I am Elizabeth of the Trinity, that is to say, Elizabeth disappearing, submerged in the 'Three'. Let us give ourselves up to Them, sacrificing ourselves every moment without seeking for anything extraordinary. Let us make ourselves small, allowing Him Who is our all to carry us in His arms as a mother does her child.

"Yes, we are weak—indeed, I may say we are nothing but misery; but He well knows that He delights in forgiving and raising us up, in bearing us in Himself; in His purity and infinite sanctity. In this way He purifies us by continual contact with Him. He wishes us to be stainless, and He Himself will be our purity! We must allow ourselves to be transformed into His image, which will be accomplished simply by loving Him ceaselessly with such a love as causes unity between those who love. I wish to be a saint that I may glorify my Divine Master; I ask Him to make me live for love alone, which is my vocation. Let us unite ourselves to Him, so that our days may be in continual communion with Him; let us awake in love, deliver ourselves to love all day by doing the will of the good God, in His sight, with Him, in Him, for Him alone; let us give ourselves incessantly in the way in which He wishes; then, when night comes, after a colloquy of love in our heart throughout the time, let us sleep again in love. Perhaps we may know of faults and infidelities on our part; let us abandon them to love which is a consuming fire, and thus we shall have our purgatory."

Again she writes: "Since we aspire to become 'victims of charity', like our holy mother Saint Teresa, we must allow

[8] St. Jn 8:29.

The Inner Life

ourselves to become rooted in the charity of Christ, as Saint Paul says in the beautiful epistle of today. How is that to be done? In living—raised above all that is around us—with Him Who dwells within us, and Who is charity. He thirsts to give us all He is, to transform us into Himself. Let us rouse our faith and remember that He is within us, and wishes us to be true to Him. How many acts of self-denial we can offer unknown to all but Him! Let us lose none of them. It seems to me that the saints are souls completely oblivious of self, lost in Him Whom they love, with never a thought of self or of creatures, so that they are able to say with Saint Paul: 'I live, yet not I, but Jesus Christ liveth in me.' No doubt we must immolate ourselves in order to be so transformed, but we love sacrifice because we love the crucified God. Oh, let us be in earnest about it! Let us give our soul to Him, telling Him that we long to love but Him alone; let Him do all, for we are feeble and childish, and it is such joy to be the little babe of the good God!"

Chapter Ten
Sister Elizabeth and Her Family Circle

The first anniversary — All Souls' Day, 1902 — Filial affection — Divine Providence — "My two lovely lilies" — The mystery of Divine adoption.

Intermingled with her spiritual sayings are touching words addressed to those whom Sister Elizabeth said she had never loved so deeply as since she became a nun. Her correspondence with her relatives delights as much as it helps us, while completely refuting the prejudice felt by the world against those who sacrifice the ties and joys of home for the sake of God.

The following letter was written by the little novice in August, 1902, on the first anniversary of her entrance into Carmel.

"Dear Mamma,

"Just a year ago I gave to God the best of mothers, yet the great sacrifice has not separated our souls! Do you not realize that they are more united now than ever before? Oh, let me tell you how happy I am! The good God has been too kind to me; my whole soul is filled with gratitude and love to Him and to you. I thank you for having given me to Him. When I remember the anguish of those last hours, I thank Him Who upheld us both.

"Marguerite was radiant the other day. I have not seen her so happy for the last year; she has lost her little heart. . . . I assure you that she who is enamoured of Christ is no less happy. My Bridegroom is so beautiful! I love Him passionately, and am

The Praise of Glory

transformed into Him by loving Him; besides, it is such joy to have Him always with me. We love one another so dearly! Ah! But for that, I should still be with you. I feel the sacrifice, yet I am perfectly happy.

"Tell the engaged couple that I continually pray for them."

Three months later, All Souls' Day revived sad memories in her mother's heart. Sister Elizabeth consoled her by the radiant hope of her own faith.

"November 1, 1902

"My Dear Mamma,

"Our reverend mother, who knows you must be feeling lonely, has given me leave to tell you how closely united my soul will be to yours during the next few days, and that, one in our faith and love, we shall find the dear ones who have left us and have gone to paradise. I never before felt them so present with me. They are glad I am in Carmel, for it is very near heaven; indeed, we Carmelites are already in heaven by faith.

"When you hear the bell toll for the Office of the Dead, join your prayers to mine; whatever I do is done by you too; that agreement has been made with the good God.

"The Divine Master says today: 'Blessed are they that mourn, for they shall be comforted.'[1] 'God shall wipe away all tears from their eyes'[2] in heaven. Dear Mother, I have often seen you weep; your life has been full of sorrow and sacrifices; but you know that the more God asks, the more He gives.

"The Lamb Whom the blessed adore in the Vision is He to Whom your Elizabeth is betrothed, and Whose bride she

---

[1] St. Matt 5:5.
[2] Apoc 7:17.

The Family Circle

longs to become. Oh, how beautiful a lot is mine! All heaven belongs to me; my life is centered where, even in this world, I follow my 'Lamb wherever He goeth.'

"If you could only know how happy I am, you would thank Him Who has chosen me! Listen to what He says to you: 'Whosoever shall do the will of My Father that is in heaven, he is My brother and sister and mother.'[3] Remember, you are not alone; the Divine Friend is with you, and with Him your Elizabeth!"

All her letters are in the same strain of supernatural tenderness.

"February, 1902

"My Dear Marguerite,

". . . I address my letter to Luneville, as I think you are there now. Give all sorts of kind messages to Mademoiselle A— and tell her that the grille of Carmel, which made her blood freeze and seemed so melancholy to her, looks gilded to me. Ah, if we could only raise the curtain, what a prospect we should see on the other side! Infinitude itself! And that is why it enlarges every day. Carmel, which is solitude with Him we love, is heaven beforehand. Do not be jealous; He alone realizes the sacrifice I made in leaving you. I know that I could never have made it unless His love had upheld me, for I love you so dearly—more dearly every day, for He makes it supernatural.

"These carnival days are delightful and full of God. The Blessed Sacrament is exposed; I am before Him nearly all day, and Marguerite, whom I seem to keep in my soul, is there with me. We are in darkness, for the grille is open and all the light comes from Him. I like to see the grating between us. He

[3] St. Matt 12:50.

The Praise of Glory

is a prisoner for me and I for Him.

"Since Mamma is interested in my health, tell her that I am quite well. I should never notice it was winter but for the pretty curtains with which the good God covers our windows. How charming the cloister looks with its decorations of hoar-frost!

"Live close to God; we are one in Him."

"Do you remember", she writes to her mother about August 1, 1903, "how cunningly your Elizabeth used to hide to make a pretty surprise present for you? This year, too, I am making my preparations, my secret plans, with my Divine Spouse. He opens all His treasures to me, and I have taken this lovely bouquet from them, a crown which will shine on your brow for all eternity. Your little daughter will rejoice some day in heaven, thinking she has helped the Divine Master to make it; that she set it with glowing rubies, the blood of your heart and her own!

"I am writing in our little cell, which is full of silence, and, above all, full of God. I feel tonight that I must thank you again, for you well know that I should never have left you without your *fiat*, and He wished me to sacrifice you for love of Him. Carmel is like heaven; we must separate ourselves from all to possess Him Who is the All, but I love you as we shall love in our fatherland. There can never be any greater separation between us than there is now, for He Whom I possess within me dwells in you, so that we are united.

"And now, dear Mamma, I only have time to wish you one thing: that God, Who has taken me for Himself, may, as time goes on, be more and more the one Friend Who is your solace at all times. Live on intimate terms with Him, heart to heart, as we live with one we love; that is the secret of the happiness of your child, who embraces you with all the tenderness of her Carmelite heart—the heart that is all your own, for it is all

The Family Circle

His, and belongs to Him and to the Blessed Trinity."

When Elizabeth met her relatives in the parlor, she generally spoke to them of recollection, of intimacy with God, and of the joys of divine love. Her fervor made her delight in raising the souls she loved to greater heights.

"I am overjoyed at seeing what the good God is doing for Mamma and Marguerite", she wrote to Canon A——. "He has taken me that He may give Himself more fully."

Again: "I long to send my dear mother to you. You will see how God is carrying out His work in her, so that I cry for joy and gratitude sometimes. How happy it is to share one's mother's religion, to feel that she is all His, to be able to speak to her from one's soul, and to be understood! It is well for us to confide in God and to abandon the care of self and those we love to Him. . . ."

Heaven repaid her self-abandonment by showering blessings upon the home still dear to her. Her young sister married a man who was all her faith could desire. The wedding gave her an opportunity of explaining her own happiness to her mother.

"Marguerite and her husband came to see me. They seem very happy. I thanked God on their account . . . and on my own. From a worldly point of view my lot seems nothing but self-sacrifice, yet, believe me, I have the better part. In spite of the tears it cost her, a mother ought to rejoice at having given a Carmelite to God, for, after a priest, I know of nothing more holy upon earth. The name of Carmelite implies that the soul is angelic. Ask our holy mother, Saint Teresa, whom you taught me to love while I was a young child, that I may become a saintly Carmelite. You should rejoice at being loved by the little heart that is wholly given to God. If I love Him, it is you who led me to Him; you prepared me so well for our

The Praise of Glory

first meeting on that great day when we gave ourselves to one another! Thank you for all you have done! I long to make Him loved, and to give Him to souls as you have done.

"I give my crucifix a kiss for our Lord to take to you from His bride, your fond little daughter."

"November, 1903
"The kingdom of God is within you."[4]

"Dear Marguerite,

"What pleasure you gave me on my feast by your pretty message and your lovely photograph! St. Elizabeth must have let you know what I wanted most. Your likeness makes me become recollected, and then it seems as if we two were both close to our Lord. It is really true that He is in our souls, and that we are always near Him like Martha and Mary. While you are busy I keep you at His feet. You know that when we love Him, outside things cannot distract our thoughts from Him, and so Marguerite is Martha and Mary at the same time!

"How I enfold you in my prayers, you and the dear little creature who is already in the mind of God! Let yourself be given up to and possessed by His Divine life, so that the little one will enter this world enriched with blessings.

"I hope it will be very pretty, and am delighted to think what happiness it will bring with it, thank God! I share your joy in the midst of the solitude I love so well."

The following charming lines were written on the birth of little Elizabeth:

"I feel full of reverence before this little temple of the Blessed Trinity; her soul seems to me like a crystal through which God shines. If I were with her, I should kneel to adore Him Who dwells within her. . . . How I should like to nurse

---
[4] St. Luke 17:21.

The Family Circle

her! But the good God has called me to the mountain to be her angel and to protect her by my prayers, and I joyfully sacrifice all the rest to Him for her sake. How happy I feel at thinking that you are a mother! I confide you and your little angel to the care of Him Who is Love itself. I adore Him with you and embrace you in His heart."

"March, 1904

How good God is!

"Dear Grandmamma!

"How glad I am that I can call you by this sweet name, and that the dear little one is called Elizabeth! Thank God for giving her to me, so that I may be her angel I have adopted her as my own property. I prayed much for her before her birth, and now my prayer and self-denial will be the two wings beneath which I shall shelter her.

"I offered a novena of Masses that she might be washed in the Precious Blood. The novena ended today—the Feast of the Five Wounds of our Savior—and the little angel has come to us from the wound of His Heart; is it not touching?

"Let me know the day of her baptism, so that I may accompany my little darling to the font, where the Holy Ghost will descend into her soul. Your Carmelite would have been delighted to see you, yet sacrifice is sweet, especially when it is our heart we offer. You gave your Elizabeth to God, He has sent you a second, and we shall try which of us can love you best. . . ."

The Praise of Glory

"July 20, 1904

The eye of God is upon her; His love encircles her like a rampart.

"Dear Little Sister,

"'Echo of my soul', as Thérèse of the Infant Jesus called one of her sisters. I love to give you this sweet name on the eve of your feast.

"My darling flower, my Marguerite, I beg God to grant all the wishes of your great 'heart of gold', to send down on you the fire of His love, that beneath these divine rays you may grow and bloom, and that in the shadow of your 'great white petals', another little flower very dear to my heart may open its tender bud.

"How pretty your little 'Sabeth' is! She made me all sorts of charming little signs yesterday from the arms of her delighted grandmother. She looked so sweet with her eyes closed and her hands folded on her heart. I made our reverend mother smile by telling her that my niece was an 'adorer'; that is her calling as the 'House of God'."

"August, 1904

God is Love.

"My Darling Little Sister,

"Yes, I do indeed find you at the feet of Jesus, and I never leave you, but share the joy of His Heart at finding a Marguerite wherein He can rest. Be His paradise in this land where He is so little known and loved; open your heart wide that He may enter as your Guest, and when He is in the little cell of your soul, love Him, Marguerite! He thirsts for love: bear Him company. . . . I am pleased with you, and the Master loves His little blossom.

The Family Circle

"It seems a long time ago since we climbed the mountains together; I remember what a lovely view we had from our room. Does not such scenery lead you to God? Enjoy beautiful Switzerland and our dear mother's companionship. I can understand that you are making a sacrifice in going so far from George. It is the law of this life: sacrifice and joy go side by side. The good God wishes to remind us that we have not yet reached our final happiness.

"Still, we have turned in that direction, and He Himself will carry us there in His arms. There in heaven, little Sister, He will satisfy all our cravings. Meanwhile, let us dwell in the heaven of our soul, where we can be so happy even here."

"Easter, 1905
Alleluia!

"Dear Marguerite,

"We have sung the Alleluia, and I am writing to tell you how I rejoice in your happiness of motherhood. I am so glad to be made an aunt a second time, especially of a little niece, for I think there will be the same sisterly love in your happy home as there was between you and me, and 'Sabeth' has an Odette, as Aunt Elizabeth had a Marguerite. 'Sabeth' was born on the Feast of the Five Wounds of Jesus, and now Odette has arrived on the day the Master was sold to save her little soul. Is it not touching ?

"I bore your soul with me wherever I went during this great week, especially during the night of Maundy Thursday; and since you could not go to Him, I asked Him to go to you. During the silence of prayer I whispered to my 'Guite' the words addressed by the Père Lacordaire to Magdalen when she went to seek her Master on the morning of the Resurrection: *'Ne le*

The Praise of Glory

demandez plus à personne sur la terre, a personne dans le ciel, car Lui c'est votre âme, et votre âme c'est, Lui!" [5]

"What blessings He is showering on your little nest, and what love He shows you by entrusting to you the two little souls which 'He chose in Him before the foundation of the world, that they might be holy and unspotted in His sight in charity!'[6] It is you who must guide them to Him and make them all His own.

"Tell George from me how my heart shares all your joys, for which I thank 'the Father', from Whom comes 'every perfect gift'.[7]

"Good-bye. I keep close to your babies with you. Each has a beautiful angel beside her who sees the Face of God; let us ask them to lead us to the Love which is unchangeable and keep us there.

"I send Odette a medal which has touched the miraculous Infant Jesus of Beaune; fasten it to her cradle, so that He Who so dearly loves the little ones may bless and protect her."

Later on she writes to Elizabeth and Odette themselves— a charming way of pleasing and touching the soul of their mother, which is so faithful an echo of her own.

"My dear little nieces, my lovely pure white lilies, whose calix contains Jesus Himself, if you only knew how I pray that He may overshadow and protect you from all harm! You look very tiny in your mother's arms, but to your aunt, who sees you with the eye of faith, you partake of infinite grandeur for you have been present in the mind of God from all eternity, since He 'predestinated you to be made conformable to the image of His Son', and has clothed you with Himself in baptism, making you both His children and His living temple.

---

[5] It was thought best to leave this sentence untranslated, as it hardly admits of an English rendering apart from its context.—Translator
[6] Eph 1:4.
[7] St. James 1:17.

The Family Circle

"O dear little sanctuaries of love! When I see the splendor which shines within you, though as yet it is only the daybreak, I am silent, and adore Him Who has created such marvels!"

"August, 1905

"He who is joined to the Lord is one spirit.[8]

"My Dear Little Sister,

"Today is Sunday, the happiest of days, for I spend it before the Blessed Sacrament exposed in the oratory, excepting the time when I am at the turn, of which I take advantage to have a chat with you, beneath the eyes of Him we love. I have chosen a large sheet of paper, for I have so many things to say to my 'Guite'!

"I have lately been reading some splendid things by Saint Paul about divine adoption, and I naturally thought of you. Being a mother, you know what depth of love for your children God has put into your heart, so you can understand how great is the mystery of our being the children of God. Does it not make you tremble, Marguerite? Listen to what my dear Saint Paul says: 'God chose us in Him before the foundation of the world. . . . Who hath predestinated us into the adoption of children . . . unto the praise of the glory of His grace.'[9] Which means that, almighty as He is, it does not seem as if He could have done anything more grand. Again: 'If a son, an heir also through God.'[10] And what is this inheritance? 'God hath made us worthy to be partakers of the lot of the saints in light.'[11] And then, as if to show that it does not mean in the far future, the apostle adds: 'Now, therefore, you are no more strangers and foreigners, but you are fellow-citizens

---

[8] 1 Cor. 6:17.
[9] Eph. 1:4, 5, 6.
[10] Gal. 4:7.
[11] Col. 1:12.

The Praise of Glory

with the saints, and the domestics of God.'[12] O Marguerite! This heaven is the center of our soul; as Saint John of the Cross says, when we are in its deepest center, we are in God. How simple and consoling it is! In the midst of all your motherly cares and occupations you can retire into this solitude and give yourself up to the Holy Ghost, so that He may transform you into God, impressing the Divine image of His beauty on your soul, in order that, when the Father looks down on you, He may see nothing but His Christ, and may say: 'This is my beloved daughter in whom I am well pleased!' Little Sister, I shall rejoice in heaven at seeing the beauty of my Christ shining in your soul. I shall not be jealous, but shall say to Him, with a mother's pride: 'It is I, wretched creature as I am, who brought her forth unto Thy life.' Saint Paul spoke so of his converts, I should like to imitate him. What do you think about it?

"Meanwhile, let us 'believe in His love, and the charity which God hath to us',[13] like Saint John. Since we possess Him within us, what does it matter if our heaven is obscured by night? If Jesus seems to sleep, let us rest beside Him; let us be calm and silent; do not let us wake Him, but wait in faith. I do not think that 'Sabeth' and Odette trouble themselves much as to whether there is sun or rain, while they are in their mother's arms; let us imitate the little ones and rest as simply in the arms of God.

"I was always fond of a large park, for solitude is a delight. I think you appreciate it. Will you make a retreat with me for a month ending on September 14? Our Mother has given me this little holiday from the turn so that I shall not have to talk or think about it; I am going to bury myself

[12] Eph. 2:19.
[13] 1 St. John 4:16.

The Family Circle

in the depths of my soul, that is, in God. Will you imitate me in this very simple action?

"When your many duties distract your attention, I shall try to compensate for you, and you, if you like, will enter each hour into the center of your soul where your Divine Guest dwells. You might think of the beautiful words I quoted to you: 'You are the temple of God, and the Spirit of God dwelleth within you',[14] and those of the Master: 'Abide in Me, and I in you'.[15] It is said that Saint Catharine of Siena always dwelt in her cell even when in the midst of the world, for she lived in that inner dwelling place in which Marguerite, too, knows how to live. . . ."

[14] 1 Cor. 3:16.
[15] St. John 15:4.

Chapter Eleven
"*Sola Soli*"

Letters of condolence — "How simple it is to die!" — Thirst for self-sacrifice — Retreat of 1905 — Impressions of the last hour — A presentiment.

The same freshness and high tone of feeling characterizes all of Sister Elizabeth's correspondence. Her refined, delicate style, graceful and inspired by supernatural feeling, gives an indescribable charm to every subject she treats, so that it has been said of this daughter of Saint Teresa, as of her seraphic mother, that she cannot be thoroughly known except by her letters. Were it not for fear of making our story too long, we should give the reader all that have been preserved; however, we select a few which presage the final state of her soul, which was already raised above this world and had begun to mount towards God.

"I have heard of the painful sacrifice God asks of you", she wrote to Monsieur l'Abbé X— when his father died. "I think that, at such times, our only comfort can come from the Master Whose divinely loving Heart 'was troubled' at the tomb of Lazarus, so that we can weep with Him and, leaning on Him, find fresh strength and peace. I pray a great deal for your father's soul. He was indeed the 'just man' of whom the Scriptures speak, What a consolation, when his course was run, to look back upon his life so full of good works! For him the veil has fallen, the darkness of mystery has disappeared: he has seen ! . . . Let us follow him by faith into the regions of peace and of love, for all must end in God, Who some day will say His *veni* to us also; then, like the little babe on its

The Praise of Glory

mother's breast, we shall sleep in Him, and 'in His light we shall see light.'[1]

"Good-bye, Monsieur l'Abbé. Let us live on the heights far away . . . in Him . . . in our hearts, and as the communion of saints brings us into intercourse with those who have left us, let us pray together for the soul of your dear father, so that if he has not yet attained to it, he may soon enjoy the eternal vision of God. It is beneath this radiance of the presence of God that I remain at one with you!"

She wrote to a friend urging her to rise above her grief:

"I can understand your sorrow. What an impenetrable mystery death is! Yet, at the same time, how simple for the soul that has lived in faith, for those who 'look not at the things which are seen. . . . For the things which are seen are temporal, but the things which are not seen are eternal.'[2] Saint John, whose pure soul was radiant with divine light, gives in a few words what seems to me a most beautiful definition of death: 'Jesus knowing that His hour was come, that He should pass out of this world to the Father . . . '.[3] Is not the simplicity of these words touching? When the final hour sounds for us, we must not suppose that God will come before us to judge us, but that we shall remain for all eternity in the state in which God finds us then, and our degree of grace will be our degree of glory. By the fact of being delivered from the body, the soul can see Him without a veil within itself, as it has possessed Him all its lifetime, though unable to contemplate Him face to face. This is perfectly true; it is theology. Is it not a comfort to think that He Who is to be our Judge dwells within us

[1] Ps 35:10.
[2] 2 Cor 4:18.
[3] St. John 13:1.

"Sola Soli"

throughout our miseries, to save us and to forgive our sins? Saint Paul affirms positively that we are 'justified freely by His grace, through faith in His blood'.[4] How rich we are in the gifts of God, predestinate by divine adoption, and so heirs of the heritage of His glory!"

She whose soul found heaven so near and death so simple, approached the end of her exile; the thirst for immolation, the grace of her childhood, was a divine call to the Calvary now appearing on the horizon.

Sister Elizabeth's health had been maintained, with the help of a little management, until the spring of 1905, after which our Observance had to be modified for her—a supreme renouncement for this true Carmelite, who wished to keep her Rule until death, "until she died of very love"!

"It was very painful to me to be taken care of because I keenly longed to follow my Master in His self-sacrifice", she confided to the mother prioress shortly before she died. "I remember now what a severe sacrifice you asked of me one day. It was the beginning of Lent, and I begged you, as a favour, to let me have no more than usual at collation. You answered, giving me no hope of obtaining what I asked: 'You will eat whatever is given you.' Your reply seemed a refusal, and I submitted, but not without regret. On entering the refectory in the evening I longed to look at my place, but I offered this and my eagerness to our Lord as a renewal of the sacrifice made in the morning. But when I slipped along the bench of our table there was the meagre little collation I wanted! I cannot tell you how glad I was! No epicure was ever so pleased with a sumptuous dinner as I was with the frugal little meal! How happy I was, and how thankful to God and to you, my mother!"

[4] Rom 3:24, 25

The Praise of Glory

Alas! She would never enjoy that happiness again. She could not fast, but the doctor gave us hopes that, with rest and fresh air, she would recover.

She was taken from the office of portress, and henceforth, "alone with the One", we saw her fully correspond to grace in her complete solitude.

"Our kind mother, who watches over your Elizabeth with true maternal love", she wrote to her mother, "insists upon my living out of doors, so instead of working in our little cell, I install myself like a hermit in the most deserted part of our immense garden, where I spend a delightful time. Nature seems to me full of God: the wind rustling among the trees, the songs of the little birds, the beautiful blue sky, all speak to me of Him. O Mother! I must tell you that my happiness continually increases, is becoming infinite, like God Himself; yet it is so calm and sweet. I should like to tell you my secret.

"Saint Peter says in his first epistle: 'You believing, shall rejoice with joy unspeakable.'[5] The Carmelite draws all her happiness from this divine source of faith. She believes, as Saint John says, in the 'charity the Father hath bestowed on us';[6] she believes that this charity drew Him to earth and into her own soul, for He Who is called 'the Truth' has said: 'Abide in Me, and I in you.'[7] She obeys this most sweet commandment in all simplicity, living in intimacy with the God Who dwells within her, Who is more present to her than she is to herself. This is not all imagination or sentiment, dearest Mother, it is pure faith; and your own faith is so strong that God might say to you as He said to another: 'O woman, great is thy faith!' Yes, it was great when you led your Isaac

[5] 1 St. Pet 1:8.
[6] 1 St. John 3:1.
[7] St. John 15:4.

"*Sola Soli*"

to sacrifice him on the mountain! The good God has registered this heroic act of a mother's heart in the great book of life. I think your page will be well filled, and that you can await the hour of divine judgment in peaceful confidence.

"It is your feast on Tuesday, Mother dear, and though as a rule we do not write on such occasions in Carmel, our reverend mother has allowed me to make my letter coincide with the date so dear to me. You will feel sure that I send you my tenderest wishes. Do you remember how I used to enjoy preparing my surprises for that day? I have offered all such things on the altar of my heart to Him Who is a 'Spouse of blood'. It would be far from true to say that it has cost me nothing. Sometimes I wonder how I could have left so good a mother, but the more we give to God, the more He gives, as I realize better every day. So I wish you a happy feast! I should be very glad if our Lady, on the Feast of the Assumption, were to take with her all your cares, past, present, and to come, for you have only too many, and your Elizabeth cannot bear to see a shadow pass over your dear face."

The "most sweet commandment—'Abide in Me,'" of which Sister Elizabeth of the Trinity reminds her mother, was the source of changeless peace to herself in spite of the lassitude caused by her failing health. She knew how to raise herself above her feelings.

"I press towards the mark . . . Christ Jesus",[8] she said, and she spoke the truth. Later on she owned to her prioress that she used to look at her sometimes on leaving midday recreation, in the hopes of seeing a little gesture of invitation which would have been a ray of sunshine in the gloom. "As you did not notice me, Mother, I went back to our cell with my trials." "What did you do there?" "I used to try to raise myself above,

[8] Phil 3:14.

The Praise of Glory

or creep under them. I read Saint Paul, who had always brought me grace—although purely in the spirit of faith at such times, I assure you. I went over my favorite passages, or asked my Master to lead me to fresh pastures, and by ruminating over what I found there I got the better of my troubles in the end. But if you only knew what God wants of me! He will not allow me to cast a glance at anything but Him, although He hides Himself entirely. He requires real heroism of me.

"I am starting this evening on a long journey, which is nothing less than my private retreat", she wrote on October 8, 1905, to Monsieur l'Abbé X—, a recently ordained priest. "I shall be in absolute solitude for the next ten days, with several extra hours for prayer, and shall wear our veil down when walking about the convent. I shall be more like a hermit of the desert than ever. Before entering my Thebaid, I feel a real need of asking for the help of your holy prayers; above all, for a special intention in the Holy Sacrifice of the Mass. When you consecrate the Host in which Jesus, Who alone is holy, is about to become incarnate, will you consecrate me with Him as a victim of praise of His glory, so that all my aspirations, my movements, my actions, may be a homage to His sanctity?

"'Be ye holy, because I the Lord your God am holy.'[9] I concentrate my thoughts upon this sentence, beneath the light of which I shall make my divine journey. Saint Paul comments upon it for me when he says: 'He chose us in Him before the foundations of the world, that we should be holy and unspotted in His sight in charity.'[10] This, then, is the secret of virginal purity: to dwell in love—that is to say, in God. 'God is charity'.[11]

[9] Lev 19:2.
[10] Eph 1:4.
[11] St. John 4:16.

"*Sola Soli*"

"Pray much for me during these ten days, for I trust in your doing so. Indeed, it seems to me quite simple, for God has united our souls so that we should help one another. Has He not said: 'A brother that is helped by his brother is like a strong city'?[12] This is the mission I entrust to you. Monsieur l'Abbé: will you offer for me Saint Paul's fervent prayer for his loved Ephesians?—'that the Father . . . would grant you, according to the riches of His glory, to be strengthened by His Spirit with might unto the inward man, that Christ may dwell by faith in your hearts; that being rooted and founded in charity, you may be able to comprehend, with all the saints, what is the breadth, and length, and height, and depth. To know also the charity of Christ, which surpasseth all knowledge, that you may be filled unto all the fulness of God?'[13]

"'Sanctify the Lord Christ in your hearts'[14] so as to realize what David sang under the influence of the Holy Ghost: 'Upon him shall My sanctification flourish.'"[15]

This retreat might be termed the crown of all the rest.

"God has given me such light on our holy vocation," she said, when giving an account of these days of grace: "I have learned to realize its height and sublimity so deeply, that I beg Him not to let me live long, for it seems so difficult for such a coward as myself to mount so high, and to remain there. He can find many substitutes for the deficiency of the glory His little 'praise' could have rendered Him in this world, and can make a few days equal the long career I might have had. He knows how I love Him and long to suffer for Him."

[12] Prov 18:19.
[13] Eph 3:16-19.
[14] 1 St. Pet 3:15.
[15] Ps 131:18.

The Praise of Glory

After this retreat we could see that she was rapidly approaching the state in which the soul lives for God alone. The young nuns who were her neighbors at recreation said that they could no longer follow her spiritual flight. Truly she dwelt in higher regions, as was evident to all who had to deal with her.

Her inner feelings imparted a striking modesty and dignity to her appearance. A novice who met her in the cloisters, seeing her so deeply absorbed in God, was afraid to ask her for some service that was required.

There was much during the latter part of her life that resembled her postulancy, but her continual progress in recollection and prayer gave this privileged soul a maturity, and a grace for helping others, which raised our highest expectations.

Sister Elizabeth of the Trinity was about to leave the noviceship and to devote herself still more to the community, where her influence would naturally be more widespread.

As we witnessed her treasures of grace, we said to ourselves that God intended either to make her a great saint, or to accomplish His work rapidly. The latter conjecture was soon forced upon us. Our hopes were obliged to concede to her ardent longings. Did the Divine Master give her any secret presentiment of it? While she was preparing the crib at Christmas time, she was heard to say to the Divine Infant: "Ah! My little King of love! We shall see one another nearer next year!" "How do you know that?" her companion asked. She looked at her, gave her usual angelic smile, and spoke no more.

Part III
The Threshold of Eternity

Love has been the beginning and the middle of thy course; it must also be the end. Thou canst not live without it: it is thy life in this world and in the next, for it is I.

Dialogues of Saint Catharine of Genoa.

Chapter Twelve
God Calls *Laudem Gloriæ* to Himself

Saint Joseph, the patron of a happy death — A helpful retreat — Lent and Saint Paul — The Venerable Marguerite of the Blessed Sacrament — Palm Sunday — Self-surrender — A sudden improvement in health — Letters to relatives.

When we drew our patron saint for the year at recreation on New Year's Day, 1906, Saint Joseph fell to the lot of Sister Elizabeth of the Trinity. She was very pleased. "Saint Joseph is the patron of a good death," she said; "he is coming to take me to the Father." No one believed it. Indeed, we smiled at the hope which so delighted her. One of the elder nuns playfully scolded her for expecting eternal rest so soon. Elizabeth made a little sign of conviction, or rather, of intuition.

During the same month she attended with the rest of the community a retreat given by a Jesuit father which strengthened her resolution of uniting her will to that of God, so that she was quite ready to enter the *via dolorosa*, or rather, it was the viaticum in the strength of which she courageously walked forward in the path on which she had already started.

Sister Elizabeth owned, later on, that for some months she had felt an utter weariness beneath which she must have succumbed but for the help of God.

Before leaving the office of portress, she had sometimes found it difficult to walk quickly when she heard herself summoned at some little distance. On one particular occasion, when the bell rang as she was at the foot of the stairs, it cost her a severe effort to mount the first flight; she simply could not get any farther, but, like our first mothers, the generous

The Praise of Glory

young nun drew strength from her infirmities. "I can do all things in Him Who strengtheneth me"[1], she exclaimed, and her body so responded to the fortitude of her soul that no one would have guessed the grave state of affairs. Even those who were most anxious, and with grave reason, about her health, were not yet aware how seriously it had broken down. Sister Elizabeth of the Trinity, fearing lest she might exaggerate her sufferings, minimized her symptoms when she was told to describe them. Everything possible was done to cure her, but, to our great grief, nothing succeeded.

"After saying the Hours in the morning," she owned when speaking of her condition, "I used to feel thoroughly exhausted, and wondered how I should get through the day. My cowardice reached its height after Compline, and I was sometimes tempted to envy a sister who was told to rest from Matins." "Did you not think it a want of simplicity to keep silent about your sufferings?" interrupted the prioress, overcome at what she heard. "The idea of telling you never entered my head, Mother, as your care for me and the exceptions in the Observance you made for me had no effect, I saw clearly that it was the will of God. Besides, I was always afraid of listening to nature, and what more could you have done for me? When you made me rest, it did not refresh me; I was thoroughly broken down, and could find no position that gave me any comfort, nor could I sleep soundly, so that it was a question whether the night or day was the more exhausting.

"Prayer was the best remedy for my ills. I passed the time of 'the great silence' in real agony, which I united to that of my Divine Master, keeping close to Him, pressed against the grille of the choir. It was an hour of unmixed suffering, but it won me strength for Matins, when I had a certain facility for

[1] Phil 4:13.

The Divine Summons

keeping my mind on God. After that, I was as powerless as before, and unseen, thanks to the darkness, crept back to our cell as best I could, often leaning against the wall."

The mother prioress adds: "Sister Elizabeth of the Trinity was moved to tell me some touching details of her life, to which I listened, deeply moved, recalling the words of the apostle: 'Oh, the depths of the divine counsels!' as I wondered at the ways of God with this girl, still so young, yet already perfected in virtue. Quoting Sister Thérèse of the Infant Jesus, she declared that many pages of her history would only be read in heaven; indeed, some of them could not be understood in this world, 'but', she said, 'the mercies of the Lord I will sing forever'[2] as regards His elect, for we shall see, in the light of God, that His will for us was always a will of love."

Alone with the One, our little sister was journeying to her Calvary, anxious to complete her supreme sacrifice. Had she not for a long time been invited to the more intimate union for which that suffering prepares us? Knowing that "there is an interchange of love that takes place on the cross alone", she longed to mount it.

She wrote to her saintly friend in January, 1906: "How strongly one feels the need to sanctify one's soul, and to forget self to forward the interests of the Church. Poor France! I love to cover it with the Blood of the Just One, He Who is 'always living to make intercession for us.'[3] What a sublime mission the Carmelite has! She ought to meditate with Christ, to be another humanity, in which He can perpetuate His life of reparation, sacrifice, praise, and adoration. Pray that I may respond to my vocation, and may not abuse the graces He

[2] Ps 88:1.
[3] Heb 7:25.

The Praise of Glory

showers upon me. What misgivings I feel about it sometimes! Then I cast myself upon Him Whom Saint John calls 'Faithful and True',[4] and beg Him to be answerable for my fidelity."

With such thoughts did she fortify her soul while her body grew visibly weaker. After having spoken of her family, Sister Elizabeth ends her letter with the words: "How full of happiness I felt on returning to our cell after Mass on Christmas night, as, remembering the joys of the past, I said to myself with the apostle: 'For Him I have suffered the loss of all things.'[5] Ask Him to make me self-forgetful, that I may be immersed in God. The Sunday in the Octave of the Epiphany will be the third anniversary of my nuptials with the Lamb, so when you consecrate the Host in which Jesus will become incarnate, will you consecrate your little child to Almighty Love, that He may transform her into the 'Praise of Glory?' . . ."

When Sister Elizabeth of the Trinity heard her young companions make their plans for Lent, she did not feel drawn to contemplate the Savior's Passion. But could she keep to her usual mode of prayer? When she went to her cell after recreation, she questioned Saint Paul, and on opening his epistles haphazard, the first text she lit upon was the passionate cry of the great apostle: "That I may know Him and the fellowship of His sufferings, being made conformable to His death."[6]

She was startled at the words. Was not he, whom in her simplicity she termed the "father of her soul", announcing her speedy deliverance to her? She thought so, and later events soon convinced her that she was called to honor the

[4] Apoc 19:11.
[5] Phil 3:8.
[6] Phil 3:10.

The Divine Summons

sufferings and death of her Divine Master by imitation rather than by devout meditation.

The symptoms of a serious disease of the stomach showed themselves towards the middle of Lent, and a few days after the feast of her holy patron of the year, Sister Elizabeth was installed permanently in the infirmary. "I knew Saint Joseph would come to fetch me this year!" she cried joyfully; "and he is here already!"

Feeling a presentiment that, unless a miracle occurred we should lose the young nun on whom we had built so many hopes, we began a regular crusade of prayers. The process of the beatification of the Venerable Marguerite of the Blessed Sacrament was then being brought forward in Rome.[7] Her special devotions were the Mysteries of the Holy Infancy and the sorrowful Passion of the Son of God, Who called her His "little bride". A striking miracle was required to bring the cause to a successful ending, and we hoped the servant of God would perform it for us, as we recalled the divine favours she had won for the Carmel of Dijon in the old days, when she held her mystic intercourse with the Infant Jesus. One of her relics was worn by our dear little invalid until she died, and we made novena after novena.

But God decreed otherwise, and the "bride of the holy Infant Jesus" leant towards her little sister to lead her on the way of suffering, which was to stamp on Elizabeth, as it had on Marguerite, a resemblance to their crucified God.

We realized it as we watched the progress of the disease, while the dear little nun, knowing that she was loved with an unspeakable love, was overwhelmed with gratitude. "My illness seems to me rather mysterious", she said; "I call it 'love's ailment', since it is He Who is tormenting and wearing

[7] A Carmelite nun of Beaune, 1619-1648.

The Praise of Glory

me away. I give myself up and am resigned to it, for I rejoice beforehand in whatever He will do to me."

Palm Sunday brought her a welcome relief and solace. She had a fainting fit in the evening which so rapidly increased her weakness that we thought it best for her to receive the sacrament of extreme unction. The crisis was past when the priest entered the infirmary. He asked her whether she willingly accepted her sufferings. "Oh, yes!" she answered: "I am glad to suffer." She received the sacrament of extreme unction with touching devotion, as a fresh consecration to suffering of whose "divine dispensation" she was to receive so large a share. How beautiful she looked, as with lustrous eyes, and clasped hands, she held her profession crucifix, exclaiming again and again: "O Love! Love! Love!"[8]

She had the happiness of receiving the Holy Viaticum, a touching coincidence with Saint Teresa's account of how she always prepared herself specially for her communion of Palm Sunday as a tender attention to her Master. The saint grieved at seeing that, though the Jews of Jerusalem strewed palm branches on His path, yet there was not one who offered Him food and shelter for the night. She watched Him on His way to Bethany, and, troubled at the thought of His weariness, she begged Him to stay within her heart and take some rest.[9] Sister Elizabeth, who shared this devotion, had felt very disappointed at not receiving holy communion in the morning, but now she was fully rewarded. At the very hour of the evening in which our Lord had asked His friends at Bethany to compensate for the forgetfulness of His people, He had

---

[8] "How sweet death is in Carmel!" exclaimed the priest as he left the convent. "If I were younger I would become a religious." Our account is supplemented by his letter to Madame Catez, printed at the end of this volume. See Appendix.

[9] Historire de sainte Thérèse d' après les bollandistes, chap. xx. Also Kelation N., Baker., 1911.

The Divine Summons

come to repose in her heart and in her suffering love—in His little house. The happy little nun could not find words to express her bliss next day.

Later on she wrote: "I have been in the infirmary since the end of March, with nothing to do but to love God. A dangerous crisis occurred in my illness on Palm Sunday, and I thought the hour had come for me to enter eternity and contemplate the Blessed Trinity unveiled. I received extreme unction and the visit of my Divine Master in the calm and silence of that night, and it seemed as if He were waiting that moment to break my bonds. The days I spent expecting the great Vision baffle description. Our Reverend Mother kept beside me, preparing me to meet the Bridegroom, and my longing to go to Him made Him seem tardy. How sweet and gentle death is for those who have loved none but Him, and who, as the apostle says, 'look not at the things which are seen . . . for the things which are seen are temporal: but the things which are not seen are eternal!'"[10]

These days which "baffled description" were a real ascent of Mount Calvary for Sister Elizabeth of the Trinity; acute pain, added to her already grave suffering state, gave her more intimate share in the Mystery we were celebrating. Absorbed in the contemplation of "Christ in anguish", she kept herself united to Him as a gentle victim who rejoiced to have been chosen for the sacrifice. Her patience never failed for a moment, and her self-surrender was complete. When she was told that an operation had been decided upon, she said with a quiet smile:

"Yes! An operation—The doctors talk of nothing else; however, they may do what they like with me. I leave myself in their hands as in the hands of God." When a contrary

[10] 2 Cor 4:18.

The Praise of Glory

decision was arrived at a few days later, she accepted it with the same simplicity. Having, as it were, passed from self into God, her peace was truly heavenly.

Her family asked for two consultations during her illness. "While the doctors were deliberating together," she said afterwards, "I united myself to the Divine Master before the tribunals when the judges were debating whether He should live or die."

Her sufferings and exhaustion were so severe that on Good Friday we thought she was dying. Thank God, our fears were not realized! Next night, she felt as if some change was being worked within her, and in the morning she was evidently better. Her infirmarians found her kneeling on her bed, though for the last week she had been incapable of any movement. Sister Elizabeth of the Trinity took a little nourishment, although previously unable to swallow, and, saying that she was cured, she asked to be allowed to go down to the choir for the great Office of Holy Saturday. It would have been impossible for her, yet we hoped soon to see her among us again, and our Alleluias were sung in hearty thanksgiving. Eastertide had never been more joyful for us.

No one had a greater share in our happiness than the poor mother, as she knelt in our chapel and thanked God for having preserved the daughter she thought never to have seen again in this world.

Their last interview before Lent had given her no warning of the severe trial awaiting her. Her loving child had carefully concealed the real state of her health from Madame Catez, who was ill herself and required great care. Lent passed without anyone daring to tell the latter of the rapid progress of the malady, the existence of which she knew nothing. When she was informed of the real state of affairs on the Monday of Holy

The Divine Summons

Week, her faith inspired her with the courage needed to bear the cross imposed upon her, the pain of which was increased by her enforced separation from the child she loved so dearly. The depth of her Christian feeling appeared in her beautiful letter to Sister Elizabeth, who read and re-read it continually, and replied as follows:

"My Dear Mother,

"I never felt so near you. Your letter has been a solace and a joy to me. I have kissed it as a relic, and thanked the good God for having given me such a matchless mother. If I had gone to heaven, how I should have kept beside you! I should never have left you, and should have made you feel that your Elizabeth was close to you.

"As I know you will understand me, I will own to you in confidence what a deep disappointment it was not to go to Him I love so dearly. Think what an Easter Day your daughter would have spent in heaven! . . . But that was self-love, and now I obey and ask to be cured. I do so in union with you, Marguerite, and my dear little angels, whom I should have delighted in protecting had I taken my flight.

"If you only knew how kind our mother is! She is a real mamma to your daughter; and I assure you that, on the night of my crisis, I needed to hear her voice and feel her hand in mine, glad as I was to go to God, for, in spite of that, it is such a solemn moment one feels so little and so empty-handed."

"Canon A— joined us in storming heaven with prayers that the life might be prolonged of the saintly young nun who opened her heart to him in return for his fatherly letter: "I know that I can tell everything to you, who have always been my confidant. My soul is filled with joy at the thought that I shall soon gaze on the unspeakable beauty of Him Whom I love, and shall be immersed in the Blessed Trinity. Oh, how dear it would cost

The Praise of Glory

me to come back to the world which seems so vile to me after my lovely dream! God alone is perfectly pure and holy. Fortunately, we can dwell in Him even in this our earthly exile. However, my Master's pleasure is mine: I yield myself to Him to do as He pleases with me.

"Will you, His priest, consecrate me to Him as a little sacrifice of praise, who desires to glorify Him either in heaven, or in the midst of as much suffering in this world as He chooses. . . . If I go, you will help to free me from Purgatory. How clearly I realize how miserable and stained with sin I am in every way! I need my kind mother to rid myself of it. She comes to make her thanksgiving every morning beside my little bed. I communicate, too, within her soul, and the same love flows into the soul of both mother and daughter.[11] She prays so fervently that I may be cured, that I ask her to let me go and be her guardian angel in heaven. How much I should pray there for you, too; it would delight me to do something for my dear canon!

"Good-bye; it is sweet to wait the coming of the Bridegroom. Pray for me, that I may be completely surrendered to Him in the suffering He sends me, and that, even here, I may live for love alone."

The improvement in Sister Elizabeth's health continued, but as she was still too weak to go to the parlor, she wrote to console her family.

"Dear Mamma,

"Your little invalid wants to speak to you from her heart, that heart so full of tenderness for you.

---

[11] At the beginning of Sister Elizabeth's illness the mother prioress used to come and make her thanksgiving beside the bed of the little invalid, to console her for being deprived of frequent communion. It was a great comfort to the dear child, who used to prepare herself for these morning visits as if she were really about to receive the hidden God Whom she adored within the soul of her mother. She used to call this time the sunshine of her day.

The Divine Summons

"I know that you are ill, and my kind mother inside the convent, who is always near me, tells me all about your health. You cannot imagine what care she lavishes upon me, with all the tenderness and delicacy of a mother. How happy I am alone in my little infirmary! My Master is here with me, and we live heart to heart, day and night. I appreciate the happiness of being a Carmelite more than ever, and I pray to God for the darling mother who gave me to Him. I have been drawn nearer heaven since this illness; I will tell you all about it some day.

"Oh Mother! let us prepare for eternity; let us live with Him, for He alone can accompany and help us on this great journey. He is the God of love; we cannot understand how dearly He loves us—above all, when He sends us trials."

She was afraid to tell all to her mother, who would have been injured by any strong emotion, but spoke unreservedly to her sister.

"I do not know whether the hour has come for me to pass from this world to my Father, for I am much better, and the little saint of Beaune seems to wish to cure me. Yet at times it seems as if the Divine Eagle were about to swoop down upon His little prey and carry it off to where He lives in the realms of dazzling light.

"You have always forgotten your own interests when your Elizabeth's happiness was concerned, and I am sure that if I go, you will rejoice at the thought of my first meeting with Divine Beauty. When the veil falls, how gladly shall I pass to Him, into the very secret of His face! There shall I spend my eternity, in the bosom of the Trinity, where I dwell already in this life.

"Only think, Marguerite, what it will be to contemplate the splendor of the Divine Being in His own light; to penetrate all

The Praise of Glory

the depths of His mystery; to be one with Him we love; to sing unceasingly of His glory and His love; to be 'like Him, because we shall see Him as He is'![12]

"Little sister, I shall rejoice to go to heaven to be your angel there, and I shall be zealous for the beauty of your soul that I love dearly even in this world.

"I leave you my devotion to 'the Three'. Live with Them in the heaven of your soul; the Father will overshadow you, making a cloud between you and the things of this world, to keep you all His own. He will communicate His power to you, so that you will love Him with a love as strong as death. The Word will imprint in your soul, as in a crystal, the image of His own beauty, and you will be pure with His purity, luminous with His light. The Holy Ghost will transform you into a mystic lyre. Beneath His divine touch your silence will send forth a magnificent canticle of love. Then you will be the praise of His glory as I dreamed that I should be in this world. You will take my place. I shall be *Laudem Gloriæ* before the throne of the Lamb, and you will be *Laudem Gloriæ* in the center of your soul. So shall we be united throughout eternity.

"Always keep your faith in the love of God. If you have to suffer, it will be because you are more deeply loved; so whatever happens, love and chant your thanksgiving.

"Teach the little ones to live in the sight of God. I should like Elizabeth to have my devotion to the Holy Trinity. I shall be present at their First Communion, and will help you to prepare them for it.

"You must pray for me. I have offended my Master more than you think. But, above all, thank Him, and say a Gloria every day. Forgive me for the bad example I have often set you.

[12] 1 St. John 3:2.

The Divine Summons

"Farewell! How I love you! Perhaps I shall soon go to the home of love. What does it matter? Let us live in love, and to glorify Love, whether we are in heaven or on earth! . . ."

Sister Elizabeth of the Trinity spoke the truth, the Divine Eagle was about to swoop down upon His prey, to bear it away to the regions of eternal light. Marguerite of the Blessed Sacrament did not finish the work she had begun. She had shown her interest in our cause by dispelling all idea of an operation, but was it not best for our little sister to hasten her flight towards the end for which she longed so fervently?

During May her life was again in danger through a second crisis. "Heaven seemed opened again!" she cried; "and you prayed so ardently that I am still a prisoner, but a happy prisoner who praises the love of her Lord day and night within her heart.

"He is so good! Anyone would suppose that He had no one to love or think about but me, from the way in which He gives Himself to my soul. He does so that I, in my turn, may give myself to Him for His Church and His interests; that I may care for His honor, like my holy mother Saint Teresa.

"Oh, pray for me, that I, too, may be *caritatis victima* !"[13]

---

[13] Hymn for the Office of St. Teresa.

Chapter Thirteen
Transformed into Jesus Christ

The altar of sacrifice — Past and present —Touching interview — Letters — The glories of Carmel — A royal palace.

Sister Elizabeth of the Trinity was indeed a victim of divine love. While we made our novenas, she remained bound upon the altar of sacrifice, fully convinced that our prayers would not wrest her from it. "'I rejoice in my sufferings,' she said with Saint Paul, 'and fill up those things that are wanting of the sufferings of Christ in my flesh.'[1] Yes, I am glad to take part in the work of redemption; I suffer, as it were, a continuation of the Passion—'That I may know Him . . . and the fellowship of His sufferings, being made conformable to His death,'"[2] she repeated incessantly, applying to herself the word of the great apostle which had struck her so forcibly at the beginning of Lent.

We have watched her, since the impression made upon her by her first confession, in her persistent warfare against herself; then, drawn by the Spouse of virgins, giving Him her heart at their first meeting; again, after her vow at the age of 14, withdrawing into herself to realize the gift of God within her; finally, establishing herself, by the light of faith, in union with the Three Divine Persons. Such shall we see her still, in this last phase, as, true to her guiding light, she gazes on the Cross and completes her transformation into Jesus crucified.

"I have never been so happy as since God has deigned to

[1] Col 1:24.
[2] Phil 3:10.

The Praise of Glory

let me share the pangs of the Divine Master", she wrote. In a letter to her mother she says: "You fear that I am destined to be a victim of suffering; I beg you not to grieve over what would be so beautiful a lot. I feel unworthy of it! Think what it would be to take part in the agony of my crucified Bridegroom; to go to my passion with Him; to share His work of redemption! . . ."

The mother prioress, fearing that Sister Elizabeth of the Trinity would never be able to walk again, had her carried into the parlor to console her relatives. The meeting was very touching. Madame Catez could not take her eyes off the emaciated but radiant face of her dearly-loved daughter, who did not conceal her regret at having come back to life. She asked to see her mother and sister separately, urged them to sanctify their souls, and prepared them for the coming sacrifice by leading them to where she dwelt herself—beneath the divine Light which had been the joy, as well as the sanctity, of her career.

The letters, which were often obliged to supply the place of interviews behind the grille, allow us to read Sister Elizabeth's soul during the last stages of her illness.

"What a consolation it is to be able to open my soul to my mother, and to feel that hers is at one with mine!" she wrote, after seeing her in the parlor. "I feel as if my love for you were not only that of a child for the best of mothers, but that of a mother for a child as well. I am the little mother of your soul. You consent, do you not? We are going into retreat for Pentecost—I into a more thorough retreat than the rest, alone as I am in my little cenacle. I am asking the Holy Ghost to reveal to you the presence of God within you of which I spoke. You may believe what I said, for it is not my own idea. If you read the Gospel of Saint John you will see

Transformed into Jesus Christ

that the Divine Master constantly insists upon this commandment: 'Abide in Me, and I in you.'[3] And again: 'If anyone love Me . . . My Father will love him, and We will make Our abode with him.'[4]

"Saint John, in his epistles, hopes that we shall have 'fellowship' with the Blessed Trinity: what a sweet and simple term to use! Saint Paul says that to believe is sufficient. 'God is a Spirit'[5] and it is by faith that we approach Him. Realize that your soul is 'the temple of God', as Saint Paul teaches: the Three Divine Persons dwell within it during every instant of the day and night. You do not possess the Sacred Humanity except when you receive holy communion, but the Divinity, the Essence which the blessed adore in heaven, resides within your soul. When once we realize this, a most delightful intimacy is established, and we are never again alone."

Madame Catez, who was going to Paris to be present at the ceremonies following the beatification of the sixteen Martyrs of Compiègne, received the following lines:

"Your Carmelite's soul will take part with your own in the triduum of our blessed Martyrs. What a joy it would be to your daughter if she too could offer God the witness of her blood! Then it would be worthwhile to have stayed on earth and seen her dream of heaven fade away! But what I want of Him above all things is the martyrdom of love which consumed my holy mother Teresa, and since Truth Himself has declared that the greatest proof of love is to give our life for Him we love, I give Him mine, which has long been His, that He may do as He wills with it. If I am not a martyr of blood, I wish to be a martyr of love. Dear Mother, let us love God,

---

[3] St. John 15:4.
[4] St. John 14:23.
[5] St. John 4:24.

The Praise of Glory

and live with Him as with one we love, from whom we cannot be separated. Tell me if you are becoming more recollected, for I care immensely for your soul. Remember the words of the Gospel: 'The kingdom of God is within you.'[6] Enter this little kingdom to adore the Monarch Who resides in it as in His own palace. He has such love for us! He has given you many a proof of it by asking you often, on your path of life, to help Him bear His cross.

"P.S.—Do not forget to pray while you are in the train on Thursday. I remember that it is a very good time for prayer."

"You must erase the word 'discouragement' from your dictionary of love", she wrote to her sister. "The greater your weakness and difficulty in recollecting yourself and the more our Lord seems hidden, the more joyful you ought to be, for then you are giving to Him, and when we love, is it not better to give than to receive?

"God said to Saint Paul: 'My grace is sufficient for thee, for power is made perfect in infirmity.'[7] The great saint had mastered that truth, for he says: 'Gladly, therefore, will I glory in my infirmities, that the power of Christ may dwell in me.'[8]

"What does it matter what we feel? It is He Who is unchangeable; He loves you today as He loved you yesterday and will love you tomorrow, even if you have grieved Him. Remember, 'deep calleth on deep'![9]

"The abyss of your misery attracts the abyss of His mercy. God has made me understand this truth, and we must share it between us. He has also drawn me strongly to suffering and to self-surrender; is not that the crowning-point

---

[6] St. Luke 17:21.
[7] 2 Cor 2:9.
[8] *Ibid.*
[9] Ps 41:8.

of love? Let us lose no sacrifice; there are so many we can make in the day. You have many opportunities with the babies. Oh! Give them all to the good Master! Do you not find that affliction binds us more closely to Him? So, if He takes away your sister, it will be to give Himself more to you. Help me to prepare for eternity: I do not think my life will last much longer. You love me well enough to be glad that I am going to rest where I have lived so long. I like to tell you these things, 'little echo of my soul'. I am selfish, for perhaps I shall grieve you, yet I want to lift you above all that can die. . . into the bosom of infinite Love. That is the fatherland of the two little sisters: there they will meet to part no more.

"Oh, Marguerite! As I write to you this evening my heart is overflowing; I feel the 'exceeding charity' of my Master, and I wish I could put my soul within your own, that you might always believe in this charity—above all, in your hours of deepest trial. When you wake in the night, unite yourself to your Elizabeth. I should like to ask you to come to me here; there is such silence and mystery about this little cell, with its white walls on which hangs the bare cross of black wood. It is mine, the cross on which I ought to immolate myself each moment so as to resemble my crucified Bridegroom! I am the good God's little recluse; I love solitude with 'the One', and lead a delightful hermit's life. I, too, am often incapable of doing what I wish; I need to seek my Master Who hides carefully from me. Then I arouse my faith, and am content to relinquish the joy of His presence to give Him the joy of my love.

"I have been thinking of the Feast of Saint Margaret for a long while, and I shall try to do more for you than anyone does, for I shall give you nothing perishable, but what is divine and eternal. I am preparing for the day by a great

The Praise of Glory

novena. Every morning I say Sext for you, which is the hour consecrated to the Word, in order that He may so stamp His likeness in your soul that you may be another Christ. Then I give you None, which I dedicate to the Father, that He may own you as His beloved daughter; that with the 'might of His arm'[10] He may lead you in all your ways, and may turn your steps more fully towards that abyss wherein He dwells, in which He wishes to be hidden with you.

"Farewell! May the 'Three' bless my three little offerings, and make their heaven and the place of their rest within each of them! O Abyss! O Love! This is our chant on our lyres as being the praise of glory, and this shall finish my letter."

"June, 1906

"It is I, myself, who am telling my dearest mother that her little invalid still feels better. She has more strength for sitting up in bed, her head is fairly strong, but her legs will not support her, otherwise I think she would be able to do something for herself. Her infirmarians eagerly supply all her wants most charitably and affectionately.

"Our mother gave me the great pleasure today of hearing Mass from the tribune and of spending a full hour afterward before the Blessed Sacrament. I was nearly on a level with Him, like a queen at the right hand of her spouse.

"I spent a great part of yesterday on the terrace. As it is near the choir I could hear Benediction. Our mother herself led me there. I tell her sometimes that she takes so much care of me that she stops my going to heaven.

"Your letter was very interesting. How beautiful the ceremonies of our blessed martyrs must have been, and how thankful you ought to be to the good God for having led me to

[10] Ps 88:14.

Transformed into Jesus Christ

the Mountain of Carmel, an order made illustrious by so many saints and martyrs!"

How she loved her order! She felt a holy pride in belonging to it, and was delighted when a vocation commended to her prayers was fulfilled, as the following letter to a Carmelite novice shows.

"I thank Him, Who has willed to unite us so closely in Himself, for having 'exalted you with His right hand',[11] and led you to Mount Carmel, which is lighted with the rays of the Sun of Justice. There, in the track of our holy mother Teresa and all the saints of our order, our two souls, called by the Master to Himself, ought to be transformed into the 'praise of glory' of which Saint Paul speaks.

'With zeal have I been zealous for the Lord God of Hosts!'[12] This device of all our saints made our holy mother a 'victim of charity', as we sing in her beautiful Office. It seems as if the good God were leaving me on earth that I, too, may be a victim of love, zealous for His honor. Will you obtain grace for your sister to fulfil this divine plan; she, like you, longs to become a saint, that she may give glory to her adored Master.

"Saint Paul, whose magnificent epistles I read constantly, says that God 'chose us in Him before the foundation of the world, that we should be holy and unspotted in His sight in charity'.[13] Has not Elias, who exclaimed in the fervor of his faith: 'As the Lord liveth, the God of Israel, in Whose sight I stand!'[14] left this living in the Divine presence as the heritage of the children of Carmel? If you are willing, our souls, traversing space, will meet together to sing this great war cry of our father's. We will ask him on his feast-day for the gift of

---

[11] Ps 117:16.
[12] 3 Kings 19:10.
[13] Eph 1:4.
[14] 3 Kings 17:1.

prayer, which is the essence of the Carmelite life—the 'heart to heart' which never ceases, because, when we love, we are no longer our own, but are given to the Beloved, in Whom we live more than in ourselves.

"Our holy father, Saint John of the Cross, has written divinely on this subject in his *Spiritual Canticle* and *Flame of Divine Love*. I delight in the solid teaching of his books.

"It is good news that you are to enter the novitiate, and I beg the Queen of Carmel to give you the double spirit of our dear and holy order: the spirit of prayer and penance, for complete self-sacrifice and immolation are needed in order to live in continual contact with God. Like the saints, let us long for suffering and, above all, let us prove our love for God by our fidelity to our holy rule, cherishing a sacred passion for it; and if we keep it, we shall be kept by it, and it will make us saints—that is, such souls as our seraphic mother desired—who serve God and His Church"

Sister Elizabeth of the Trinity fed her faith continually on the writings of Saint Paul, so that even during the doctor's visits, which were frequent towards the end of her life, she managed to introduce the subject of the great apostle. The doctor, surprised at her remarks, used to ask as he entered the infirmary: "Well, Sister, what does Saint Paul say today?" "She is wonderful!" he said on leaving. "What intelligence and poetry!" His admiration was particularly excited by the heroic courage with which so young a nun bore sufferings whose intensity he realized better than anyone else. "I never saw such fortitude and serenity in suffering; she is enduring a veritable martyrdom", he remarked later on.

Her ideal for which she had so generously striven sustained her in this martyrdom. "I want to reach heaven not only with the purity of an angel," she confided to the mother

Transformed into Jesus Christ

sub-prioress, "but transformed into Jesus crucified. Suffering has a growing attraction for me; the desire of it almost overmastered the Lord of Heaven, strong as He is."

She wrote to one who could understand her feelings: "David said of Jesus, 'His sorrow is immense.' I have made my home in this immensity—the royal palace in which I dwell with my crucified Spouse.[15] I choose it for a trysting-place with you, who appreciate the happiness of suffering and know how to look on it as a revelation of 'exceeding charity'. Oh, how I love it! It has become my peace, my repose. Pray God to increase my capacity for pain."

She wrote to her mother: "The good God takes pleasure in immolating His little victim (*hostie*),[16] but the Mass He is saying with me, of which His love is the priest, may last

[15] One day Sister Elizabeth put in the prioress's cell a little card with a picture of a fortress with a drawbridge. Near the closed door was pasted a print of our Lady of Lourdes as *Janua Cœli*. We shall see later on the reason for this name. From one corner of the embattled tower floated a small flag with the device: "Fortress of pain and holy recollection, the dwelling of *Laudem Gloriæ* while awaiting her entrance into her Father's house." Beneath the drawbridge were written the following lines:

> "Where shall we find the Master?" wrote a saint.
> Where is His home, save in the midst of pain?
> There would I dwell, my mother and my priest,
> To magnify the Cross where He was slain.
>
> But yet I need thee, 'neath thy shelt'ring wing
> To enter this fair palace of my Lord,
> This fortress, the strong citadel of God,
> Which to the soul doth changeless peace afford.
>
> David hath sung: "Christ's sorrow is immense!
> In this immensity my home I make,
> In sacred silence, self I immolate,
> Transformed into love's victim for His sake.

[16] Here, as elsewhere, the word "*hostie*" is used, which in French signifies the Sacred Host in the Mass as well as an ordinary victim. The word "victim" or "sacrifice" does not render the meaning of this passage in the original.

-Translator.

The Praise of Glory

some time longer. The victim (*hostie*) does not find it long in the hands of Him Who sacrifices her. She can say that, though she treads the track of suffering, she is the more set upon the road of happiness, of truth, of Him Whom no one can take from her, dearest Mother. Your motherly heart ought to leap for joy at the thought that the Master has deigned to choose your daughter, your own child, to aid Him in His great work of redemption; that He has signed her with the seal of the Cross, and suffers in her as an extension of His Passion. The bride belongs to the Bridegroom; mine has taken me for His own. He wishes me to be a second humanity in which He can suffer still more for His Father's glory and to succour the needs of His Church. The thought consoles me greatly. Our mother often speaks of it to me; I shut my eyes and listen, and, forgetting that it is she, feel as though the Master were beside me, encouraging and teaching me how to bear His Cross.

"This kind mother, so eloquent about self-sacrifice, thinks of nothing but relieving my pain, as I often say to her; however, I submit to it like a child. Our Lord told Saint Teresa that He preferred her obedience to the penances of another saint, so I take Marguerite's little dainties when my stomach allows me, and they relieve it more than anything else.

"I kiss my Master's Cross at each fresh pang, saying: 'I thank Thee, but I am not worthy of it', remembering that suffering was the comrade of His life, and that I do not deserve that His Father should treat me as He treated His Son.

"A saint, writing of Jesus, said: 'Where did He dwell,

---

[17] Sister Elizabeth's soul was wounded afresh with love by this saying of Saint Angela of Foligno's. I never went near her without repeating it, knowing that it would delight her. Then she used to speak to me in feeling accents of the Savior's Passion, and of her joy at dwelling with Him through suffering.

-Note by Author.

save in anguish?'[17] Every soul that is bruised by affliction of whatever kind can exclaim to itself: 'I dwell with Jesus; we live in intimacy, sheltered within the same home.'

"The saint of whom I speak teaches us that the sign which proves that God dwells in us and that we are possessed by His love is that we take what hurts us not only patiently, but gratefully. To reach this state we must long and lovingly contemplate Christ crucified; this contemplation, if genuine, must infallibly lead us to a love of suffering.

"Dear Mother, view every trial and contradiction you meet with in the light that shines from the Cross; thus you will please God and grow in love. Oh, thank Him for me! I am so happy! I wish I could shed some of my happiness on those I love!

"Adieu! I cannot hold my pencil any longer, but my heart remains with you. I appoint the shadow of the Cross as our trysting-place, there to learn the science of suffering.

"Your happy daughter,

"'Elizabeth of the Trinity'"

Chapter Fourteen
Close to the Sanctuary

The "Angel of Lisieux" — A night of grace — The Queen of Virgins and Martyrs — *Janua Cœli* — The little tribune — August 2, 1906 — Last retreat.

Sister Elizabeth had expressed her regret at returning to life. Her longing aspirations were unfavorable to our efforts, and heaven seemed to side with her. The mother prioress tried to make her wish to be cured by persuading her that her zealous work for the community would be a proof of gratitude for the graces received in religion. Sister Elizabeth accepted this view, which struck a tender chord in her sensitive heart. But one day, while repeating to her Divine Master the obedience she had received, she thought she heard, in the center of her soul, the words: "Earthly offices are no longer for you", which filled her with peace and joy. Her thirst for eternity so increased that she asked her prioress for leave to yield entirely to it, and to stop the prayers which opposed her hopes and deferred her happiness. They were no longer mentioned in her presence, but suspecting that we were continuing them secretly, she had recourse to the "Angel of Lisieux", for Sister Thérèse of the Infant Jesus had been homesick for heaven, and would understand her trouble and show her pity. With full confidence in Sister Thérèse, our little sister asked her, as a guarantee against her fears, that she might be able to walk. Her prayer was granted, to her great joy, and she felt certain she would not recover.

"My stomach is still refractory," she wrote to her mother;

The Praise of Glory

"but only think, I am beginning to walk! I cannot understand it, for I am no stronger than when I could not even sit up.

"The other day, when our mother came to see me, I felt so exhausted that I told her I was going. 'It would be much better if you would try to walk instead of talking like that', she answered. I love to obey her, so when I was alone, I tried to walk by the side of the bed, but it hurt me dreadfully. After asking Sister Thérèse of the Infant Jesus not to cure me, but to give me the use of my legs, I was able to walk. I am like an old woman doubled up over her stick. Our mother takes me on her arm to the terrace.[1] I am quite proud of my journeys, and am longing to show you how I make them; I am sure you would laugh, for they are very comic. I am very glad to tell you the good news, as I know it will please you.

"Do not grieve about your Elizabeth; the good God will leave her here with you a little longer, and when she is in heaven she will watch constantly over her mother, the kind mother she loves more dearly every day. Oh, darling Mother, let us look above! It rests the soul to think that heaven is our Father's house; that we are expected there as if we were dearly loved children returning home after exile, and that He makes Himself our travelling companion to lead us there."

We never cross that little terrace without picturing Sister Elizabeth of the Trinity as she sat there, especially in the early morning, when she came to refresh her poor head, worn out by sleeplessness. She had hardly reached her armchair and thanked her dear infirmarian with a smile, when her eyes closed, and she seemed lost to all around her. "*Laudem Gloriæ* is absorbed in contemplation again", we said to ourselves; indeed, she had not been distracted from it even

---

[1] A passage open to the air, connecting the two wings of the convent, which is used as a promenade by the sick.

Close to the Sanctuary

during the night. She kept her breviary beside her so as to join in the recitation of the Little Hours. She held in her arms a statuette of our Lady from which she had never parted since a certain night when, during her divine colloquies, she happened to glance at a picture on the wall which represented the Mother of Sorrows. Touched at the sight, she felt conscious of an affectionate reproach and a tender, maternal urging to ask more of a mother's love. She owned to having thought less frequently of the Blessed Virgin for some time past, but since then her devotion to the Mother of heaven had redoubled. She asked her mother to give her a statuette of our Lady of Lourdes, from which she remembered having received many favours as a young girl, so that she who had "kept" her "coming in" might also "keep" her "going out".[2] From that time she always called our Lady, *Janua Cœli*.

After this nocturnal visit the invalid wrote: "The Queen of Virgins is the Queen of Martyrs too; but the sword transpierced her heart, for with her all passed within her soul.

"Oh, how beautiful she is in her long martyrdom! How majestic in her strength and sweetness! It is because she learned from the Word Himself how those whom the Father selects as victims, those whom He chooses as associates in the great work of the Redemption, ought to suffer.

"She is there, at the foot of the Cross, standing, strong and valiant, and my Master says to me, '*Ecce Mater tua*'.[3] He has given her to me for my Mother. And now that He has returned to the Father, and has put me in His place on the Cross, our Lady is there to teach me to suffer as He suffered.

"When I have said my '*Consummatum est*', it will be she, *Janua Cœli*, who will introduce me into the eternal courts,

[2] Ps 120:8.
[3] St. John 19:27.

The Praise of Glory

whispering to me the mysterious words: '*Laetatus sum in his quae dicta sunt mihi, in domum Domini ibimus*'.[4]" Meanwhile, Sister Elizabeth of the Trinity entrusted the Queen of Angels with the custody of the entrance to her heart, which was already heaven on earth.

"Today I gave you with all my heart to our Lady", she wrote to her sister on the Feast of Mount Carmel: "I never was so fond of you before. I weep for joy at remembering that the Blessed Virgin, full of peace and light as she is, is my Mother. I delight in her beauty, being her child, and feel a daughter's pride in it. I am strongly attracted to her, and have made her queen and guardian of my heaven and of yours, too, for I do everything for both of us together."

Janua Cœli became the "wall and the bulwark" of Sister Elizabeth of the Trinity's favorite sanctuaries, so that we often found the little statuette on the threshold of a small tribune which overlooked the chapel. We knew when we saw the figure of the Immaculate Conception that our little sister must be near.

"I make long visits to my Master several times a day," she wrote to her mother, "and thank Him for enabling me to walk to Him. What a joy it is to me!"

It was indeed a great consolation to her to be able to reach the infirmary tribune. How often mother prioress found her there, bent double with pain! One day, when it was too dark to see her, the prioress called her by her favorite name, *Laudem Gloriæ*. The poor child, who was huddled together with suffering, tried to sit up, and with tearful eyes but smiling face answered: "I came to take refuge in my Master's prayer, for I need His divine strength; I am suffering so intensely."

[4] Ps 121:1. This letter is an extract from the short retreat mentioned later on.

Close to the Sanctuary

The same thing often happened. "I met her one day on the landing of the infirmary, looking like a ghost", relates one of the nuns. "I asked her for some information, which she gave with her usual sweetness, as if she were quite well. I heard afterwards that she was on her way to the tribune to seek for strength to endure an almost unbearable attack.

"I often looked up at the tribune on passing it, but it seemed empty. Unless quite close to it, our dear little sister, crouched on the ground in a dark corner, could not be seen. She seemed to me a personification of prayer and pain."

The state of the little invalid grew worse; she found more difficulty every day in taking any food. Through incessant headache and sleepless nights she kept up her courage by continual prayer.

"Your dear letter gave me very great pleasure", she wrote to her venerable friend. "I like the thought of Saint Paul you sent me. I think it is realized in me, on this little bed, the altar on which I immolate myself to Love. Pray that my likeness to the adored Image may be more perfect every day. The thought haunts me and brings strength to my soul in suffering. You have no idea how I feel the work of destruction being carried out throughout my whole being! It is the road to Calvary set before me, on which I walk joyfully, like a bride, by the side of the crucified God.

"I shall be 26 on the eighteenth of this month. I do not know whether I am to end this year in time or in eternity. I beg you again, as a child does its father, to consecrate me at Holy Mass as a sacrifice of praise to the glory of God. Oh, consecrate me so thoroughly that I may be no more myself but Him, Jesus! and that the Father may recognize Him when He looks at me. May I be 'made conformable to His death,'[5] and

---
[5] Phil. 3:10.

suffer what is wanting in His Passion! Then bathe me in the Blood of Christ, that I may be strong with His strength. I feel so insignificant, so weak!

"Farewell, dear Canon A——, I ask you to bless me in the name of the Holy Trinity, to Whom I am specially dedicated. Will you also consecrate me to the Blessed Virgin? It was she, Mary Immaculate, who gave me the habit of Carmel, and I beg her to clothe me with the robe of 'fine linen',[6] which the bride puts on to go to the Supper of the Lamb.

"P.S.—On August 2 I shall have spent five years in the religious life."

On that day, August 2, she wrote the following lines to the Reverend Father V——:

"Dear Reverend Father,

"I think that next year I shall keep your feast and Saint Dominic's in the 'kingdom of the saints, in light'. This year I retire again into the center of my soul to keep your feast there, and I want to tell you so. I also want to ask you, Reverend Father, to pray for me that I may be faithful and may climb my Calvary in a way worthy of the bride of Christ 'For whom He foreknew, He also predestinated to be made conformable to the image of His Son.'[7] How I love this saying of the great Saint Paul! It brings peace to my soul. I think that, in His 'exceeding charity', He has 'foreknown', 'called', and 'justified'[8] me, and while waiting for Him to 'glorify' me,[9] I wish to be the continual 'praise of His glory'. Father, ask this of Him for your little daughter. Do you remember? Five years ago today I knocked at the door of Carmel, and you

[6] Apoc. 19:8.
[7] Rom 8:29.
[8] *Ibid.*, 29, 30.
[9] *Ibid.*, 30.

Close to the Sanctuary

were there to bless my entrance into solitude. Now I am knocking at the 'eternal gates',[10] and I ask you to bend down again and bless my soul on the threshold of my Father's house. When I am in the great furnace of love, in the bosom of the 'Three' to Whom you guided me, I shall not forget all you have done for me, and in my turn I long to give you to my Father, from Whom I have received so much. May I venture to tell you what I wish? I should be so glad to receive a few lines from you, showing me how to realize the divine plan for me, and to be conformed to Christ crucified.

"Good-bye, Reverend Father. I beg you to bless me in the Name of the 'Three', and to consecrate me to Them as a little 'Praise of glory'."

August 2

"Dear Mother,

"Do you remember this day five years ago? I remember it and so does He! He has gathered up the blood of your heart in a chalice which will weigh heavy in the balance of His mercy!

"Yesterday I was recalling our last evening together, and how, as I could not sleep, I took my place by the window and remained there until nearly midnight in prayer with my Master. Last night was heavenly. The sky was so blue and calm, the convent in utter silence . . . and I thought over these five years so filled with graces. Dear Mother, never regret the joy you have given me. Thanks to your *fiat*, I was able to enter this home of sanctity and, alone with God, I have enjoyed a foretaste of the heaven to which all my soul is drawn.

"Tonight I have made a second offering of your sacrifice of five years ago, that it may rain blessings upon her who is dearest to me. Live with Him. Ah! How I wish I could make

[10] Ps 23:7.

The Praise of Glory

known to every soul what a source of strength, of peace, and of happiness, as well, they would discover did they only consent to live in this intimacy. But they will not wait. If God does not give Himself to them in a way that they can feel, they leave His sacred presence, and when He comes laden with gifts, He finds no one; the soul has gone out to exterior things and does not dwell within itself. Recollect yourself from time to time, dear Mother, then you will be quite close to your Elizabeth . . . ."

Our little invalid felt that her end was near, and prepared her poor mother, who was also seriously ill, for the great sacrifice.

"Dear Mother,
"How well it is to speak of Him, and to rise above all that is passing and that will come to an end, especially suffering and separation . . . to rise to where all is everlasting! How it consoles your Elizabeth to be able to talk to you of her plans for eternity! Do not forget that you promised, at the Elevation during holy Mass, to stand at the foot of the Cross with our Lady, that you may each offer God your child together!

"How much we need trials to do the work of God within our soul! The good God has an immense desire to enrich us with His graces but we regulate their measure, which is in proportion to our submission to His immolation of us—a joyful immolation, and a thankful one, like that of Jesus, in which we say with Him: 'The chalice which my Father hath given Me, shall I not drink it?'[11] The Divine Master called the hour of the Passion 'the cause for which He had come'[12] and for which He had longed. When some great suffering or

---
[11] St. John 18:11.
[12] *Ibid.* 12:27.

Close to the Sanctuary

insignificant sacrifice offers itself, let us think at once that this is our hour, the hour in which we are to prove our love for Him Who has loved us with an 'exceeding charity'. Glean them all, darling Mother; offer a large sheaf, by never losing the smallest sacrifice. Your offerings will each be a ruby in the splendid crown your God is preparing for you in heaven. I shall go and help Him to make your diadem, and shall come with Him, on the day of our great meeting, to place it on the head of my dearest mother.

"Adieu! Let us love Him in very truth. We must draw courage from our union with Him. The soul that dwells in His presence is clothed with His strength, valiant in suffering."

At this time Sister Elizabeth of the Trinity was fascinated by the beauty of some of the finest passages of the Apocalypse, which brought before her visions of eternity that drew her towards the heights where the Spirit and the bride beckon one another. Feeling the need of more complete solitude, she asked permission to make a retreat which she began on August 15, as a preparation for her eternal retreat. She announced the good news to one of her sisters in the following terms:

"*Janua Cœli, ora pro nobis*!

"*Laudem Gloriæ* enters her novitiate of heaven this evening in preparation for her clothing with the habit of glory, and is anxious to recommend herself to the prayers of Sister A—. I want to learn to identify, to conform myself with my adored Master, Who was crucified by love. Then I shall be able to fulfil my office of 'praise of His glory' and sing the eternal *Sanctus* here while waiting my entrance to chant it with the choir of heaven. Sister, let us fix our eyes on our Master so that the simple, loving gaze of faith may separate us from all else, and may set a cloud between us and the things of this world. Our inner being is too richly

The Praise of Glory

endowed to be possessed by any creature. Let us keep all for Him and sing to our lyre with David: 'I will keep my strength to Thee.'"[13]

During these days of blessings Sister Elizabeth was drawn to Calvary. Her loved Master spoke to her, not in words, but by giving her fresh light regarding the love hidden in the cross. He showed her that her dreams of union would find their realization in suffering. The generous young nun, more inflamed with love than ever, was intoxicated with the divine chalice whose bitterness was changed for her into unspeakable sweetness. She finished her retreat on the Feast of the Dedication of Churches of the Order, August 31. Sister Elizabeth, "House of God", had a special devotion for Feasts of the Dedication; she renewed her consecration to the Three Divine Persons, and her love and zeal for their glory.

A special grace had been reserved for this last Dedication.

On the Feast of the Ascension, as the mother prioress, whose morning visit to the infirmary had been delayed, was explaining the matter to the invalid, she noticed that her face was transfigured with joy.

"Oh, Mother!" answered the little nun, "never mind about me. The good God has granted me such a favor that I have lost all idea of time. Early this morning I heard within the depths of my soul the sentence: 'If anyone love Me . . . My Father will love him, and We will come to him, and will make Our abode with him,' [14] and at the same instant I realized its truth. I could not tell you how the Three Divine Persons revealed Themselves, but I saw Them, holding Their counsel of love within me, and I seem to see Them still. Oh! How great God is, and how He loves us!"

---

[13] Ps 58:10.
[14] St. John 14:23.

Close to the Sanctuary

"Until that time," adds the mother prioress, "Sister Elizabeth had hoped that our visits would not be postponed; now she said to me: 'Do not feel anxious any longer about disappointing me. When you cannot come, you will know that I am with my Divine Guests. I cannot and ought not to care for anything else except to live in intimacy with Them. I feel so clearly that They are there', she said, clasping her hands above her heart.

"Henceforth, whenever I recommended any particular intention to her, she used to answer: 'I will speak to my Almighty Counsellor', as, after the Feast of the Ascension, she called the Three Divine Persons."

This intimate manifestation of the Holy Trinity crowned her life of persevering recollection with the grace of the Mystery which she ceaselessly adored within herself, in that center of our being where Saint John of the Cross shows It hidden, but carrying on Its divine operation. This seems to have been the supreme dedication of this little "tabernacle", whose translation into the eternal Temple was soon to take place; so that the Feast of August 3, 1906, was, above all, a feast of thanksgiving.

As this would be the last retreat of the daughter she so dearly loved, the mother prioress said she would like her to note down any striking thought that occurred to her. Sister Elizabeth would have found it difficult to describe the graces received by her from God in the simple, yet profound manner of which we have spoken. She guessed what her mother wanted, and left her this keepsake of her prized solitude. "The last retreat of *Laudem Gloriæ*", she said, as she gave the prioress, on a certain anniversary, the manuscript prepared with the delicate instinct of a daughter's heart.

At a first glance, the pages, written during a course of

The Praise of Glory

exhausting and sleepless nights and such torturing pain that the poor child felt faint with agony, seem only simple notes on what she read in the Holy Scriptures, with her personal reflections on them; but they are more than that. Sister Elizabeth told the mother prioress one day that she had striven in this little manuscript to explain how she understood her office of "praise of glory", and realized that while on earth we can live the life of heaven. This is the leading idea of her retreat as it was of her life. While scanning its pages we seem to read the predestined soul, which might have called them: "Reminiscences of a Soul" (*Souvenirs intimes*).

Chapter Fifteen
Joy in Sacrifice

Nocturnal Lauds — The school of the saints — Confidential letters — Strong advice — Thirst for self-abasement — Humiliations — A characteristic letter — Life echoed in a letter.

The spirit of praise which penetrated Sister Elizabeth of the Trinity made the office of Lauds her especial favorite. When deprived of her much-needed sleep, she passed the first hours of the night near her little window, where, with eyes gazing into the starry sky, her soul mounted with the sacred canticles into the presence of the "Three". When autumn began with its chilly evenings she was obliged to give up her long vigils, yet she used to rise for this part of the Divine Office until the last week of her life. She declared that it soothed her and brought speedy sleep. She evidently intended to give God all she could "extract" from her exhausted frame. "My Master makes me feel that He is pleased with my nightly Lauds, which encourages me to continue them as long as possible", she said. Everything in her beautiful soul was regulated by faith and charity, whose light made her value the most insignificant daily duties. She owned one day that the only thing that reconciled her to the thought of being cured was her resolution of making her self-oblation more entire by keeping the most minute details of our holy Rule. The sincerity of her determination was shown during her last two months of exile by her growing eagerness to keep every observance that she possibly could.

The Praise of Glory

In spite of her declining strength, Sister Elizabeth of the Trinity punctually followed the services in choir from the infirmary tribune. One night, when suffering more than usual and thoroughly exhausted, she "felt tempted" to go back to bed. When told that she should have done so, and there joined the prayers of the community, she replied in impressive tones: "I thought it would be cowardly, Mother, so I left my armchair and knelt to pray with stronger faith on account of my lack of courage. My Master strengthened me so divinely that I never found it easier to put off resting until after Compline." She belonged, indeed, to the school of the saints, who seek strength and rest in prolonged sacrifice and suffering.

When anyone tried to ease her pain, she used to say: "It is not worthwhile; my days are almost over. God has taught me that, as I shall soon see Him face to face, *Laudem Gloriæ*, far from resting, ought to extract from herself all possible prayer and suffering."

In such a frame of mind she found fresh joy in every new occasion of self-immolation. The doctors tried the stomach-pump, which, as her state of utter exhaustion reacted on her nerves, was veritable torture to her. "I have often prayed for martyrdom," she said; "I can no longer hope for it, but at least I prepare myself in that spirit for these painful operations." She fortified herself against her natural dread by kissing her crucifix, and then submitted calmly and peacefully.

When asked how she had passed the night, she used to answer simply, "As a sick person does", and at once began to inquire about the other invalid nuns, or to speak of God. Yet her infirmarian used to take her prioress such notes as the following:

Joy in Sacrifice

"Eleven o'clock
[From the Palace of Pain and Bliss]

"Mother,

"Your little 'Praise of glory' suffers. I cannot sleep, yet how calm my soul feels, in spite of my anguish! Your visit brought me this heavenly peace. I long to tell you so, and pray for you incessantly in gratitude. Oh, help me to climb my Calvary! I feel the power of your priesthood over my soul so strongly, and have such need of you! Mother, I feel my 'Three' so close to me that I am more overcome by happiness than by pain. My Master has reminded me that pain is my dwelling place, that it is not for me to choose my sufferings. I plunge with Him into immense suffering. . . ."

"September 30

"My Darling Mother,

"Your little 'Praise of glory' is suffering very, very much; it is the 'exceeding charity', the divine dispensation of pain. I think that from now to the ninth I have just time to make a novena of suffering for you with my Master. Will you be willing to accept it to gratify my love? I have fled for refuge to my Jesus's prayer, and confide in His omnipotence."

"I feel that my will is developed and strengthened by suffering", she said, in giving an account of her inner life. "Sometimes I used to hesitate before doing what was more perfect lest it might annoy any of my sisters. Now such fears are powerless to stop me; I am ready to pass through fire to perform the will of God more perfectly."

All her words and writings reveal this virile courage. Formerly she drew souls to recollection; now her influence led them to practice the most heroic virtues. "When you are

The Praise of Glory

blamed," she said to a novice who questioned her, "you should not only submit, but be glad, and say 'Thank you'." To another: "We must accept our difficulties rather than wish to be freed from them; accepting them frees us. In the same way we must be willing to undergo the consequences of our faults or faithlessness as being due to God, Who will know how to derive from them glory to Himself and profit to us . . . ." To another sister she said: "How we deceive ourselves regarding genuine union with God! Souls that think they have reached it because they enjoy sensible consolations are like children playing with ashes that the wind carries away. No, no! True union does not consist in delights, but in privation and pain."

"You know how I love my vocation, my Carmel", she said one day to the mother sub-prioress. "Well, I so long for abjection that, if our mother told me I was unworthy to wear the holy habit, unworthy of being a Carmelite, and drove me away, I believe I should be overwhelmed with joy at being treated as I deserve."

"Oh I if you only knew what heavenly days I spend!" she wrote to a friend. "I am growing weaker, and I feel that it will not be long before the Divine Master comes to fetch me. I know and experience joys hitherto unknown to me. How sweet and soothing are the joys of suffering! I hope that before I die, I shall be transformed into Jesus crucified, and the thought brings me strength in my pain. Our sole ideal should be to conform ourselves to this Divine Model. What fervor we should bring to our self-sacrifice and self-contempt, were our eyes always turned on Him! Jesus Christ dwelt in sorrow during the 33 years He passed on earth, and He shares His lot only with privileged souls. What inexpressible joy it is to think that the Father has predestinated me 'to be made conformable to the image of His Son'![1] Saint

---
[1] Rom 8:29.

Joy in Sacrifice

Paul has made known to us this divine election, which seems to be my lot.

"The good God has made me see many things by the light of eternity, and I wish to tell you, as coming from Him, not to fear sacrifice and struggle, but rather to rejoice at it. Do not feel sad or discouraged if your nature wars upon you or is the field of battle; I would even say, love your own misery, for it is the subject of God's mercy. When the sight of it saddens you or throws you back on self, the cause is self-love. In times of discouragement take refuge in the prayer of the Divine Master; He saw you and prayed for you on the Cross. This prayer of His lives and is present eternally before His Father; it is that which will save you from your miseries. The more you realize your weakness, the more confident you should feel, for then you depend on Him alone."

Her little friend N—, who had not heard from Sister Elizabeth of the Trinity for several months, was deeply grieved at the thought of no longer receiving the advice and encouragement which had so greatly helped her. The warm-hearted invalid drew strength from her affection to answer the young girl's many questions in the following beautiful letter, the echo of her own life:

"At last Elizabeth has come with her pencil to be close to her little N—; I say 'with her pencil', for we have been together, heart to heart, long ago, have we not? How fond I am of these evening meetings! They are the prelude to the intercourse there will be between our souls when I am in heaven and you on earth. I feel as if I bent over you like a mother over her favorite child. I raise my eyes and look at God; then I lower them on you, shedding on you the rays of His love. I say nothing to Him, but He understands me and prefers my silence. My darling child! I should like to be a saint to help you while on earth until

The Praise of Glory

I can do so from paradise. What would I not suffer to obtain for you the needed grace of fortitude!

"Now I will answer your questions. Let us speak first of humility. I have read splendid passages on this subject. A devout writer says that 'the humble soul finds its keenest joy in the feeling of its powerlessness before God'. Dear little friend, pride is not a thing that can be destroyed with the blow of a sword. No doubt some heroic acts of humility, such as we see in the lives of the saints, weaken it considerably, if they do not cause its death, but we have to slay it every instant. 'I die daily!' cried Saint Paul.[2] This doctrine of dying to self—the law for every Christian soul ever since Christ said: 'if any man will come after Me, let him deny himself and take up his cross daily'[3] — this doctrine, which seems so austere, is sweet and delightful when we consider that this death puts the life of God in the place of our life of sins and miseries. That is what Saint Paul meant when he wrote: 'Stripping yourselves of the old man with his deeds and putting on the new . . . according to the image of Him that created him.'[4] This image is God Himself. Do you not remember how plainly He expressed it on the day of creation: 'Let us make man to Our image and likeness'?[5]

"If we reflect seriously upon our origin, the things of this world will seem so petty that we shall despise them. Saint Peter wrote in one of his epistles that we are 'made partakers of the Divine nature'.[6]

"The soul that realizes its own grandeur enters 'the liberty of the glory of the children of God',[7] that is, it passes beyond all things, self included.

"Saint Augustine says that we have two cities within us—the city of God and the city of self; as the one is enlarged, the other

[2] 1 Cor 15:31. [3] St. Luke 9:23.
[4] Col 3:9, 10. [5] Gen 1:26.
[6] 2 St. Pet 1:4. [7] Rom 8:21.

Joy in Sacrifice

will be destroyed. A soul that lived in faith in the presence of God, which had the single eye of which Christ speaks in the Gospel—that is, a pure intention, aiming solely at God, directed solely to God—would also be a humble soul. It would recognize what were the gifts He had bestowed on it, for humility is truth, but would appropriate nothing to self, referring all to God as did our Lady. The movements of pride you feel within you only become faults when your will consents to them; they may cause you great suffering, but they do not offend the good God. The faults into which you tell me you slip inadvertently no doubt denote self-love, but that, dear little friend, is part of everyone's nature. What God wants of you is never wilfully to dwell upon any thought of pride or to perform any action inspired by pride, which would be wrong. But if you find you have done such a thing, you must not be disheartened, for that only comes from irritated pride, but, like Saint Mary Magdalen, confess your miseries at the Master's feet and ask Him to free you from them. He delights in seeing a soul recognize its own helplessness; then, as a great saint said: 'The abyss of God's immensity is confronted with the abyss of the creature's nothingness, and God embraces this nothingness.'[8]

"I deeply pity those who live for nothing higher than this world and its frivolities; they seem to me slaves. I should like to say to them: 'Shake off the yoke that weighs you down. Why wear fetters that chain you to self and to things less than self?' The happy people in this world are those with enough self-contempt and self-forgetfulness to choose the cross for their lot. What blissful peace we enjoy when we place our joy in suffering!

"Have you ever seen the pictures of death mowing the harvest with his sickle? Well, that is my condition! I seem to feel

---

[8] St. Angela of Foligno.

The Praise of Glory

him destroying me. It is painful to nature, and I assure you that, did I not rise above it, I should be nothing but a coward in my trials. But this is the human way of looking at it, and I quickly 'open the eye of my soul to the light of faith', which tells me that it is Love Who is destroying me and slowly wearing me away; then I feel an immense joy, and yield myself as His prey.

"When we meditate on our eternal predestination visible things seem so contemptible! Listen to what Saint Paul says: 'Whom He foreknew He also predestinated to be made conformable to the image of His Son.'[9] That is not all. You will see, my darling, that you are among the number of the predestinated. 'And whom He predestinated, them He also called.'[10] It is baptism that made you a child of adoption, that stamped you with the seal of the Blessed Trinity. 'And whom He called, them He also justified.'[11] How often have you been justified by the sacrament of penance and by the many touches of God upon your soul, without your knowing it! 'And whom He justified, them He also glorified.'[12] That awaits you in eternity; but remember, our degree of glory will be the degree of grace in which God finds us at the moment of death. Allow Him to complete the work of His predestination in you, and listen to Saint Paul again—he will give you a rule of life: 'Walk in Jesus Christ, rooted and built up in Him.'[13]

"Yes, little child of my soul, 'walk in Jesus Christ'. You need that spacious way; you are not made for the narrow, cramped by-ways of this world. 'Be rooted in Him.' For this you must be uprooted from self, or act as if you were, by denying self wherever you meet it. Be 'built up in Him', far above all that is passing, where all is pure and full of light.

[9] Rom. 8:29.
[10] *Ibid.*, 30.
[11] *Ibid.*
[12] *Ibid.*
[13] Col 2:6, 7.

Joy in Sacrifice

Be 'confirmed in the faith', that is, act by the light of God alone, never by your own impressions and imagination; believe that He loves you, and will help you in your struggles; believe in His love, in His 'exceeding charity'. Support yourself by the great truths of faith which show us how rich we are, and what is the end for which God has created us. If you dwell in these truths, yours will be real devotion. The truth, the truth of love, is so beautiful! 'He loved me and delivered Himself for me.'[14] That, dear little friend, is the truth! Finally, grow in gratitude. That is the last rule I give you; it is only the result of the rest. If you are 'rooted in Jesus Christ . . . confirmed in faith', your life will be full of thanksgiving, in the 'charity of the children of God'. I wonder to myself how a soul which has fathomed the love of God's heart for it can help being joyful, whatever its suffering or grief.

"I also wonder what our reverend mother will think of this long epistle. She will not let me write at all now, as I am extremely weak and constantly feel faint. Perhaps this letter may be the last your Elizabeth will send you. It has taken her a great many days to write, and that will explain its incoherence, yet I cannot bring myself to leave you this evening. I am alone; it is half-past seven; the community is at recreation, and I feel as if I were almost in heaven already, alone with the One, bearing my cross with my beloved Master. My happiness increases with my sufferings. If you only knew what sweetness there is at the bottom of the chalice prepared by our Father in heaven!

"Adieu, my little darling! May He 'protect you beneath the shadow of His wings'[15] from all evil."

---

[14] Gal 2:20.
[15] Ps 16:9.

Chapter Sixteen
Last Consolations

Overflowing charity — October 4 — The triduum — With Him she loved — Preparing for a clothing — The ceremony — The "consuming fire".

We have reached the last weeks of the life of our poor little Sister Elizabeth of the Trinity. Her stomach was so ulcerated that it was difficult to know how to sustain the fervent victim, consumed as she was by the fire of love and of pain. "I do my best for love of the good God not to starve to death", she wrote to her relations, who were taxing their ingenuity to find something that would do her good.

Notwithstanding her extreme exhaustion, she remained out of bed the greater part of the day. She made more frequent and lengthy visits than ever to the Blessed Sacrament, begging to be allowed to spend at least half an hour before It. When, at last, obliged to own herself vanquished by illness, she passed her time in arranging fresh flowers for the sacristy and in rendering a thousand little services to those around her, all that she did being marked with the perfect neatness which characterized her.

Sister Elizabeth, overflowing with charity like her Divine Master before He left His disciples, found strength to pour out her devoted love on those who had a claim on this final consolation. Her last letters, here grouped together, are like fragrant spices collected to make some delicious perfume, for the incense that *Laudem Gloriæ* was to give forth comes freely from these pages as from a "lighted censer".

The Praise of Glory

To a Carmelite Nun:

"Before I go to heaven, I want to tell you that I shall pray much for you in our Father's house. I appoint as our meeting-place the Furnace of Love; there I shall pass my eternity, and you can begin yours already, even here below. Dear Sister, I shall be zealous for your beauty. Are we not anxious for the well-being of those we love? I think that my mission in heaven will be to draw souls to interior recollection by helping them to go out from self and to adhere to God in great simplicity and love; also to keep them in that silence of the soul which allows God to imprint Himself upon it and transform it into Himself. Dear little Sister, I seem to see all things now in the light of the good God, and were I to begin my life over again, I should strive not to lose a single instant. We brides of Christ in Carmel must not do anything except for love and for God. If by chance, from the great center of light, I see you forsake this one occupation, I shall come to call you to order at once. Would you not like me to do so? Pray for me, help me to prepare for 'the Marriage Supper of the Lamb'.[1] Dying entails great suffering, and I reckon on your aid. I will help you at your death in return. My Master urges me on; He speaks to me of nothing now except of eternity . . . of love. . . . It is so serious—so grave a matter!

"Good-bye! I have neither strength nor leave to write much, but you know Saint Paul's saying: 'Our conversation is in heaven.'[2] Little Sister, let us live by love, that we may die of love, and glorify the God Who is all love!

"Laudem Gloriæ"

---

[1] Apoc 19:9.
[2] Phil 3:20.

Last Consolations

She wrote to a postulant whose angel she had been, and who had been obliged to return to her family for special reasons:

"Dear Little Tobias,

"My angel's heart was deeply touched by your letter. I am glad you so fully realize the truth that I am not really leaving you. My prayer and sufferings are the wings beneath which I shelter you 'to keep thee in all thy ways'.[3] How gladly would I undergo the greatest tortures to win you more love and faithfulness! You are the dear child of my soul, and I want to help you, to be your angel, unseen but always present, to succour you.

"Dear little Sister, I think it is love which shortens our stay here below—in fact, Saint John of the Cross states it plainly. He wrote a wonderful chapter describing the victims of love, and the last assaults it makes upon them.

"'Our God is a consuming fire'[4] if we always keep united to Him by a simple and loving gaze of love. If, like our adorable Master, we can say at the end of each day: 'I do always the things that please Him',[5] He will know how to consume us, and we shall fly, like two little sparks, to be lost in the great Furnace where we shall burn joyfully for all eternity.

"You wish me to ask the good God for some sign to show whether we shall meet again, and whether you will take your place beside your little angel; but, glad as I am to please you, I cannot do this. It is not in my way; I should feel that I was not leaving all to God. What I can assure you of is, that our Master loves you, loves you dearly, and wishes you to be His own. He feels a divine jealousy regarding your soul—the jealousy of a Spouse. Keep Him in your heart

[3] Ps 90:11.
[4] Heb 12:29.
[5] St. John 8:29.

The Praise of Glory

alone and separate; let love be your cloister; you will bear Him with you everywhere and find solitude in a crowd.

"Good-bye! Everything reminds me that I am going to heaven. If you only knew with what serene joy I wait to see God face to face! In the midst of the dazzling light, I shall still be bent over my child to preserve her like a pure lily for the Divine Master, so that He may gladly gather her for His garden of virgins, and may rest His glowing gaze upon the flower grown for Him with such deep love."

To the Same:

"I never before felt such need of enveloping you in my prayer. When my anguish is most keen, I feel so impelled to offer it for you that I cannot do otherwise. Are you suffering in any way? I give you all my pain to dispose of as you choose.

"How happy I am at thinking that the Master is soon coming to fetch me! Death is ideal for those whom God has kept!

"In heaven I shall be your angel more than ever. I know my little sister's need of protection in Paris where her life is passed. Saint Paul says that God wishes us to be 'holy and unspotted in His sight in charity'.[6] Ah! How fervently I shall beg Him that this great decree may be accomplished in you! To attain this, listen to the same apostle's advice:

"'Walk ye in Him; rooted and built up in Him, and confirmed in the faith . . . abounding in Him.'[7] While contemplating the ideal Beauty by His own brilliant light, I shall beseech Him to imprint it in your soul, so that even while on this earth, where all is stained, you may be beautiful in His beauty, luminous with His light.

[6] Eph 1:4.
[7] Col 2:6, 7.

Last Consolations

"Adieu! Thank Him for me, for my joy is immense. I appoint as our meeting place the 'lot of the saints'.[8] There, in the choir of virgins pure as the light, we shall sing the canticle of the Lamb, the eternal *Sanctus*, beneath the light of the Face of God; then we shall be 'transformed into the same image from glory to glory'."[9]

To a Friend:
"October 1, 1906
"The hour draws near when I am 'to pass from this world to my Father'. Before leaving, I wish to send you a word from my heart, a legacy of my soul. The Divine Master's love never overflowed as it did at the last moment when He was about to leave His own. He seems to have put something of this feeling in the heart of His little bride in the evening of her life, for I feel a flood of affection rise from my own heart towards yours.

"We see the true value of things by the light of eternity. Oh, How empty all is that has not been done for God and with God! I beg you to mark all your doings with the seal of love; it is the only thing that lasts ! . . . What a serious thing life is! Each minute is given us for the purpose of rooting ourselves more deeply in God, according to Saint Paul's expression, so that we may attain a more striking likeness to our Master, a closer union. The secret of realizing this plan, formed by God Himself, is to forget, to forsake self, no longer making any account of it; to look upon the Divine Master and on Him alone; to receive joy or sorrow indifferently, as both coming from His love. This establishes the soul upon the summits where all is peace.

---

[8] Col 1:12.
[9] 2 Cor 3:18.

The Praise of Glory

"I leave you my faith in the presence of God, Who is all love, dwelling within our souls; I entrust it to you. This intimacy with Him within me has been the lovely sun that irradiated my life, making it a foretaste of heaven, and it sustains me now in my suffering. I do not fear my weakness, which strengthens my trust in the 'Mighty' One Who is within me, and His omnipotence works, as the apostle says, 'above what we could hope for'.

"Adieu! When I am in heaven, will you let me help you, and even find fault with you because of my love for you, if I see that you do not give all to the Divine Master? I will protect your two darling treasures, and will ask for all you need to make their souls beautiful, true daughters of Love. May He keep you all His own, faithful in all things. I shall always be yours in Him!"

Sister Elizabeth kept her most charming little attentions and pregnant sayings, such as bring with them both light and life, for her sisters in the cloister. The little note she placed in a cell on the anniversary of a profession is a sample. With great tact, she wrote in the person of our Lady, whose picture forms the heading of these lines on recollection:

"Jesus made His first oblation to the Father in my arms, and He sends me to receive yours. I bring you a scapular[10] as a pledge of my protection and love, as a 'sign' of the mystery which is to be worked in you. I come, my daughter, to finish 'clothing you with Jesus Christ', that you may be 'rooted in Him' in the depths of the abyss with the Father and the Spirit of Love; that you may be 'built up in Him', your Rock and your Fortress; that you may be 'confirmed in the faith' in the immense love which rushes into your soul from the great Furnace. This all-powerful love will work

---

[10] The little vestier, influenced as she was by faith, with characteristic charm, waited for this opportunity to give her sister the blessed scapular of our Lady.

Last Consolations

great things in you. Believe my word, the word of a mother, and of a mother who thrills with joy at seeing with what special tenderness you are loved. Oh! Dwell within the depths of your own soul!

"The Bridegroom is here! He comes with all His gifts; the abyss of His love clothes you as with a vestment.

"Silence! Silence! . . ."

The month of October held in reserve the last joys of Sister Elizabeth of the Trinity's earthly exile. She very much wished to take part in the community festivities that yearly honor the blessed death of our seraphic mother. She confided her longing to the saint, and it was granted against all likelihood. Sister Elizabeth took the opportunity of putting on a new habit, in the afternoon of that day, to ask leave to renew the ceremony of her clothing, which took place near the tribune where she was accustomed to pray before the tabernacle. Full of faith, she observed the most minute details of the ceremonial, and did not dispense herself from the great prostration.

We were much affected at seeing her at choir in the evening, after an absence of seven months. Frail and trembling, she could hardly be perceived in the dim light, and was lost to all around in fervent prayer which she knew would be the last she would make in the place associated with so many graces and cherished memories. She felt a calm joy in prostrating before the grille in commemoration of her oblation on December 8,[11] and her consecration on January 21.[12] Her whole soul went with the *Suscipe* which our holy mother was to offer as a "praise of glory" to the Blessed Trinity. Then, serenely radiant, she regained her "dear solitude" to complete the gift so sincerely renewed.

---

[11] Her clothing.
[12] Taking the veil.

The Praise of Glory

Her sister and brother-in-law, who had promised to help us with the music of the festivals we were preparing in honor of our Blessed Martyrs of Compiègne, came to practise in the chapel in the evening. Sister Elizabeth noticed how unselfishly her dear Marguerite accompanied her husband, trying to bring him forward, while keeping in the background herself.

"I ought to be, like her, an instrument from which the Divine Master can draw the melodies He loves best," she said, "effacing myself to give Him all the glory, only seconding His action by co-operation with His grace." The most insignificant matters thus raised her to God, or rather, nothing brought her down to earth. "Her feet rest on this world; her heart, her soul, and her spirit are in heaven," said one of the nuns to her mother.

Sister Elizabeth was able to take part in our beautiful festivities from her little sanctuary, to which the picture of the Blessed Martyrs was fastened. By the numerous Masses celebrated during the triduum she united herself more closely with the Sacred Host. She was almost on a level with the Blessed Sacrament, and delighted in applying to herself the words of the Psalmist: "The queen stood on Thy right hand",[13] saying: "I take advantage of the place I hold beside Him Who made me queen to draw many graces from His heart."

Her thoughts centered on the young Levites who came to hear the spiritual and profound sermons with which we were favored. She besought her "Almighty Counselor" to infuse that unction into the depths of their heart which, in bygone days, had so powerfully penetrated her own from the same source.

On the 15th, the Feast of Saint Teresa, our bishop and most revered father, Monseigneur Dadolle, announced the beatification of the Blessed Martyrs, to whose robes of virgin-

---

[13] Ps 44:10.

Last Consolations

white was added the purple of their sacrifice of blood. The coincidence of the two feasts led his lordship to speak of our seraphic mother's life as also that of a martyr, since she gave the greatest possible gift . . . supreme love. He developed this idea in a remarkable sermon which moved the hearts of all his hearers. When Sister Elizabeth of the Trinity quitted her sanctuary she felt irresistibly impelled to give the Divine Master her whole love by an absolute sacrifice. The bishop willingly gave her, at the parlor grille, his blessing as father and pontiff, which little "praise of glory" looked upon as her final consecration.

When she confided her desire of suffering to the reverend father, he told her not to limit herself to that, but to yield herself in all simplicity to God, leaving Him free to act in any way He chose.

From that time her soul, turned towards the regions raised above all suffering, seemed to grow daily more full of light and, notwithstanding her pain, our little sister appeared to dwell already in the heaven of glory. "I feel love standing beside me as though it were a living being!" she exclaimed; "and it says to me: 'I wish to live in thy companionship; therefore, I desire thee to suffer without thinking that thou art suffering, submitting thyself simply to my action upon thee.'"

One more memory of this month of October. It shows us Sister Elizabeth of the Trinity unselfish in her charity to the very end. A lay sister postulant, her companion in the novitiate, was about to be clothed; the invalid offered to make her white head-dress, upon which she expended her affection and the remnant of her strength. No one who witnessed the exquisite taste with which she arranged everything, and her forethought about the smallest details, in order that nothing might disturb the recollection of the young novice on the morning of the great day, would have supposed that Sister Elizabeth would take to her bed next week, never to leave it again. Yet the exhaustion of her poor body, which was almost reduced to a skeleton and required all her mental energy to urge to the slightest movement, showed that the end was not far off. Her fingers could hardly hem the linen and often fell helpless on her little table. The poor child used to smile, but would allow no one to do her task; her great charity sustained her, for she knew how delighted her little sister would be if she did the work.

She remained in her usual place, wrapt in contemplation, on October 22, during the clothing, deeply happy in the thought that she would soon be laid, for another ceremony, in the very place where the young novice now prostrated. Alas! In three weeks her hope was realized.

She wrote that evening for the last time from the "palace of pain":

"My Dearly Loved Priest,[14]

"Your little victim is enduring very, very much; she is in a kind of physical agony, and feels so cowardly—cowardly enough to scream! But He Who is the fulness of love visits her and makes her live in company with Him, while intimating to her that as long as He leaves her on earth He will give her suffering. I wish, Mother, if you will allow me, to prepare a great festival for you on All Saints' Day: to begin a novena of pain for you, during which we shall come every night, out of affection for you, to visit you while you are asleep."

Her tortures were now increased by severe interior inflammation; she was literally scorched and could hardly speak,

---

[14] Towards the end of her life *Laudem Gloriæ*, who had now become a "victim of praise", addressed as her priest her by whose hands her oblation had been made and through whom the supreme sacrifice was now being perfected.

Last Consolations

but her face was radiant with joy. "God is a consuming fire," she said; "He is acting upon me."

"I shall never forget the impression your angel-daughter made upon me when I gave her holy communion, three weeks before she died", wrote a religious in a letter to us. "Although I had been told about it beforehand, I was so unnerved that my hand trembled when I placed the Sacred Host upon her tongue, which was as red as fire. I consider that having been allowed to give holy communion to her whom He was about to crown in heaven is one of the greatest favors shown me in my ministry by the Sacred Heart of Jesus. Our Lord seemed to intimate to me that the love which inflamed the soul of His saintly victim was burning her more fiercely than the heat which consumed her poor body."

This was indeed the fact, and Sister Elizabeth of the Trinity yielded herself so entirely to the "living flame of love" kindled within her heart, that it wounded her divinely. She greeted her prioress one morning with the words: "O Mother! A little more and you would never have found *Laudem Gloriæ* on earth again!"

"How was that?"

"Yesterday evening my soul was undergoing a kind of prostration, when I suddenly felt myself, as it were, invaded by Love. No words could express what I experienced; it was a fire of infinite sweetness which, at the same time, gave me a mortal wound. I think that, had it lasted any longer, I should have succumbed."

Thus ended this life wholly given up to love, which may be epitomized in the words of the Gospel concerning Saint Mary Magdalen: "She hath loved much."[15]

Saint John of the Cross says of these predestined souls: "The death of such souls is most full of sweetness, beyond that

---
[15] St. Luke 7:47.

The Praise of Glory

of their whole spiritual life, for they die of the sweet violence of love, like the swan which sings more sweetly when death is nigh. This is why the psalmist said, 'Precious in the sight of our Lord is the death of His saints',[16] for then the rivers of the souls' love flow into the sea of love, so wide and deep as to seem a sea themselves; the beginning and the end unite together to accompany the just departing for His kingdom."[17]

The inner history of Sister Elizabeth of the Trinity concludes with the end of our holy father's commentary.

"O flame of the Holy Ghost! penetrating so profoundly and so tenderly the very substance of my soul, and burning it with Thy heat, since Thou art so gentle as to manifest Thy desire of giving Thyself wholly to me in everlasting life; if formerly my petitions did not reach Thine ears, when I was weary and worn with love, suffering through the weakness of sense and spirit, because of my great infirmities, impurity, and little love, I prayed to be set free—for with desire hath my soul desired Thee—when my impatient love would not suffer me to submit to the conditions of this life according to Thy will—for it was Thy will that I should live—and when the previous impulses of my love were insufficient in Thy sight, because there was no substance in them; now that I am grown strong in love, that body and soul together do not only follow after Thee, but that 'my heart and my flesh rejoice in the living God'[18] with one consent, so that I am praying for that which Thou willest that I should pray for . . . break Thou the slender web of this life that I may be enabled to love Thee hereafter with that fulness and abundance which my soul desires, without end for evermore."[19]

[16] Ps 115:1.
[17] *The Living Flame of Love*, stanza 1:27, 28 (Lewis's translation; Baker, 1912).
[18] Ps 83:3.
[19] *The Living Flame of Love*, stanza 1:3, 35.

Chapter Seventeen
From Calvary to Heaven

The last visit to the parlor — Love and glory — Extreme unction — The dying nun — A symbolic dream — The Angelus — Heaven — The Feast of the Dedication.

On Monday, October 29, Sister Elizabeth of the Trinity saw all her relatives in the parlor. Her two little nieces were brought to her, and their mother made them kneel before the grille. "Then, with a majesty which was quite impressive," says Madame Catez, "she held up her large crucifix, and after having looked lovingly upon them, gave them her blessing. Did she feel a presentiment that she would never see them again?. . . We thought she was almost better—she spoke with greater ease, and talked to us for a long while, making her last requests. Doubtless God had pity on us, and let us fancy we should see our dear little Carmelite once more. She summoned courage to say to me as we made our farewell: 'Mother, when the out-sister comes to tell you that my sufferings are over, you must kneel down and say: "My God, Thou didst give her to me; I give her back to Thee. Blessed be Thy holy Name!"'"

Next day, Sister Elizabeth of the Trinity could not leave the infirmary. "I visited her during the day," relates the mother prioress. "She was very pale, but happy. She pointed to a picture hanging on the wall, and said: 'I was looking just now at our holy mother, and meditating on her glory, and I thought that her poor little daughter would be a long distance from her in heaven. At the same instant it was said to me in the depths

The Praise of Glory

of my soul that Saint Teresa's glory was less the reward of her great deeds than of her love, which was a great consolation to me. We have loved one another so deeply', she said, pressing the crucifix of her profession day to her heart. 'At the end of my life this teaching confirms all my special devotions. . . . Now I wish to live solely for love.'"

Thus prepared for the last stage of her life, which was to begin on that very day, she kept herself "in company with love" during the whole of her long and painful agony.

Madame Catez came on the evening of the 30th to ask after her daughter. The portress, who found the mother prioress in the infirmary, says: "I took the opportunity of recommending several matters about which I was deeply concerned to Sister Elizabeth of the Trinity. Without giving me a precise answer, she replied affectionately, yet with simple and deep gravity. She might have been dictating her last testament, and she made me promises which have since been fulfilled. 'Do not talk to me any longer, dear sister, you are tiring yourself,' I said; 'besides, I must take your message to your mother.' 'Tell her I am dying,' replied the invalid; 'I can say no more.' Stupefied at hearing her speak thus, I was impressed afresh by her energy in having so mastered her suffering in order to console me.

"When she was urged to lie down to rest she answered: 'Oh, no! I am so exhausted that I am afraid I should never be able to sit up again.'"

Towards the end of Matins that night, the prioress felt impelled to go and see the daughter she so dearly loved. The poor little one was awaiting her in an anguish of expectancy, fearing lest she might die in her mother's absence, for she had been seized with a fit of shivering, which shook her in her bed. When her fears were allayed, and her sufferings calmed

From Calvary to Heaven

by remedies, she became drowsy. Towards three o'clock in the morning the mother Prioress heard a slight noise, and hastened to the sick bed. Sister Elizabeth, who was in acute pain, thought the longed-for end had come, and poured out her soul to the mother who watched beside her. It was an hour never to be forgotten. Heaven seemed open to the gaze of the happy young nun so perfectly detached from all things and ready to respond to the summons of the heavenly Bridegroom.

Her weakness was extreme, and she received the last sacraments again on the morning of October 31,—the vigil of a feast dear to her faith.

Sister Elizabeth of the Trinity, who always took a special delight in the beautiful Office of All Saints, hoped that she was now to join the great multitude beheld by Saint John before the "throne of the Lamb".[1]

When the bells of the different churches sounded the Angelus at noon she exclaimed: "O Mother, they are ringing for '*Laudem Gloriæ's*' departure! All the bells in the town sounded for my profession, and now they are pealing for my journey from the Church militant to the Church triumphant. Those bells will make me die of joy! Let me go, then", and she held out her arms towards heaven.

Shortly before ten o'clock on the morning of All Saints' Day we thought her last hour had come. The community assembled in the infirmary to recite the prayers from the Manual. Sister Elizabeth of the Trinity recovered from her collapse, looked round to see that all were present, begged their pardon in touching terms, and then, in answer to a question asked, she said: "Everything passes! . . . At the end of life love alone remains. . . . We must do all for love, and unceasingly forget self; the good God is so pleased when we

[1] Apoc 7:9.

The Praise of Glory

are self-regardless. . . . Ah! If I had always done so! . . ." she added with a humility that went to our hearts. . . . Holy little one! It was your own special grace you were revealing to us, and the secret of your rapid attainment of perfection.

The bells pealed all day, to the delight of our little sister, though she did not hear the divine summons she expected.

"If our Lord offered me the choice of dying either in an ecstasy or in the abandonment of Calvary, I should prefer the latter—not on account of its merit, but that I might glorify and resemble Him", she had confided to us a few days earlier. We reminded her of her wish, and she was consoled by the thought that it was about to be realized.

Faith, the strength of the martyrs, had so developed in her, through her firm resolution of believing that all things are sent to us by the hand of Love, that she was divinely sustained throughout her own martyrdom, with its helplessness and crucifying feelings of abandonment which recalled the dereliction of Calvary. "It seems as though my body were suspended and my soul in darkness," she said one day; "but it is the action of Love, and knowing that, my heart rejoices."

This jubilation of the higher part of her soul did not prevent the sensitive part from adding to the trials the poor child was already enduring. It was delivered over to a kind of agony. "If I had died in my former state of soul, death would have been too sweet", she declared. "I depart in pure faith, and I prefer it, for I resemble my Master more closely, and it is more real."

Her longing to conform to God crucified made her welcome every fresh suffering with an angelic smile.

Towards the end of October her stomach, which was almost completely worn out, could hardly retain a few barley-sugar

From Calvary to Heaven

drops.[2] After All Saints' Day Sister Elizabeth took nothing. She could not even swallow a drop of water without suffering severe pain; her mouth, which had been parched with thirst for the last three weeks, was dried up for want of moisture. The keen thirst, the torments of which we could do nothing to quench, was particularly trying to her. "It resembles what our Lord suffered on the Cross", we told her. "Oh, yes! It is delightful!" she exclaimed. "His love is so infinitely tender, He never forgets anything that would make me share His pains!"

She received holy communion for the last time on November 1, as she could not swallow the smallest particle of the Sacred Host in the state we have just described. When someone spoke to her of the great sacrifice the deprivation of her God must be to her, she answered: "I find Him on the cross; it is there He gives me His life."

Her special love for cleansing her soul in the precious Blood of the Savior had, for some years, given her a strong desire of receiving the sacrament of penance, a grace which our chaplain frequently renewed during this last trying week of her life. His words of comfort, which had so often benefited her during her religious life, supported her now through her severest trials.

Acute cerebral pains seemed to threaten meningitis, but the danger was averted by constant applications of ice which melted instantly on coming in contact with the intense heat she endured in her head; she felt as if her brain were on fire. The poor child's eyes, terribly bloodshot, remained closed until the last moments. At times her speech was almost indistinguishable. It was then that we fully realized how deeply

---

[2] Sister Elizabeth had taken nothing but milk since the beginning of her illness: a glassful sufficed for what she called her four meals. Angel on earth as she was, she was nourished by God, Who visibly communicated His divine strength to her.

The Praise of Glory

her soul, which had always mastered her physical state, was immersed in God. Hitherto, in spite of the pain that racked her, it was possible to understand the interior concentration of her mind. Now she could hardly control her thoughts, yet divine union had become so habitual to her that it was maintained throughout her sufferings.

One of the nuns, seeing her state of prostration, was about to offer her some little encouragement, but was intensely surprised at hearing her murmur words whose depth revealed how fully, though in appearance all but dead, she lived to God. The same impression was felt by many others during those nine days. It was the grace left us by the little seraph, which remained imprinted in our souls, an ideal to be realized and never to be forgotten.

During her extreme exhaustion, Sister Elizabeth of the Trinity was grateful to anyone who would recite the prayers known as "The Exercises of Saint Gertrude" to her. She gave signs of finding comfort in them, and used to try to whisper, when they were ended, "Gertrude!" that the reader might resume. The sighs and transports of a heart thirsting for union fitly expressed her own yearning—"O Love! Love! Tarry not to accomplish my nuptials! . . . O Love! Hasten to satisfy my longing. . . . Finish what Thou hast begun!"

At the words: "Praise Thyself in Thee; praise Thyself in me and by me!" she trembled with emotion and murmured: "Oh! That is what I wish!"

"It was rather consoling than fatiguing to watch beside our little sister's sick bed", writes one of her infirmarians. "It was a real pleasure to go near her. Whenever I touched her innocent body, I seemed impregnated with the perfume of purity exhaling from it. So strongly did I realize our Lord's presence in her that I used to kiss her hands with the same reverence

From Calvary to Heaven

and respect that I should have shown to the crucified Jesus. She let me do so in all simplicity, exclaiming: 'It is for Him!'

"The last moments before her holy death are always in my mind. She gave me the impression of a victorious champion finishing the race. She seemed to cry with Saint Paul: 'I have fought a good fight, I have finished my course,'[3] 'I am a queen for all eternity!'"

A queen she was already, as, with a striking dignity preserved until the very last, she climbed her Calvary at the right hand of the divine King. "Our Lord wishes me to go to my passion with the majesty of a queen", she had said some months before, when speaking of the way in which the brides of Christ should suffer. It was thus she bore her cross, always controlled by the divine strength which freed her from the commonplace cares usual to the sick.[4]

Her power of speech returned to her at intervals, and she made use of it to praise God and console her sisters. One day, a nun to whom she had confided the grace she had found in her name—*Laudem Gloriæ*—asked her to give her a name for herself to be her strength and guidance. On October 30, Sister Elizabeth caused a slip of paper to be put in her cell on which were written the words: "*Abscondita in Deo*".[5] "I longed," the sister says, "to return to her to learn more of it, but her illness increased so rapidly that I feared I should never speak to her again. What was my astonishment; on

---

[3] 2 Tim 4:7.

[4] She said to one of the nuns a short time before: "One night, when my pains were overwhelming, I felt that nature was getting the upper hand, but I roused my faith and said to myself, 'That is not the way in which a Carmelite should suffer!' Then I thought of Jesus in His Agony and, offering Him my pain to console Him, I felt strengthened. That is how I have always acted during my life—in every trial, small or great, I contemplate what our Lord went through resembling it, that I may lose my suffering in His and myself in Him."

[5] Col 3:3.

The Praise of Glory

November 5, when alone with her for a moment, to feel her clasp my hand and to hear her say in a gasping, almost dying, voice: 'You are *Abscondita*, are you not?' 'Yes!' 'Well! It is He Himself Who gave you that name; I understood it. Oh, What a vocation! *'Abscondita in Deo'* means separation from all earthly things, a continual ascension to Him. What mortification, what prayer, what self-effacement that name requires! I cannot tell you all, but I will help you from heaven', and whenever I saw her she repeated: 'I will help you.'"

"I shall never forget the impression made upon me by those last nine days", says the mother sub-prioress. "On the one hand, I felt deeply touched at watching the poor body, perfectly unrecognizable, recalling the descent from the Cross; and on the other, I was struck with profound admiration for the soul so engrossed by the great mystery of the next world that it was impossible for her to describe what dawned upon her.

"Whenever our mother entered the infirmary she was greeted by a smile of indescribable sweetness. Sister Elizabeth used to try to open her eyes to look at her. If the mother prioress seemed tired from watching by her sick-bed, she used to try to persuade her to rest, showing her anxiety about her mother's health in numberless ways. Sister Elizabeth said to her one day: 'When I reach the good God, my first prayer will be for your health.' 'No, no! Pray for my soul first, that is much more urgent and important.' 'Certainly the soul comes before the body, but I think that in heaven we shall be able to care for a great many things at once, for heaven is Unity.' When our mother did not come to see her, she used to say to me: 'The victim is about to be sacrificed, and cannot do without the priest.'"

The dear child used to find comfort in the help given her by mother prioress whose hand she held in her own, saying:

From Calvary to Heaven

"Do not leave me, I stand in great need of your aid to finish climbing my Calvary. Oh! to think that the time will come when I must traverse that mysterious, solemn passage alone!" "But our Lady will be there, and will take you by the hand; you will have nothing to fear with such a Mother." "Yes, that is true! *Janua Coeli* will be sure to let little *Laudem Gloriæ* pass through. But what a serious thing it is when we come to this state! The thought of heaven thrills my soul, I seemed to have dwelt there for a long time, yet it is quite unknown to me! . . . Oh! How we ought to pray for the dying! I would willingly spend my eternity near them to help them. There is something terrifying about death. . . . How formidable it must be for those who have spent their lives in pleasure and are attached to so many things in this world! Even though I am detached from everything, I have an indescribable feeling, an intuition of the justice and sanctity of God. I realize that death is a punishment, and I feel so insignificant, so wanting in merit. . . . How we ought to encourage those in their last agony! . . ."

The impressions of the dying nun, angelic in her innocence, added to the sufferings of her whole frame, resulting from the many complications of her disease, reminded us of her ardent wishes when, as a young girl, she offered herself as victim for the sins of the world. Her prayers had been heard, and it was evident to those beside that little bed—a genuine altar of sacrifice—that the High Priest was completing the oblation of His innocent victim.

"You are clothed with the Man of Sorrows", someone said to her one day. "You are completely conformed to Jesus crucified." "Yes, indeed!" she replied simply, in accents of genuine joy.

At times her appearance reminded us of certain pictures of the Holy Face; her mournful expression touched and

The Praise of Glory

impressed us with reverence and recollection. At other times our little sister looked like a young child. She really had the character and simplicity of infancy, which developed during her illness and gave a wonderful charm to her whole person, even during her severest sufferings. We used to love to visit her and collect the sayings which seemed addressed to us from the threshold of eternity, so luminous and appropriate were they; she appeared to see into our souls. We were surprised at her presence of mind during the acute pain of her last few days. She might have answered, as did the Venerable Marguerite of the Blessed Sacrament when questioned as to the help she received from God: "The Divine aid is immense!"

"O Love! Love!" Sister Elizabeth had cried after a violent crisis, "Thou knowest whether I love Thee and desire to contemplate Thee! Thou knowest also what I suffer! Let it be for thirty, forty years longer if Thou wilt; I am ready. Spend all my substance for Thy glory; let it distill drop by drop for Thy Church." She remained in this disposition of soul until the end.

One evening, her infirmarian, seeing that she was in torture, said to her: "You can bear no more, my poor little sister?" "Oh, no! I can bear no more!" "Do you wish to go to heaven?" "Yes! Until now I have abandoned myself to Him, but I am His bride, and now I have the right to say to Him: 'Let us go!' We love one another so dearly, we are impatient to see one another. Oh! How I love Him!"

One day her expression revealed that the state of her soul was changed—in fact, the darkness that had her during those first days of agony had given place to light, but she was not permitted to explain the secrets heard in those regions so near to the vision of God.

From Calvary to Heaven

A little later on she spoke of a happy dream she had had. "I saw a beautiful palace, all white and gold, and in this palace a bride. She was excessively tall, but so well proportioned that she was very graceful; she had a matchless dignity." "Perhaps it was *Laudem Gloriæ*."

"I don't know", she answered, smiling; "I did not see her face, but she was beautiful—beautiful! And the dream has made me as happy as if I were in heaven." How often have we thought how it applied to our dear little sister, the bride of Christ developed by suffering, adorned with innocence and grace, about to be introduced to the courts of heaven for the eternal nuptials!

One morning she peered beneath her half-closed eyelids, leaning forward as though to examine something. "What are you doing?" we asked her.

"I see a palm", she said, putting out her hand as if trying to grasp it.

"A palm?"

"Yes, a beautiful palm."

"Is it for you?"

"I don't know, but I am not selfish; I should like each of my sisters to have one."

Later on she exclaimed, with a gesture that showed she saw herself surrounded with radiance:

"It is full of light! It is grand! . . . It is . . . ." She could not finish her sentence.

On the eve of her death she found strength to express her happiness. At her request the doctor had just told her of the extreme weakness of her pulse. "In two days I shall probably be in the bosom of my 'Three'; is not that joy enough? *Lætatus sum in his quæ dicta sunt mihi!* It is our Lady, full of light, pure with the divine purity, who will take

The Praise of Glory

me by the hand to lead me into heaven—that realm of dazzling brightness!"

She did not try to hide from the doctor the overflowing delight her faith produced. He was so astonished at her happiness that she tried to explain it to him by a comparison which led her to speak in a touching manner of the divine adoption, and the tears stood in the eyes of many of her listeners.

Exhausted by her efforts, she entered for the last time into her cherished silence. Yet we heard her murmur in a sort of chant: "I am going to the light, to love, to life! . . ." They were her last intelligible words.

The night between the eigth and the ninth of November was a very painful one, as suffocation was added to her other complaints. Towards morning her acute sufferings abated. Calm and silent, the wise and prudent virgin peacefully awaited the coming of the divine Bridegroom, aided by the prayers of her mothers and sisters who knelt around her. The bell of the convent sounded the first Angelus. The Queen of Carmel, present though invisible, succoured the child she dearly loved until the hour when, all being finished, she was to conduct her to heaven. Sister Elizabeth of the Trinity, leaning on her right side, her head thrown back, her eyes wide open now and fixed upon a point slightly above our heads, seemed rather in ecstasy than in agony. Her face was wonderfully beautiful; we could not look away from her, and she seemed to gaze upon the eternal hills already.

With this radiant expression she left us, without its being possible to say when she drew her last breath. All was over now! . . . *Laudem Gloriæ* no longer sang on this earth; our hearts sought her in the great Furnace of Love, the bosom of the "Three". She had said: "I shall hardly

From Calvary to Heaven

have reached the threshold of paradise when I shall rush there like a little rocket, for a 'praise of glory' can have no other place to all eternity."

And it was the morning of a feast of a Dedication. August 2, 1901, had commemorated one of these solemnities.[6] On that day Sister Elizabeth of the Trinity had consecrated herself to a life of perfection and praise on Mount Carmel. On November 9, 1906, (the Dedication of the Basilica of Saint Savior), she mounted with gladness to the house of the Lord, bearing her sheaves and singing "Glory be to God!"[7] The first Office sung in the presence of her remains in the choir was another feast of a Dedication, that of the churches of France, whose beautiful liturgy was chanted opposite this little "House of God", which had always reflected His divine glory.

How touching were some of the allusions in this majestic Office! "The Lord has sanctified His tabernacle. My house is a house of prayer. . . ."

Was not Sister Elizabeth of the Trinity also "the stone hammered with many blows, polished by the chisel in the hands of the divine Sculptor"?[8]

Our hearts vied with one another in saying to her, in the words of Holy Church, "O bride! How blessed is thy lot! Thou art dowered with the glory of the Father, filled with the grace of the Bridegroom, espoused to Christ, thy King!"[9]

For three days we enjoyed the pleasure of keeping her virginal body among us, of surrounding it with our prayers

[6] The Dedication of our Lady of the Angels, where the Seraph of Assisi received the Portiuncula indulgence, and where, according to Saint Bonaventura, "he began the evangelical life with which he has inspired his whole Order."
[7] Office of the Dedication.
[8] *Ibid.*
[9] From the primitive text of *Urbs Jerusalem beata*.

The Praise of Glory

and loving veneration. The exteme alteration in her features revealed her martyrdom. She had indeed "spent all her substance" for her God, and passed from this world to her Father transformed into the image of Jesus crucified. Her dream was realized.

As soon as the news of her death became known in the town, people crowded to Carmel, eager to look upon "the little saint", as everyone called her, and carrying with them numerous rosaries and medals. Everybody thought that any souvenir of her would bring a blessing with it.

Her funeral was a genuine triumph. An imposing circle of 24 priests surrounded the humble child who, retired and silent, had immolated herself for Holy Church and her consecrated Levites.

Numerous friends accompanied her to her last resting-place. They agreed in saying that their feelings, as they followed in procession, were less of mourning than of hope. For us, the pain of sacrifice seemed outweighed by the joy of having offered God a gift which we knew would be perfectly pleasing to Him. The divine peace shed upon our Carmel was both a pledge and a reflection of that into which our dearly-loved sister had entered for all eternity

"I should like to keep myself, as a little vase, close to the divine source, so that I might communicate life to souls, by letting the waters of infinite charity overflow upon them," Sister Elizabeth of the Trinity had said one day.

The saintly child, plunged in the very ocean of eternal life, can now fully satisfy her heart's longing. We rejoice to contemplate her leading souls into the profound silence which wholly absorbs her in the embrace of uncreated Love, thus fulfilling her celestial "mission". By revealing what was the strength and happiness of her life in this earthly

From Calvary to Heaven

exile, our seraphic sister still teaches the divine science of intimacy with Him "Who delights to be with the children of men",[10] and Whose Heart gave utterance at His Last Supper to the burning words: "If any man love Me. . . My Father will love him, and We will come to him, and will make Our abode with him."[11]

---

[10] Prov 8:31.
[11] St. John 14:23.

Appendix

Lord, the thought of man shall give praise to Thee: and the remainders of the thought shall keep holiday to Thee. (Ps. 75:11.)

Appendix
The Last Retreat of
Laudem Gloriæ[*]

First Day

Nescivi! "I knew not."[1] So sings the bride of the *Canticles* after having been brought into the inner cellar. That, it seems to me, should be the song of a "praise of glory" on the first

---

[*]We have kept the titles and divisions of these pages, although they do not contain a retreat in the strict sense of the word, that at a first glance appear to be a commentary on the Holy Scriptures, is in reality the dear child's revelation of the secret of her sanctity, the ideal fully realized by her before her life was ended. These confidential notes admit us into the "Holy of Holies" of the "little House of God".

Sister Elizabeth's was indeed a soul of one idea: to be a "praise of glory" to the Blessed Trinity. This meant for her that heaven began on earth, as she wrote the day after her profession: "Heaven in faith, with suffering and self-immolation for Him I love." And later on: "I have found my heaven while on earth, for heaven is God, and God is in my soul. On the day I realized this all things were seen by me in a new light. . . ."

In this "retreat" she lifts the veil, and contemplating the action of the blessed as they gaze upon the Beatific Vision, she exclaims "It seems to me that it would give immense joy to the Heart of God if we were to imitate, within the heaven of our soul, the ceaseless occupation of the blessed . . . living in the bosom of the tranquil Trinity, in the inner abyss, the invincible fortress of holy recollection spoken of by Saint John of the Cross."

Like her incomparable Father, the greater the heights to which Sister Elizabeth rises, the more practical she becomes. After having seen in the light of God how infinite is His sanctity, how wondrous the work His grace desires to accomplish in us, and how sublime the union to which we can attain while yet on earth, she became merciless regarding any movement of nature that could prove an obstacle, and pursued self into its last strong-holds.

The same idea is followed every day in connection with a different text of Holy Scripture, the same end aimed at, the same means given to attain it: Nescivi! To know naught but Him.

May not these pages be called her Canticle, and the prelude to the eternal *Sanctus*?

[1] Cant 6:11.

The Praise of Glory

day of her retreat, when the Master makes her sound the depths of the abyss, that she may learn to fulfil the office which will be hers in *eternity*, but which she also ought to perform in *time*, which is the beginning of eternity.

Nescivi! I know nothing, I desire nothing but "that I may know Him . . . and the fellowship of His sufferings, being made conformable to His death".[2] "Whom He foreknew, He also predestinated to be made conformable to the image of His Son,"[3] Who was crucified by love. When I become identified with this Divine Example, dwelling wholly in Him and He in me, I shall fulfil my eternal vocation, by which God chose me in Him, *in principio*, which I shall fulfil *in aeternum*, when, in the bosom of the Trinity, I shall be the ceaseless "praise of His glory", *in laudem gloriæ ejus*.[4]

"No man hath seen God at any time: the only begotten Son Who is in the bosom of the Father, He hath declared Him."[5] It might be added that none has penetrated the mystery of Christ in all its depths, unless it be our Lady. Saint Paul often speaks of the "knowledge"[6] he had received of it, yet all the saints dwell in shadow, compared with our Lady's light! The secret she kept and pondered in her heart is unspeakable; no tongue can tell it, no pen express it.

This Mother of grace will so shape my soul that her little child may be a living, striking image of her "Firstborn",[7] of the Son of the Eternal, the perfect "Praise of the glory" of His Father.

---

[2] Phil 3:10.
[3] Rom 8:29.
[4] Eph 1:12.
[5] St. John 1:18.
[6] Eph 3:4.
[7] Col 1:15.

The Last Retreat

Second Day

"My soul is always in my hands."[8] This was the song of my Master's soul, and that is why, in the midst of all His anguish, He remained calm and strong. "My soul is always in my hands." What does that mean except perfect self-control in the presence of the Prince of Peace?

"I will keep my strength to thee",[9] is another song of Christ's in which I desire to join incessantly. My Rule tells me: "In silence shall be your strength." To "keep our strength" for the Lord is to keep our whole being in unity by interior silence; to collect all our powers, to occupy them in the one work of love, to have the "simple eye" which allows the light of God to enlighten us.

A soul which listens to *self*, which is preoccupied with its sensibilities, which indulges in useless thoughts or desires, scatters its forces. It is not completely under God's sway. Its lyre is not in tune, so that when the Divine Master strikes it, He cannot draw forth celestial harmony; it is too human and discordant.

The soul which reserves anything for self in its interior kingdom, whose powers are not all "enclosed" in God, cannot be a perfect "praise of glory"; it is unfit to sing the *canticum magnum* continually, because it is not in unity. So that, instead of persevering in praise, in simplicity, whatever may happen, it is often obliged to tune the chords of its instrument which have lost their tone.

How necessary is this blessed unity for the soul that craves to live here below the life of the blessed—that is, of simple beings, of spirits! Did not the Divine Master mean to teach this to Saint Mary Magdalen when He spoke of the

[8] Ps 118:109.
[9] *Ibid.*, 58:10.

unum necessarium? How well that great saint realized it! She had recognized her God by the light of faith under the veil of His humanity, and in the silence, the unity of her powers, "she heard His word"[10] and could sing: "My soul is always in my hands", and also the little word *Nescivi!*

Yes! she knew nothing but Him: whatever noise and bustle there was around her: *Nescivi!* She might be blamed: *Nescivi!* Neither care for honor nor exterior things could draw her from her sacred silence.

Thus it is with the soul dwelling in the fortress of holy recollection. By the light of faith she sees her God present, dwelling within her; and He, on His part, is so present to her in her beautiful simplicity that He guards her with a jealous care. Then, whatever turmoil there may be outside or tempests within, however her honor may be assailed: *Nescivi!* God may hide Himself, withdraw His sensible grace: *Nescivi!* . . . "For Him I have suffered the loss of all things!"[11] she exclaims. Henceforth the Master has full liberty—liberty to infuse Himself within her, to give Himself *in His own measure*, and the soul, thus simplified, unified, becomes the throne of Him Who changes not, because unity is the throne of the Blessed Trinity.

Third Day

"In Whom we are also called by lot, being predestined according to the purpose of Him Who worketh all things according to the counsel of His will. That we may be unto the praise of His glory".[12]

[10] St. Luke 10:39.
[11] Phil 3:8.
[12] Eph 1:11, 12.

The Last Retreat

It is Saint Paul who makes known to us this divine election—Saint Paul, who penetrated so deeply into the secret hidden within the Heart of God. Let us listen to him as he enlightens us regarding "this vocation to which we are called".

"God," he says, "chose us in Him before the foundation of the world, that we should be holy and unspotted in His sight in charity."[13]

On comparing these two explanations of the divine plan, I conclude that, if I am worthily to fulfil my office of *Laudem Gloriae*, I must keep myself, whatever happens, in the *presence of God*. The apostle also says *"in caritate"*, that is to say, in God, *"Deus caritas est"*, and it is contact with the Divinity which will make me "holy and unspotted in His sight".

I apply this to the beautiful virtue of simplicity "which gives to the soul the repose of the abyss"—that is, rest in God—the unfathomable abyss, the prelude to the eternal Sabbath of which Saint Paul speaks: For we who have believed shall enter into rest."[14]

Glorified souls have this "rest in the abyss" because they contemplate God in the simplicity of His Essence. "They know even as they are known"[15] by Him—that is, by intuitive vision, and they are "transformed into the same image from glory to glory, as by the Spirit of the Lord."[16] There they are a ceaseless praise of glory to the Divine Being, Who contemplates His own splendor in them.

I believe that we should give an immense joy to the Heart of God by imitating, in the heaven of our soul, this occupation of the blessed, adhering to Him by the simple

---

[13] *Ibid.*, 4.
[14] Heb 4:3.
[15] I Cor 13:12.
[16] 2 Cor 3:18.

The Praise of Glory

contemplation which resembles the state of innocence in which man was created.

"God created man to His own image."[17] Such was the plan of the Creator, that He might view Himself in His creature, and might see His own perfections and beauty reflected through him as through a pure and flawless crystal. Is not that a kind of extension of His own glory?

The soul, by the simplicity of gaze which it fixes upon its Divine Object, is separated from all around it, and above all from self. Henceforth it is resplendent with "the light of the knowledge of the glory of God",[18] because it allows the Divinity to reflect Himself within it. Such a soul is truly "the praise of glory" of all His gifts; it sings without cessation whatever happens, and during the most commonplace employments, the *"canticum magnum"*, the *"canticum novum"*, and this canticle thrills God to His very depths.

"Thy light," we may say to this soul, "shall rise up in darkness, and thy darkness shall be as the noonday: And the Lord will give thee rest continually, and will fill thy soul with brightness, and deliver thy bones: and thou shalt be like a watered garden, and like a fountain of water, whose waters shall not fail. . . . I will lift thee up above the high places of the earth."[19]

Fourth Day

Yesterday, Saint Paul raised the veil a little way so that I could catch a glimpse "of the lot of the saints in light", and ascertain how they employ themselves, and that I might try, as far as possible, to conform my life to theirs, and fulfil my vocation of *Laudem Gloriæ*.

[17] Gen 1:27.
[18] 2 Cor 4:6.
[19] Isa 58:10-14.

The Last Retreat

Today it is Saint John who will partly open the "eternal gates"[20] for me, that my soul may rest in "Jerusalem the holy", the sweet "vision of peace"![21] He tells me, to begin with, that "the city hath no need of the sun, nor of the moon, to shine in it. For the glory of God hath enlightened it, and the Lamb is the lamp thereof."[22]

If I wish my interior city to agree with, to resemble that of the "immortal King of ages",[23] and to shine with the great illumination given by God, I must first extinguish every other light, so that the Lamb may be its only Lamp.

Here faith, the fair light of faith, appears to me. That, and no other, ought to enlighten me to go to meet the Bridegroom. The psalmist sings that "He made darkness His covert,"[24] but seems to contradict himself by saying elsewhere that He is "clothed with light as with a garment".[25] This apparent contradiction appears to mean that I ought to plunge into the sacred darkness, keeping all my powers in night and emptiness; then I shall meet my Master, and the light which "clothes Him as a garment" will enwrap me too, for He wishes His bride to be luminous with His light, and with His light alone, "having the glory of God".[26]

It is said of Moses that "he endured as seeing Him that is invisible";[27] such should be the attitude of a "praise of glory" who desires to persevere in her hymn of thanksgiving whatever happens; to be enduring in her faith, as if she saw Him

---

[20] Ps 23:7.
[21] Office of the Dedication.
[22] Apoc 21:23.
[23] 1 Tim 1:17.
[24] Ps 17:12.
[25] Ps 103:2.
[26] Apoc 21:2.
[27] Heb 11:27.

The Praise of Glory

Who is invisible; enduring in her faith in His "exceeding charity"! "We have known and have believed the charity which God hath to us."[28] "Faith is the substance of things to be hoped for, the evidence of things unseen."[29]

What does it matter to the soul that retires within itself, enlightened by this word, whether it feels or does not feel, whether it is in light or darkness, enjoys or does not enjoy? It is struck by a kind of shame at making any difference between such things, and despising itself utterly for such want of love, it turns at once to its Master for deliverance! "It exalts Him upon the highest summit of the heart"—that is to say, above the sweetness and consolations which flow from Him, having resolved to pass by all else to obtain union with Him it loves.

To this soul, this enduring believer in the God of love, may be applied the words of the prince of the apostles: "In Whom . . . believing, you shall rejoice with joy unspeakable and glorified."[30]

Fifth Day

"I saw a great multitude, which no man could number. . . These are they who are come out of great tribulation, and have washed their robes, and have made them white in the Blood of the Lamb. Therefore they are before the throne of God, and they serve Him day and night in His temple: and He, that sitteth on the throne, shall dwell over them. They shall no more hunger nor thirst, neither shall the sun fall on them, nor any heat. For the Lamb, which is in the midst of the throne, shall

[28] 1 St. John 4:16.
[29] Heb 11:1.
[30] St. Peter 1:8.

rule them, and shall lead them to the fountains of the waters of life, and God shall wipe away all tears from their eyes."[31]

All these elect souls, palm in hand, bathed in the light of God, must needs have first passed through "great tribulation", and known the sorrow "great as the sea",[32] sung by the prophet. Before contemplating the glory of the Lord "face to face", they have shared the abjection of His Christ: before being "transformed from glory to glory into the image of the divine", they have been conformed to that of the Word Incarnate, crucified by love.

The soul that longs to serve God day and night in His temple, in the inner sanctuary of which Saint Paul speaks when he says: "The temple of God is holy, which temple you are",[33] such a soul must be resolved to take a real share in the Passion of its Master. It is a ransom which in its turn will ransom other souls. Therefore it will sing to its lyre: "God forbid that I should glory, save in the cross of our Lord Jesus Christ! . . ."[34] "With Christ I am nailed to the cross."[35] And again: "I . . . fill up those things that are wanting of the sufferings of Christ, in my flesh, for His Body, which is the Church."[36]

"The queen stood on thy right hand."[37] Such is the attitude of this soul; it walks on the road to Calvary at the right hand of the crucified, crushed, and humbled King, Who, strong, calm, and full of majesty, goes to His Passion, to show forth "the glory of His grace".[38]

[31] Apoc 7:9, 14-17.
[32] Lam 2:13.
[33] 1 Cor 3:17.
[34] Gal 6:14.
[35] Gal 2:19.
[36] Col 1:24.
[37] Ps 44:10.
[38] Eph 1:6.

The Praise of Glory

He desires His bride to join in His work of redemption, and the way of sorrow which she treads seems to her the way of beatitude, not only because it leads there, but also because her holy Teacher makes her understand that she must pass beyond the bitterness of suffering, to find her rest in it, as He did.

Then she can "serve God day and night in His temple." Neither interior nor exterior trials can make her leave the fortress in which He has enclosed her. She no longer thirsts nor hungers, for in spite of her overwhelming longings for heaven she is satisfied with the food that was her Master's—the will of the Father. She no longer feels the "sun fall on her"—that is, she does not suffer from suffering, and the "Lamb . . . can lead her to the fountains of the waters of life", where He will, as He will, for she looks not at the path whereon she walks, but at the Shepherd Who guides her.

God, bending down towards this soul, His adopted daughter who so closely resembles His Son, "the first born of every creature",[39] recognizes it as one whom He has predestinated, called, justified; and His fatherly heart thrills at the thought of perfecting His work—that is, glorifying it by transferring it to His kingdom, there to sing through endless ages "the praise of His glory"!

Sixth Day

"And I beheld: and lo a Lamb stood upon Mount Sion, and with Him an hundred forty-four thousand, having His name and the name of His Father written on their foreheads. And I heard a voice from heaven, as the voice of many waters, and as the voice of great thunder and the voice, which I heard, was as the voice of harpers, harping on their harps. And they

---

[39] Col 1:15.

The Last Retreat

sang as it were a new canticle, before the throne, and no man could say the canticle, but those hundred forty-four thousand . . . for they are virgins. These follow the Lamb whithersoever He goeth."[40]

There are some, pure as the light, who even here on earth belong to this generation. They already bear the name of the Lamb and of the Father written on their foreheads. The name of the Lamb by their resemblance and conformity with Him Whom Saint John calls the "Faithful and True", Whom he shows us clothed in a robe stained with blood. These Christians are also faithful and true, and their robes are stained with the blood of their perpetual immolation. "The name of the Father", because He radiates the beauty of His perfection in them, all His divine attributes being reflected in such souls, which are like so many strings of an instrument, vibrating and giving forth the *canticum novum*.

"They follow the Lamb whithersoever He goeth," not only by the wide and level roads but by the thorny paths, among the brambles by the way. They are virgins—that is, free, set apart, detached. . . .

"Free from all except from their love", separated from all, above all from self, detached from all, both in the supernatural and natural order. What a going out from self does that imply! What a death to all! As Saint Paul says: "I die daily!"[41]

The great saint wrote to the Colossians: "You are dead; and your life is hid with Christ in God."[42] This is the condition: we must be *dead*; otherwise, we may be hidden in God at certain times, but we do not habitually *live* in the Divinity, because our feelings, our self-seeking and the rest, draw us forth from Him.

---

[40] Apoc 14:1-4.
[41] 1 Cor 15:31.
[42] Col 3:3.

The Praise of Glory

The soul that gazes upon its Master with the simple eye which makes the whole body full of light, is "kept from the iniquity"[43] within it. The Lord makes it enter the "spacious place",[44] which is nothing else than Himself; there all is pure, all is holy.

O, blessed death in God! O, sweet and delightful loss of self within Him Whom we love! Henceforth the creature can say: "With Christ I am nailed to the cross. And I live, now not I; but Christ liveth in me. And that I live now in the flesh: I live in the faith of the Son of God, Who loved me, and delivered Himself for me."[45]

Seventh Day

"*Caeli enarrant gloriam Dei*".[46] This is what the heavens declare: "the glory of God".

Since my soul is a heaven wherein I dwell, while awaiting the heavenly Jerusalem, this heaven, too, must sing the glory of the Eternal: nothing but the glory of the Eternal. "Day to day uttereth speech."[47] All the light, the communications from God to my soul, are this "day" which "uttereth speech" of His glory to "the day". "The commandment of the Lord is lightsome, enlightening the eyes,"[48] sings the psalmist. Consequently, my fidelity to all His commandments and interior promptings causes me to live in the light; it is also the "speech" which "uttereth" His glory. But what a sweet mystery! "Lord, he who looks upon Thee doth shine."[49] The soul

[43] Ps 17:24.
[44] Ps 17:20.
[45] Gal 2:19, 20.
[46] Ps 18:1.
[47] *Ibid.*, 2.
[48] *Ibid.*, 9.
[49] D'Eyragues, Ps 34:6.

which, by its far-seeing inner gaze, contemplates God with a simplicity that separates it from all else, "shines"; it is a "day that uttereth speech today" of His glory. "Night to night showeth knowledge."[50] How consoling this is! My helplessness, my repugnances, my ignorance, my very faults themselves declare the glory of the Eternal! And my sufferings of body and soul "show forth the glory of God"!

"What shall I render to the Lord, for all the things that He hath rendered to me? I will take the chalice of salvation."[51] If I take this chalice, crimsoned with the Blood of my Master, and in joyous thanksgiving mingle my own blood with that of the sacred Victim Who gives it a share of His own infinity, it may bring wonderful glory to the Father; then my suffering is a "speech" which transmits the glory of the Eternal.

There, in the soul which "shows forth His glory", "He has set His tabernacle in the sun". The "Sun" is the Word—the Bridegroom. If He finds my soul empty of all that is not included in the two words—His love, His glory—He chooses it for His "bridechamber". He enters it impetuously, "rejoicing as a giant to run the way", so that I cannot "hide myself from His heat."[52] This is the "consuming fire"[53] which will work that blessed transformation spoken of by Saint John of the Cross. "Each of them *seems to be the other*, and they are both but one"—a "Praise of glory" to the Father.

Eighth Day

"They rested not day and night, saying: 'Holy, Holy, Holy, Lord God Almighty, Who was, and Who is, and Who is to

[50] Ps 18: 3.
[51] Ps 65:12, 13.
[52] Ps 18:6, 7, 8.
[53] Heb 12:29.

The Praise of Glory

come. . . . ' The four-and-twenty ancients fell down before Him that sitteth on the throne, and adored Him That liveth for ever and ever, and cast their crowns before the throne, saying: 'Thou art worthy, O Lord our God, to receive glory, and honor, and power. . . .'"[54]

How can I imitate, within the heaven of my soul, the ceaseless work of the blessed in the heaven of glory? How can I maintain this constant praise, this uninterrupted adoration? Saint Paul enlightens me when he writes to his disciples: "That the Father . . . would grant you, according to the riches of His glory, to be strengthened . . . unto the inward man. That Christ may dwell by faith in your hearts; that being rooted and founded in charity. . . ."[55]

"To be rooted and founded in charity" is, it seems to me, the necessary condition of worthily fulfilling the office of a *laudem gloriæ*. The soul that enters into, that dwells in "the deep things of God", that consequently does all "by Him, with Him, in Him", with the purity of intention that gives it a certain resemblance to the one, simple Being—this soul, by its every aspiration, every action, every movement, however commonplace, becomes more deeply rooted in Him it loves. Everything within it renders homage to the thrice-holy God; it may be called a perpetual *Sanctus*, a perpetual "praise of glory".

"They fell down . . . and adored . . . and cast their crowns before the throne."

And first of all the soul should "fall down", should plunge into the abyss of its own nothingness, so sinking into it that, according to the beautiful expression of a mystic writer, "it finds the true, invincible, and perfect peace that naught can

[54] Apoc 4:8, 10, 11.
[55] Eph 3:14, 16, 17.

The Last Retreat

trouble, for it has cast itself so low that none will descend to follow it." Then, it can *adore*!

Adoration! Ah! That word comes from heaven. It seems to me that it can be defined as the ecstasy of love; love crushed by the beauty, the strength, the vast grandeur of Him it loves. It falls into a kind of swoon, into a profound and deep silence—that silence of which David spoke when he cried: "Silence is Thy praise."[56] Yes! That is the most perfect praise, for it is sung eternally in the bosom of the tranquil Trinity; it is also "the final effort of the soul that overflows and can speak no more".

"Exalt ye the Lord . . . for the Lord our God is holy",[57] as the psalm says. And again: "They shall always adore Him for His own sake."[58] A soul which meditates upon these thoughts, which understands their meaning with the "mind of the Lord", lives in heaven beforehand, above all that is passing around it, above the clouds, above itself!

It knows that He Whom it adores possesses in Himself all happiness, all glory, and "casting its crown" before Him, as do the blessed, it despises self; loses sight of self; and finds its beatitude in Him Whom it adores, whatever its sufferings or grief, for it has gone out from self and passed into Another. The soul, in this attitude of adoration, resembles the well, spoken of by Saint John of the Cross, which receives the waters flowing from Lebanon, so that those who look on it may exclaim: "The stream of the river maketh glad the city of God." [59]

---

[56] D'Eyragues, Ps 65:2.
[57] *Ibid.*, 48:9.
[58] *Ibid.*, 71:1; (French version).
[59] Ps 45:5.

The Praise of Glory

Ninth Day

"Be ye holy, because I the Lord your God am holy".[60] Who is He Who can give such a command? He Himself has revealed His name, the name proper to Him, which He alone may own. "God said to Moses: I AM WHO AM"; the One Who lives, the Principle of all being. "In Him we live, and move, and have our being."[61]

"Be ye holy, because I am holy", is, it seems to me, the wish expressed on the day of the creation by the words of God: "Let us make man to Our image and likeness."[62] The Creator's idea has always been to associate and to identify His creature with Himself.

Saint Peter writes that we are to be "made partakers of the divine nature."[63] Saint Paul recommends us to "hold the beginning of His substance firm unto the end";[64] and the apostle of love declares: "We are now the sons of God; and it hath not yet appeared what we shall be. We know, that when He shall appear, we shall be like Him: because we shall see Him as He is. And everyone that hath this hope in him sanctifieth himself; as He also is holy."[65]

To be holy, even as God is holy, is the measure for the children of His love. Has not the Master said: "Be ye therefore perfect, as also your heavenly Father is perfect"? God said to Abraham: "Walk before Me and be perfect."[66] This, then, is the means by which to attain the perfection that our heavenly Father requires of us. Saint Paul, after having penetrated the

[60] Lev 19:2.
[61] Acts 17:28.
[62] Gen 1:26.
[63] St. Peter 2:1, 4.
[64] Heb 3:14.
[65] St. John 3:2, 3.
[66] Gen 17:1.

The Last Retreat

divine counsels, reveals this to us clearly in the words: "God chose us in Him before the foundation of the world, that we should be holy and unspotted in His sight in charity, Who hath predestinated us unto the adoption of children."[67]

I seek light again from the same saint in order to walk unerringly on this magnificent way of the presence of God, in which the soul travels "alone with the One", led by the help of His "right hand",[68] "overshadowed with His shoulders, trusting under His wings . . . not afraid of the terror of the night, of the arrow that flieth in the day, of the business that walketh about in the dark: of invasion, or of the noon-day devil".[69]

"Put off, according to former conversation, the old man... and be renewed according to the spirit of your mind: and put on the new man, who according to God, is created in justice, and holiness of truth."[70]

The path is traced for us. We have but to deny ourselves, to die to self, to lose sight of self. Is not that the Master's meaning when He says: "If any man will come after Me, let him deny himself, and take up his cross, and follow Me"?[71]

"If you live according to the flesh," continues the apostle, "you shall die. But if by the spirit you mortify the deeds of the flesh, you shall live."[72] This is the death that God demands, of which Saint Paul says: "Death is swallowed up in victory."[73] "O death, I will be thy death!" says the Lord[74]—that is to say: "Soul, My adopted daughter, look on Me, and thou wilt

---

[67] Eph 1:4, 5.
[68] Ps 19:7
[69] *Ibid.*, 40:4, 5, 6.
[70] Eph 4:22-24.
[71] St. Matt. 16:24.
[72] Rom 8:13.
[73] 1 Cor 15:54.
[74] Osee 14.

The Praise of Glory

lose sight of self; flow wholly into Me. Come, die in Me, that I may live in thee!"

Tenth Day

"Be you therefore perfect, as also your heavenly Father is perfect."[75] When my Master makes me hear this sentence in the depths of my soul, I realize that He is asking me to live, like the Father, in an eternal present, with no past, no future, but, in unity of being, solely in the eternal present.

What is this present? David tells me: "They shall adore Him continually for His own sake." This is the "eternal present" in which a "praise of glory" should abide. But if her attitude of adorer is to be real, so that she can sing: " I will arise early,"[76] she must also be able to say: "For Him I have suffered the loss of all things"[77]—that is, for His sake, that I may incessantly adore Him, I have isolated, separated, stripped myself of all things, natural and supernatural, as regards the gifts of God. For unless a soul has destroyed and become emancipated from self, it must necessarily, at certain times, be commonplace and natural, which is unworthy of a child of God, a bride of Christ, and a temple of the Holy Ghost.

As a protection against living according to nature, the soul must have a lively faith, and must keep its eyes fixed upon the Master; then it can say: "I walked in the innocence of my heart, in the midst of my house."[78] It will adore God for His own sake, and will dwell like Him, as He does, by His example, in the "eternal present" in which He lives.

[75] St. Matt. 5:48.
[76] Ps 56:9.
[77] Phil 3:8.
[78] Ps 50:3.

The Last Retreat

"Be you therefore perfect, as also your heavenly Father is perfect." "God," says St. Denis, "is *the great Solitary*." My Master bids me imitate this perfection, to render Him homage by living in strict solitude. The Divinity dwells in eternal and profound solitude; He cares for the needs of His creatures without in any way leaving it, for He never goes out from Himself; and this solitude is nothing but His Divinity.

I must guard against being withdrawn from this holy interior silence by keeping myself always in the same state, the same isolation, the same retirement, the same detachment. If my desires, my fears, my joys, or my sorrows, if all the impulses coming from these four passions are not completely subjected to God, I shall not be solitary: there will be turmoil within me. Therefore calm, the slumber of the powers, the unity of the whole being, are needed.

"Hearken, O daughter, and see, and incline thine ear: and forget thy people and thy father's house. And the King shall greatly desire thy beauty."[79] This injunction is a call to keep silence: "Hearken incline thine ear." But in order to listen we must forget our "father's house"—that is, whatever pertains to the natural life, of which the apostle says: "If you live according to the flesh, you shall die."[80]

To forget our people is more difficult, for this "people" is that world which is, as it were, a part of ourselves. It includes our feelings, memories, impressions, etc.—in a word, it is self. We must forget it, give it up, and when the soul has broken with it and is wholly delivered from all it means, "the King greatly desires its beauty", for beauty is *unity*, at least as regards divine beauty.

---

[79] *Ibid.* 44:2, 12.
[80] Rom 8:13.

The Praise of Glory

Eleventh Day

"The Lord . . . brought me forth into a vast space . . . because He was well pleased with me."[81] The Creator, seeing that silence reigns within His creature which is deeply recollected in its interior solitude, greatly desires its beauty. He leads it into that immense and infinite solitude, into that "vast space" of which the psalmist sings, which is His very Self: "I will enter into the powers of the Lord."[82]

The Lord said by His prophet: "I will allure her, and will lead her into the wilderness; and I will speak to her heart."[83] The soul has now entered that vast solitude in which God will make His voice heard. "The word of God is living and effectual, and more piercing than any two-edged sword: and reaching unto the division of the soul and the spirit, of the joints also and the marrow."[84]

It is, then, this word itself which will finish the work of stripping the soul, having for its characteristic and peculiar property the operation and creation of what it makes known, provided the soul yields its consent.

To know, however, is not all that is requisite. The soul must keep the word, and by this keeping it is sanctified in the truth, according to the will of the Divine Master: "Sanctify them in thy truth. Thy word is truth."[85] To those who keep His word He has promised: "My Father will love him, and We will come to him, and make Our abode *in him*." [86]

The Three Persons of the Blessed Trinity dwell within the soul which loves Them "*in truth*"—that is, by keeping Their

---

[81] Ps 17:20.
[82] *Ibid.*, 70:16.
[83] Osee 2:14.
[84] Heb 4:12.
[85] St. John 17:17.
[86] *Ibid.*, 14:23.

word. And when this soul realizes what riches it possesses, whatever natural or supernatural joy it feels only induces it to enter within itself to enjoy the substantial good it owns, which is nothing else but God Himself. So that Saint John of the Cross declares "it has a certain resemblance to the Divinity."

"Be ye perfect, as your Father in heaven is perfect." Saint Paul tells me that He "worketh all things according to the counsel of His will",[87] and my Master asks me again to render Him homage in this manner: "To do all things according to the counsel of My will"; never to let myself be led by my impressions, by the first impulses of nature, but to control myself by my will. For this will to be free, it must be "enshrined within the will of God"; then I shall be "led by the spirit of God."[88] All that I do will partake of the divine, the eternal, and, like Him Who changes not, I shall dwell here on earth in an *eternal present*.

Twelfth Day

"*Verbum caro factum est, et habitavit in nobis.*"[89]

God has said: "Be ye holy, because I the Lord your God am holy", but He remained inaccessible and hidden. The creature needed that He should descend to it, that He should live its life, so that, setting its feet in His footsteps it might mount up to Him, sanctifying itself by His sanctity.

"For them I sanctify myself, that they also may be sanctified in truth."[90] I have now before me "the mystery which hath been hidden from the ages and generations . . . this mystery which is Christ, in you the hope of glory,"[91] says Saint Paul,

[87] Eph 1:2.
[88] Rom 8:14.
[89] St. John 1:14.
[90] *Ibid.*, 17:19.
[91] Col 1:26, 27.

adding that the mystery had been manifested to him. It is, then, from this great apostle that I shall learn this wisdom "which surpasseth all knowledge—the charity of Christ".[92]

Firstly, he tells me: "He is my peace", that "by Him we have access . . . to the Father",[93] "because in Him it hath well pleased the Father that all fulness should dwell: and through Him to reconcile all things unto Himself, making peace through the Blood of His cross, both as to the things that are on earth, and the things that are in heaven."[94] "And you are filled in Him," continues the apostle, "buried with Him in baptism, in Whom also you are risen again by the faith of the operation of God and you . . . He hath quickened together with Him; forgiving you all offences: blotting out the handwriting of the decree that was against us, which was contrary to us. And He hath taken the same out of the way, fastening it to the cross: and despoiling the principalities and powers, He hath exposed them confidently in open show, triumphing over them in Himself[95] . . . to present you holy and unspotted and blameless before Him"[96] This is the work of Christ as regards every soul of good will—the work which the Father, in His immense, His "exceeding charity", urges Him to do for me.

He desires to be my peace, so that nothing can distract my attention nor draw me forth from the invincible fortress of holy recollection. There He will give me "access to the Father", and will keep me as stable and tranquil in His presence as if my soul were already in eternity. By the Blood of the Cross He will make peace in my little heaven, that it may be indeed the place of repose of the Holy Trinity. . . .

[92] Eph 3:19.
[93] *Ibid.* 2:18.
[94] Col. 1:19, 20.
[95] *Ibid.* 2:10, 12-15.
[96] *Ibid.*, 1:22.

The Last Retreat

He will fill me with Himself; He will absorb me into Himself, making me live with Him by His life: *"Mihi vivere Christus est."*[97]

Though I may continually fall, in trustful faith I will ask Him to raise me, knowing that He will forgive me and with jealous care will cleanse me perfectly. More than that, He will strip me, will deliver me from my miseries, from all that offers an obstacle to the divine action upon me. He will draw my powers to Him and make them captive, triumphing over them as they dwell in Him. Then I shall have passed completely into Him and shall be able to say: "Now I live, now not I; but Christ liveth in me", and I shall be "holy, and unspotted, and blameless before Him".

Thirteenth Day

"Instaurare omnia in Christo."[98] Again it is Saint Paul who teaches me. He, who has just been immersed in the divine counsels, tells me that "God hath purposed . . . to re-establish all things in Christ."

The apostle comes to my aid again, to help me to fully realize this divine plan, and gives me a rule of life: "Walk in Jesus Christ the Lord, rooted and built up in Him, and confirmed in the faith, as also you have learned, abounding in Him in thanksgiving." [99]

"Walk in Jesus Christ" appears to me to mean to go out from self, to lose sight of, to forsake self, that we may enter more deeply into Him every moment—enter so profoundly as to be "rooted" in Him, and that we may boldly challenge all events with the defiant cry: "Who, then, shall separate us

---

[97] Phil. 1:21.
[98] Eph. 1:10.
[99] Col. 2:6, 7.

The Praise of Glory

from the love of Christ?" When the soul is so deeply fixed in Him as to be rooted in Him, the divine sap flows freely through it and destroys whatever in its life was trivial, imperfect, unspiritual: "Mortality is absorbed in life." Thus stripped of self and clothed with Jesus Christ, the spirit has nothing to fear from without or within; all such things, far from being an impediment, only root it more firmly in its love for its Master. Throughout whatever happens, for or against it, the soul is ready to "adore Him always for His own sake", being free, liberated from self and all else. It can sing with the psalmist: "If armies in camp should stand together against me, my heart shall not fear. If a battle should rise up against me, in this will I be confident. . . . For He hath hidden me in His tabernacle"[100]—that is, in Himself.

I think this is the meaning of Saint Paul's words, "be rooted in Jesus Christ".

Now, what is it to be "built up" in Him? The prophet continues: "He hath exalted me upon a rock, and now He hath lifted up my head above my enemies."[101] Is not that a figure of the soul "built up" in Jesus Christ? He is that Rock on which it is exalted above self, the senses, and nature; above consolations or sufferings; above all that is not Him alone! There, with perfect self-mastery, it controls self, rising above self and all else.

Saint Paul also counsels me to be "confirmed in the faith"; in the faith which never permits the soul to slumber, but keeps it watchful under the eye of its Master, recollected as it listens to His creative word in its faith in the "exceeding charity" which allows God to fill the soul "according to His fulness".

---

[100] Ps 26:3, 5.
[101] *Ibid.*, 6.

The Last Retreat

Finally, the apostle desires me to "abound in Jesus Christ in thanksgiving", for all ought to end in this. "Father, I give Thee thanks", was the song of Christ's soul, and He wishes to hear it echoed in mine. But I think that the *canticum novum* which will best please and charm my God is that of a soul detached from all things, delivered from self; wherein He can reflect all that He is and He can dispose of it as He will. Such a soul waits to be touched by Him as though it were a lyre, and all the gifts it has received are like so many strings which vibrate to give forth, day and night, the "praise of His glory".

Fourteenth Day

"I count all things to be but loss, for the excellent knowledge of Jesus Christ my Lord: for Whom I have suffered the loss of all things . . . that I may gain Christ: and may be found in Him not having my justice, which is of the law, but that . . . which is of God, justice in faith: that I may know Him, the fellowship of His sufferings, being made conformable to His death. . . . I follow after, if I may by any means apprehend wherein I am also apprehended by Christ Jesus. . . . One thing I do: forgetting the things that are behind, and stretching forth myself to those that are before, I press towards the mark, to the prize of the supernal vocation of God in Christ Jesus."[102]

The apostle has often revealed the grandeur of this vocation: "God chose us in Him before the foundation of the world, that we should be holy and unspotted in His sight in charity."[103] "We being predestinated according to the purpose of Him Who worketh all things according to the counsel of His will: that we may be unto the praise of His glory."[104]

[102] Phil.3:8-10, 12-14 [103] Eph 1:4.
[104] *Ibid* 1:1, 12.

The Praise of Glory

How are we to respond to the dignity of our vocation? This is the secret: *"Mihi vivere Christus est"*.[105] *"Vivo enim, jam non ego, vivit vera in me Christus. . . ."*[106] We must be transformed into Jesus Christ, and study this divine model, so thoroughly identifying ourselves with Him that we can incessantly represent Him before the eyes of His Father.

What were His first words on entering the world? "Behold, I come to do Thy will, O God."[107]

The first oblation of the Divine Master was a real one; His life was but its consequence. He delighted in saying: "My meat is to do the will of Him that sent Me."[108] This should be the meat of the bride, and at the same time, the sword that immolates her.

"Father, all things are possible to Thee, remove this chalice from Me, but not what I will, but what Thou wilt."[109] Then, serenely peaceful, she goes to meet all sacrifices with her Master, rejoicing at "having been known" by the Father, since He crucifies her with His Son. By never leaving Him, by keeping in close contact with Him, the secret virtue will go forth from her which delivers and saves souls. Detached, freed from self and all things, she will follow her Master to the mountain, to join with His soul in "the prayer of God".[110] Then, through the divine Adorer, she will "offer the sacrifice of praise always to God—that is to say, the fruit of her lips confessing to His Name."[111] And she will "speak of the might of His terrible acts and will declare His greatness."[112]

[105] Phil 1:21.
[106] Gal 2:20.
[107] Heb 10:9.
[108] St. John 4:34.
[109] St. Mark 14:36.
[110] St. Luke 6:12.
[111] Heb 13:15.
[112] Ps 144:6.

The Last Retreat

In the hour of humiliation, of oppression, she will remember the short sentence: "*Jesus autem tacebat*,"[113] and she, too, will be silent, "keeping all her strength for the Lord"—the strength we draw from silence.

When she is abandoned, forsaken, in anguish, such as drew forth from Christ the loud cry: "Why hast Thou forsaken Me?",[114] she will remember the prayer: "That they may have my joy fulfilled in themselves."[115] And, drinking to the very dregs the chalice given by the Father[116], she will find a heavenly sweetness in its bitterness.

Then, after having repeated again and again: "I thirst"—thirst to possess Thee in glory—she will die, exclaiming: "It is consummated,"[117] ". . . into Thy hands I commend my spirit."[118] Then the Father will come to take her into His heritage, where "in Thy light we shall see light."[119] "Know ye also that the Lord hath made His holy One wonderful",[120] sang David. Yes, in the case of such a soul, God's holy One is glorified indeed, for He has destroyed all else to clothe it with Himself, and it has conformed its life to the words of the Precursor "He must increase, but I must decrease."[121]

---

[113] St. Mark 15:5.
[114] *Ibid.*, 34.
[115] St. John 17:13.
[116] *Ibid.*, 18:2.
[117] *Ibid.*, 19:30.
[118] St. Luke 23:46.
[119] Ps 35:10.
[120] *Ibid.* 4:4. (In the French: "hath marvellously glorified His holy One.")
[121] St. John 3:30.

The Praise of Glory

Fifteenth Day[122]

Nearer than all to Jesus Christ, though at a distance which is infinite, there exists a created being who was also the great "praise of glory" of the Blessed Trinity. She responded fully to the divine vocation of which the apostle speaks; she was always holy, unspotted, blameless, in the sight of the Thrice Holy God.

Her soul is so simple, its movements are so profound, that they cannot be detected; she seems to reproduce on earth the life of the Divinity, the simple Being. And she is so transparent, so luminous, that she might be taken for the light itself; yet she is but the mirror of the Sun of justice (*Spœculum justitiae*).

"His Mother kept all these words in her heart."[123] Her whole history can be summed up in these few words. It was within her own heart that she dwelt, and so deeply did she enter it that no human eye can follow her.

When I read in the gospel that Mary "went into the hill-country with haste into a city of Juda"[124] to perform her charitable office to her cousin Elizabeth, I picture her to myself as she passes—beautiful, calm, majestic, absorbed in communion with the Word of God within her. Like Him, her prayer was always: "*Ecce!*"—"Here am I!" Who? "The handmaid of the Lord", the last of His creatures, she, His Mother!

Her humility was so genuine! For she was always self forgetful, knowing nothing, freed from self; so that she could sing: "Behold from henceforth all generations shall call me blessed. Because He that is mighty hath done great things to me!"[125]

---

[122] Although we have made several quotations from this devout meditation on our Lady, we give it entirely for the fifteenth day, consecrated to it by Elizabeth in her little retreat.
[123] St. Luke 2:51.
[124] *Ibid.*, 1:39.
[125] *Ibid.*, 48, 49.

The Last Retreat

This Queen of Virgins is the Queen of Martyrs too; but it was within her heart that the sword transpierced her, for with her everything took place within her soul.

Oh! How beautiful she is to contemplate during her long martyrdom, enveloped in a majesty both strong and sweet, for she has learned from the Word how those should suffer who are chosen as victims by the Father; those whom He has elected as associates in the great work of the redemption whom He has known and "predestinated to be conformed to His Christ", crucified by love.

She is there, at the foot of the Cross; she stands in her strength and courage, and my Master tells me: "*Ecce Mater tua.*" He gives her to me for my Mother! And now that He has returned to His Father, that He has put me in His place on the Cross, so that I may "fill up those things which are wanting of the sufferings of Christ in my flesh for His Body, which is the Church", our Lady is there still, to teach me to suffer as He did, to let me hear the last song of His soul which no one but His Mother could overhear.

When I shall have said my "*consummatum est*", it will be she again, *Janua Cœli*, who will introduce me into the eternal courts as she utters the mysterious words: "*Lætatus sum in his quæ dicta sunt mihi, in domum Domini ibimus.*"

Sixteenth Day

"As the hart panteth after the fountains of water: so my soul panteth after thee, O God. My soul hath thirsted after the strong living God; when shall I come and appear before the face of God?"[126]

[126] Ps 41:1, 2.

The Praise of Glory

"Yet, as the sparrow hath found herself a house, and the turtle a nest for herself where she may lay her young";[127] so, while waiting to be taken to the holy city of Jerusalem, *Beata pacis visio*,[128] *Laudem Gloriæ* has found her retreat, her beatitude, heaven beforehand, where she already begins her life of eternity.

"In God my soul is silent, it is from Him I expect my deliverance. Surely He is the rock where I find salvation, my citadel, and I shall be moved no more!"[129]

This is the mystery to which my lyre is tuned today. My Divine Master has said to me, as to Zaccheus: "Make haste, and come down, for this day I must abide in thy house."[130] Make haste and descend, but where? Into the innermost depths of my being, after having left self, separated from self, stripped myself of self—in a word, without self.

"I must abide in thy house." It is my Master Who utters this; my Master Who desires to abide in me with the Father and His Spirit of Love so that I may "have fellowship" with Them. "Now therefore you are no more strangers and foreigners. but you are the domestics of God,"[131] as Saint Paul says.

I think that to be a domestic of God is to abide in the bosom of the tranquil Trinity, in my inner-most depths, in the invincible fortress of holy recollection described by Saint John of the Cross.

"My soul longeth and fainteth for the courts of the Lord."[132] Such should be the feeling of my whole soul when it enters its interior "courts" to contemplate its God and keep in closest

---

[127] Ps 83:4.
[128] Vespers, Hymn of the Dedication.
[129] D'Eragues, Ps 62:2, 3.
[130] St. Luke 19:5.
[131] Eph 2:19.
[132] Ps 83:1.

contact with Him. It faints in a divine swoon before this all-powerful love, this infinite Majesty which dwells within it. It is not that life forsakes it, but the soul itself disdains this natural life and withdraws from it. Feeling such life to be unworthy of a spirit raised to such dignity, it dies to this life and flows into its God.

How beautiful is the creature thus stripped and freed! It is "disposed to ascend by steps to pass from the vale of tears to the place which is its end"[133]—that is, from all that is less than God, that "vast space" which is the unfathomable Trinity: "*Immensus Pater, immensus Filius, immensus Spiritus Sanctus.*"[134]

It rises, ascending above the senses, above nature, above self. It passes beyond all joy and all sorrow, passes through the clouds, never to rest until it has penetrated within Him Whom it loves, Who will Himself give it the "repose of the abyss". And all this will be done without leaving the "holy fortress". The Divine Master has said to it: "Make haste and come down."

Nor will the soul leave it when at last it lives, like the immutable Trinity, in an "eternal present", adoring God eternally for His own sake, and becoming, by a gaze that ever grows more simple, more unifying, "the brightness of His glory",[135] or, in other words, the ceaseless "praise of glory" of His adorable perfections.

---

[133] *Ibid.* 83:6, French version.
[134] Athanasian Creed.
[135] Heb 1:3.

The Praise of Glory

Appendix II
Prayer of Sister Elizabeth of the Trinity[1]

O my God, Trinity Whom I adore! Help me to become utterly forgetful of self, that I may establish myself in Thee, as changeless and as calm as though my soul were already in eternity. May nothing disturb my peace nor draw me forth from Thee, O my immutable Lord! But may I penetrate more deeply every moment into the depths of Thy Mystery.

Give peace to my soul; make it Thy heaven, Thy cherished dwelling-place, Thy home of rest. Let me never leave Thee there alone, but keep me there all absorbed in Thee, in living faith, adoring Thee and wholly yielded up to Thy creative action.

O my Christ Whom I love! Crucified by love! Fain would I be the bride of Thy heart; fain would I cover Thee with glory, and love Thee . . . until I die of very love! Yet I realize my weakness, and beg Thee to clothe me with Thyself, to identify my soul with all the movements of Thine own. Immerse me in Thyself; possess me wholly; substitute Thyself for me, that my life may be but a radiance of Thine own. Enter my soul as Adorer, as Restorer, as Savior!

O eternal Word, Utterance of my God! I long to pass my life in listening to Thee, to become docile, that I may learn all from Thee. Through all darkness, all privations, all helplessness, I crave to keep Thee ever with me and to dwell beneath Thy lustrous beams. O my beloved Star! So fascinate me that I cannot wander from Thy light!

O "consuming Fire!" Spirit of Love! Descend within me and reproduce in me, as it were, an incarnation of the Word, that I may be to Him another humanity wherein He renews all His mystery. And Thou, O Father, bend towards Thy poor little

---

[1] This prayer of Sister Elizabeth of the Trinity was found among her notes (see p. 115). It has no title.

Letters

creature and overshadow her, beholding in her none other than Thy Beloved Son, in Whom Thou hast set all Thy pleasure.

O my "Three", my All, my Beatitude, infinite Solitude, Immensity wherein I lose myself! I yield myself to Thee as Thy prey. Merge Thyself in me, that I may be immerged in Thee until I depart to contemplate in Thy light the abyss of Thy greatness!

November 21, 1904

Appendix III
Letters of Sister Elizabeth of the Trinity to a Friend[1]

Letter One

1901

I see that my little N— is no nearer being converted, and I assure you that it grieves me. I overlooked your fits of temper in the past, but you are no longer a baby, and the scenes you make are ridiculous. I know that you will allow your Elizabeth to say anything, so that I shall speak my mind, and you must really set to work to amend. As your nature is like mine, I know what you can do. If you only realized what it is to love God and to give Him all He asks, especially at our own cost. This is not a sermon, but the overflowing of my soul into your own, that together we may lose ourselves in Him Who loves us, as Saint Paul says, with an "exceeding love"!

---

[1] Elizabeth knew how to be firm when necessary, as the following letters prove, while at the same time they bear witness to her own struggles when, after her first confession, she resolved to give herself wholly to God.

The Praise of Glory

Letter Two

April, 1902

. . . Yes, I pray for you, and keep you in my soul near the good God, in that little inner sanctuary where I find Him at all hours of the day and night. I am never alone: my Christ is always there praying within me, and I pray with Him.

You grieve me, for I feel certain you are unhappy, and I assure you that it is your own fault. If only I could teach you the secret of happiness as God has taught it to me! You say that I have neither cares nor sufferings. It is true that I am happy, but in the way one can be while one's will is being contradicted. We must fix our gaze on God. It requires an effort at first when we are boiling with anger, but gently, with patience and the help of grace, we conquer in the end. Build a little cell within your soul as I do; remember that the good God is there, and enter it from time to time. When your nerves are upset or you feel unhappy, take refuge there at once and confide everything to the Divine Master. If you practiced it a little, prayer would not weary you.

You used to love to sit close beside me and tell me all your little secrets: that is how you ought to go to Him. If once you understood that, you would suffer no more: that is the secret of the Carmelite life.

I keep you in the little cell of my soul as you must keep me in yours; then we shall never be apart.

Letter Three

April, 1902

I have spent a good Lent. Nothing I have seen at Carmel is more beautiful than Holy Week and Easter Day—indeed, I should say that nothing can compare with them. I will tell you all about them when we meet.

Letters

What a joy it is to live in intimacy with God, our life being spent heart to heart with Him in a constant interchange of love with the Divine Master when we know how to find Him in the depths of our soul! Henceforth we are never alone and we long for solitude that we may enjoy the company of the Guest Whom we adore. You must give Him His proper place in your life, in the loving and passionate heart He has given you. If you only knew how kind, how loving He is in every way!

I am begging Him to reveal Himself to your soul, to be the Friend that you can always find; then you would see all things in another light, and life would become a joy.

This is not a sermon, but an overflowing of my soul into your own, that together we may lose ourselves in Him Who loves us, as Saint Paul says, with an "exceeding love"!

Letter Four

July 24, 1905

I still keep the long letter you wrote to me before you left. I have read it again and again, begging the Divine Ideal to take captive and wound the dear little heart He seeks and restrains as it struggles to escape Him and to live engrossed in things immeasurably below the end for which He created it and set it in this world.

I understand your craving for an ideal—that is, something to draw you out of self and to raise you higher; but that ideal is to be found in Him alone: Truth Itself. If you did but know Him in some degree as your Elizabeth knows Him! . . . He fascinates the soul; beneath His gaze the horizon becomes vast, beautiful, and luminous. I love Him passionately, and in Him I find my all. It is through Him, by His light, that I must view all things and perform every action. Will you turn with

The Praise of Glory

me to that sublime Ideal? It is no fiction, but a reality; it is my life at Carmel. Look at Magdalen and see how she was captivated. Since you need to live above self, live in Him: it is so simple. And then you must be the comfort of your dear mother. You do not know what there is in the heart of mothers such as God has given you and me. Remember, nothing better is to be found in this world, and I do not think my Master could have asked more from me than to yield Him mine. I want you to be perfectly submissive, and to dwell in God and in His peace. The more sure I feel that you are not good, the more resolved I am on winning your soul, for the Master wants it. Besides, are you not my own little child? I feel to some extent answerable for you, so do not let your conversion be too difficult. Let the Master take you in His nets, for it is well to be there.

Appendix IV
Letters to Rev. Canon A—

Letter One

Reverend and Dear Canon A—,

How good it is to spend Lent, Holy Week, and Easter in Carmel! It is like nowhere else. What joy I felt at singing the *Alleluia* in the white mantle and the dear habit which I have so long desired! It was bliss to spend Maundy Thursday near Him. I should have remained there all night, but the Master bade me go to rest. But that does not matter, does it? We find Him as much in our sleep as in our prayer, since He is in all, everywhere, always, at all times. I returned to the choir at two o'clock in the morning. You can guess how glad I was to be

Letters

there. I grow fonder every day of the grille that makes me the prisoner of His love; it is such happiness to think that we are both captives, fettered by our love for one another. More than that, we are but one victim, offered to the Father for souls "that they may be made perfect in one".[1]

Thank God, whenever you think of your little Carmelite, for having given her so blessed a lot. It is heaven already. The horizon is so beautiful! It is He! . . . What will it be above, since here below our union is so intimate? You know how homesick I feel for paradise. My longing is not lessened, but I already see heaven, since I bear it within me. One seems so near it in Carmel. Will you not come and see me some day, and chat through the grille as you used to with your little Elizabeth? Do you remember the first time I told you my secret in Saint Hilary's cloister? I have spent many a happy moment with you, and I beg God to reward you for all the good you have done me. I remember how glad I used to feel when I could spend a short time with you and talk over my great secret. I was but a child, yet you never doubted that God had called me.

Letter Two

August 2, 1903

I remember our conversations in the last holidays we spent together among the beautiful mountains, and how we used to stroll together by moonlight. on the hill by the church. How lovely it was in the calm and silence of night! Did you not feel that my whole heart went out to Him? And then Mass in the little chapel—the Mass you said!

[1] St. John 17:23.

The Praise of Glory

I shall never forget those happy times. My soul and heart follow you now, and I feel very near to you. I delight in the thought of having left all for Him; it is a joy to give when one loves, and I love so ardently the God Who wishes to have me for Himself alone. I feel His love descending on my soul! It is like an ocean into which I plunge and lose myself; my vision on earth while I wait to see Him face to face in the light. He is in me and I in Him. I only have to love and to let myself be loved every moment; to wake in love, to act in love, to sleep in love, my soul in His, my heart in His, that by His contact He may purify and deliver me from my misery. If you only knew how full I am of Him! I should like to tell you all about it as in the old days at Saint Hilary's, and then bathe myself in the precious Blood. I almost commit the sin of envy when I think of dear Mamma. I beg you, at least, at Holy Mass to put my soul in the chalice, and to ask the Bridegroom to make me wholly pure, a virgin soul, one with Him.

Letter Three

January, 1904

Since the divine "Little One" dwells in my soul, His prayer belongs to me, and I delight in directing it towards those for whom I shall always feel the deepest gratitude, so that you have a large share in my poor little prayers. Christmas, of which I have always been very fond, has a character all its own at Carmel. Instead of passing the holy vigil with Mamma and "Guite", I spent it in the great silence in the choir, close to Him, and delighted in saying to myself: "He is my All, my one and only All." What happiness and peace it brings the soul! He is the One; I have given Him all. If I look earth-wards I see only solitude, even a void, for I cannot deny that my heart has suffered; but if I keep my gaze fixed on Him, my glowing Star, oh! All else disappears, and I lose myself in Him like a drop in the ocean; all is calm and peace! Saint Paul alludes to this divine peace when he says that it "surpasses all understanding".[2]

On Sunday, the anniversary of the great day of my profession, I shall be in retreat, and shall delight in passing the day near my Bridegroom. I hunger for Him; He opens abysses in my soul which He alone can fill by leading me into profound silence where I should like to stay forever. Good-bye, Canon A——, I beg you to pray for me, for I have great need of your help. Remember your Carmelite at the Holy Sacrifice, at the altar of Him she loves. Tell the good God that she longs to be His victim, so that He may ever dwell in her, and that she may have something to give to others.

Letter Four

January, 1905

I have prayed much to my Divine Bridegroom for you, asking Him to give you the most precious of all His treasures—and is not that Himself, Jesus, the gift of God? He makes me experience more fully every day the joy of being His—His alone—and my Carmelite vocation leads me to adore and thank Him. Yes, Saint Paul's words are true: "He has loved us with an exceeding love." He has loved His little Elizabeth too much, but love calls forth love, and I ask nothing of the good God but that I may grasp that knowledge of charity spoken of by Saint Paul, of which my heart longs to sound the very depths; but I must wait for heaven to understand it, must I not? Yet it seems to me that we can begin to learn it on earth,

---

[2] Phil 4:7.

The Praise of Glory

since we possess Him, and in spite of everything, we can dwell in His love. He made me understand this during my private retreat in October. Ten days full of silence and absolute solitude! From Carcassonne you can see the happy hermit bury herself in her desert. I am indeed happy, and it does me good to say so, especially to you, for I know you still feel a fatherly affection for me.

If you only knew how unchanged my heart is—indeed, it is enlarged and dilated by its contact with the God of all love. It is in Him that I am still your own, and that I kneel to receive your cherished blessing.

Letter Five

February, 1905

Before burying myself in the solitude of the desert, our reverend mother has given me leave to let you know how happy your kind letter has made me. Mamma told me that you were suffering with your arm, but I hope from what you write that the rheumatism has gone.

Poor Mamma! She wishes the *Alleluia* had been sung already. God will reward her motherly heart for its long fast! Yes, Canon, as you say, there is much to expiate and much to plead for; so many wants need fervent and continual prayer and ardent love. The power of a soul given up to love is very great. We see it in Saint Mary Magdalen: one word from her sufficed to obtain the resurrection of Lazarus. There is an urgent call for this good God to work many a resurrection in our dear France which I love to set where the Divine Blood will flow upon it. Saint Paul says that we have "the remission of sins, according to the riches of His grace which hath superabounded in us."[3] The thought is such a help to me! Oh! What a consolation to go and be saved by Him at times when we

[3] Eph 1: 7, 8.

only realize our miseries, and how full I am of them! But the good God has given me a mother, the image of His mercy, who knows how to calm the anguish of her little one's soul in a moment, and to give her wings to fly beneath the rays of the creative Star, so that my life is spent in thanksgiving, united to the eternal praise sung by the saints in heaven, while I pass my apprenticeship on earth.... During holy Lent pray for your child; consecrate her with the sacred Host, so that nothing more may remain of poor Elizabeth," but that she may be wholly "of the Trinity". Then her prayer can become all powerful, and you will profit by it, since you have so large a share in it—which is only acquitting herself of her heavy debt of gratitude!... Good-bye, dear Canon A—! The bell is calling me to Matins. I shall not forget you there. That will be the first time.

Letter Six

Feast of the Ascension, 1905

Dear Mamma has told me that you have been very ill. I have asked reverend mother to allow me to pay you a short visit. Today the Divine Master returns to His Father, Who is our Father as well, and He will prepare us a place in His heritage of glory. I am asking Him to take all your bonds into bondage and to set you quickly upon your feet again. You must tell me if He listens to His Carmelite. We had our last recreation today before entering our retreat in the Cenacle until Pentecost. I feel that I shall be closer to you than ever during these ten days, for I shall dwell more completely in Him. Saint Paul, whose beautiful epistles I am studying, and which delight me, says: "The things that are of God no man knoweth but the Spirit of God."[4] The plan of my retreat will

---

[4] 1 Cor 2:11.

The Praise of Glory

be to hold myself by faith and love beneath the "unction from the Holy One",[5] of which Saint John speaks, since He alone "searcheth the deep things of God".[6] Oh! Pray for me, that I may not grieve this Spirit of Love but may allow Him to work all the creations of His grace within my heart! Will you also pray for my dear community, and above all, for our reverend mother and all her intentions? I ask you to help me to requite my debt of gratitude to her. If you only knew what she is to your little child! A virtue from God continually flows from her soul into mine. If, on her feast-day, you could offer her the lovely bouquet, crimsoned with the Blood of the Lamb, that so delighted her last year, I assure you I should be overjoyed. I thank you beforehand, being certain that my wish will be granted if possible. How simple I am with you! But are you not the father of my little soul?

Good-bye, dear Canon A——. Bless me and obtain for me the Spirit of Love and Light!

Appendix V
Letters to Madame——

Letter One

There is no wood like the wood of the Cross for enkindling the fire of love in the soul, and Jesus wants to be loved and to find in the world that so offends Him souls given to Him—that is, wholly yielded up to Him and His good pleasure. "My meat is to do the will of Him that sent Me."[1] Our Lord was the first to say this. The soul in communion with Him enters into

---

[5] 1 St. John 2:20.
[6] 1 Cor 2:10.
[1] St. John 4:34.

the feelings of His divine soul, and its one ideal is to fulfil the will of the Father Who has loved us from all eternity.

As you have given me leave to speak freely to you and to read something of the secrets of your heart, allow me, dear Madame—, to tell you that I see the will of God manifested in your sufferings. He has deprived you of the power of action, of seeking amusement, or doing any work, so that your one occupation may be to love and to think of Him. I tell you, from Him, that He thirsts for your soul. You are specially consecrated to Him, for, to my great joy, you wished to be His entirely while living in the world. It is very simple! He is always with you. Be always with Him, in your actions, your sufferings, and when your body is exhausted. Remain in His sight; see Him present with you, living in you.

Were I not in Carmel, I should envy your solitude—you are so secluded among your beautiful mountains. You seem to me in a little Thebaid. How delightful to wander about alone through those vast woods, to leave your books and work, and dwell with the good God, heart to heart, in closest intimacy, gazing upon Him with overflowing love! You should enjoy such happiness; it is heavenly.

Letter Two

You ask me how I can bear the cold. Believe me, I am not more generous than you, but you are ill and I am in good health. I do not feel that the weather is cold, so you see I have not much merit. I used to suffer far more from the winter at home than I do at Carmel without a fire. The good God gives us grace. Besides, it is well for us when we feel such little things, to look at the Divine Master Who also suffered the like because of "His exceeding charity" towards us; then we long to return Him love for love. We meet with many such sacrifices at Carmel, but they are sweet when the heart is made captive by love.

I will tell you what I do when I feel a little tired: I look at the crucified God, and when I see how He gave Himself for me; it seems as if I cannot do less than spend myself, wear myself out, that I may repay Him some little of what He has given me. Dear Madame, let us communicate in His spirit of suffering in the morning at Holy Mass. We are His brides: we ought to be like Him. Let us keep ourselves in Him during the day. If we faithfully live His life, if we identify ourselves with all the feelings of the soul of the crucified God, we need no longer dread our own weakness; He will be our strength, and who will dare to take us from Him? I believe that He is greatly pleased with you, and that your sacrifices must console His Heart. During Lent I appoint as our meeting-place the infinity of God, His charity. Shall not that be the desert where, with our Divine Spouse, we will live in profound solitude, since it is in this solitude that He speaks to our hearts?

Letter Three

It is well for us to look into the hearts of the saints and to follow them, in faith, until they enter heaven. There they shine with the light of God, Whom they contemplate face to face. This heaven of the saints is our own country, the Father's house, where we are expected and loved, to which some day we too may take our flight, to repose in the bosom of infinite Love! When we fix our eyes upon this divine world, which surrounds us already even in our earthly exile, in which we can spend our life, how the things of this world disappear! They are the things that are not, that are less than nothing. The saints well understood this true wisdom, which makes us leave all things, ourselves above all, to fly to God and dwell in Him alone. Dear Madame—, He abides in us to sanctify us. Let us ask Him to be Himself our sanctity. We are told in the gospel that when our Lord was on earth a secret virtue went out from Him—the sick recovered health, the dead were raised to life when brought in contact with Him. Yet He is still living—living in the tabernacle, in the adorable Sacrament, living in our souls. He Himself has told us so: "If anyone love Me, he will keep My word, and My Father will love him, and We will come to him, and will make Our abode with him."[2] Since He is there, let us bear Him company as a man does his friend. This divine union is wholly interior: it is the essence of the Carmelite life which makes our solitude so dear to us; for, as is said by our father, Saint John of the Cross (whose feast we keep today), "Two hearts that love one another prefer solitude to all else."

On Saturday, the Feast of the Presentation of our Lady, we had the beautiful ceremony of the renewal of vows. Oh! dear Madame, what a happy day it was! What a joy to bind oneself to the service of so kind a Master, to tell Him that one is His till death, the bride of Christ! I am very glad to know that you, too, are given to Him. I think our great Saint Elizabeth in heaven must bless and seal the union of our souls.

I shall never go to see your beautiful mountains, but in heart and soul I shall follow you there, asking Him Who is our "Trysting-place" to draw us to those other mountains, to those divine summits so far distant from earth that they nearly touch heaven. It is there that I remain united with you under the rays of the Sun of Love!

---

[2] St. John 14:23.

The Praise of Glory

Letter Four

Before entering the strict silence of Lent, our Reverend Mother has given me leave to tell you how earnestly I and my dear community are praying for you. I understand your dread of an operation, and beg our Lord to relieve and calm your fears Himself. The apostle Saint Paul says that "God worketh all things according to the counsel of His will;"[3] consequently we ought to receive everything as coming directly from the divine hand of our Father, Who loves us, and Who, amidst all our trials, is following out His own end—that of uniting us more closely to Himself. Launch your soul upon the ocean of trust and submission to His will; remember that whatever troubles and frightens you does not come from the good God, for He is the "Prince of Peace",[4] that peace which He has promised to men of goodwill. When you fear, as you tell me, that you have abused His graces, that is the time to redouble your trust in Him, for, as the apostle says elsewhere, "Where sin abounded, grace did more abound";[5] "God is rich in mercy, for His exceeding charity wherewith He loved us",[6] Then do not dread the hour through which we all must pass. Death is the sleep of the babe upon its mother's heart. At last the night of exile will have fled for ever, and we shall enter into possession of "the lot of the saints in light".[7] Saint John of the Cross says that we shall be judged by our degree of love, which corresponds with what our Lord said of Saint Mary Magdalen: "Many sins are forgiven her, because she hath loved much."[8] I often think that I shall have a very long Purgatory, for much will be asked of those who have

[3] Eph 1:11.
[4] Isa 9:6.
[5] Rom 5:20.
[6] Eph 2:4.
[7] Col 1:12.
[8] St. Luke 7:47.

Letters

received much, and He has been so overflowing in generosity to His little bride! However, I confide in His love, and sing my hymn of His mercies while I am still on earth.

If we were to grow more like God every day, with what confidence we should regard the hour in which we must appear before His infinite sanctity! I think you have discovered the secret. It is by self-denial that we reach this divine end; by this we die to self and give place to God. Do you remember the beautiful page in Saint John's gospel where our Lord says to Nicodemus: "Amen, amen, I say unto thee, unless a man be born again, he cannot see the kingdom of God"?[9] Let us renew ourselves in the depths of our soul—"Stripping yourselves of the old man with his deeds, and putting on the new, according to the image of Him Who created him."[10] It is to be done gently and simply by separating ourselves from all that is not God. Then the soul no longer fears nor desires anything, the will being completely lost in that of God, which produces union.

Let us pray much for one another during the holy time of Lent, retiring into the desert with our Master, and asking Him to teach us to live His life.

Letter Five

February, 1904

I have felt closely drawn to you lately while reading the life of Saint Elizabeth, your mother and my heavenly patroness. I am so fond of those words addressed to her by our Lord: "Elizabeth, if thou will keep with Me, I will keep with thee, and nothing will be able to separate us." Dear Madame did not the Divine Spouse say so to us in the silence of our

---

[9] St. John 3:3.
[10] Col 3:9, 10.

The Praise of Glory

soul when He invited us to follow Him more closely, to be one with Him by becoming His brides? During these days in which we keep the "Forty Hours", the Blessed Sacrament is exposed here. Today, Sunday, I have spent nearly the whole day before our Lord, trying by my love to make Him forget the sins committed during the carnival.

Lent will begin on Wednesday: shall we make a Lent of love together? "The Son of God loved me, and delivered Himself for me."[11] This, then, is the way love expresses itself: it gives itself, it empties itself entirely into Him Whom it loves. "Love makes the lover go out of himself; transporting him, by an ineffable ecstasy, into the Heart of Him it loves." Is not that a beautiful thought? Let it be the guiding watchword of our souls, so that they may suffer themselves to be borne away by the Spirit of Love, and beneath the light of faith may, while still on earth, join the hymn of love eternally sung by the blessed before the throne of the Lamb. Yes, dear Madame—, let us begin our heaven on earth, our heaven in love! He Himself is this love, as Saint John tells us: "God is charity."[12] Shall not this be our trysting-place?

Letter Six

January, 1905.

In the epistles of Saint Peter I came across a quotation which will express the good wishes of your little Carmelite for you: "Sanctify the Lord Christ in your hearts."[13] To do that we must carry out the idea of Saint John the Baptist: "He must increase, but I must decrease."[14] Dear Madame—, let us

---

[11] Gal 2:20.
[12] 1 St. John 4:8.
[13] St. Peter 3:15.
[14] St. John 3:30.

make God increase in our souls during this new year which He gives us to sanctify ourselves and to unite ourselves more closely to Him. Let us keep Him "alone and separate"; let Him be really King. As for us, let self disappear and be forgotten, that we may be nothing but the "praise of His glory", according to the apostle's beautiful expression.

I also wish you all the blessings of health which you need, as you suffer so severely for want of them. Remember what Saint Paul said: "Gladly, therefore, will I glory in my infirmities, that the power of Christ may dwell in me."[15] It is all the will of the good God. Rejoice, rejoice, dear Madame—, in the bodily pains which affect your soul as well, and remember that if you bear your state of helplessness faithfully and lovingly you can load Him with glory. Our holy mother Saint Teresa said: "When we know how to unite ourselves to God and to His holy will, accepting whatever He decrees, we possess everything."

I wish you this deep peace in the divine good pleasure. I understand what sacrifices your health must impose upon you, but it is sweet to say to ourselves: "He wills it." He said one day to one of His saints: "Drink, eat, sleep, do whatever you like, as long as you love Me." It is love that makes His yoke so easy and His burden so light. Let us ask the Infant God to consume us by this divine flame, by the fire that He willed to bring on earth. . . ."

Letter Seven

January, 1906

May 1906, be, for your soul, a chain of fidelity whose every link, soldered by love, may bind you more closely to the Divine Master and make you indeed His captive, "fettered to

[15] 2 Cor 12:9

The Praise of Glory

Him", as Saint Paul says. The saint, with his large and generous heart, desired for his disciples "that Christ might dwell in their hearts, that they might be rooted and founded in charity."[16] That is what I wish for you, too, dear Madame—: that the reign of love may be supreme within you, that its influence may make you totally oblivious of self, and may conduct you to that mystic death of which the apostle spoke when He exclaimed: "I live, now not I; but Christ liveth in me."[17] The Divine Master, in His discourse after the Last Supper, that last song of the love of His soul, utters to the Father the beautiful words: "I have glorified Thee on the earth, I have finished the work which Thou gavest Me to do."[18] We who are His brides, dear Madame—, ought consequently to identify ourselves completely with Him, and ought to be able to repeat these words at the close of each day. Perhaps you will ask me how we are to glorify Him. It is very simple. Our Lord told us the secret when He said: "My meat is to do the will of Him that sent Me."[19] Cling closely to the will of this adorable Master; look upon each joy and each suffering as coming directly from Him, and your life will be a continual communion, for all things will be like a sacrament coming from God to you. This really is the fact, for God is not divided. His will is His whole being. He is wholly and entirely in all things, and these things are, to a certain extent, nothing but an emanation of His love! You see how you can glorify Him in the states of suffering and languor which are so hard to bear. Forget self as much as possible; that is the secret of peace and happiness. Saint Francis Xavier exclaimed: "What touches me, touches me not; but what touches Him, touches

[16] Eph 3:17.
[17] Gal 2:20.
[18] St. John 17:4.
[19] *Ibid.*, 4:34.

me to the quick." Happy the soul that becomes so utterly detached; that is love indeed!

Appendix VI
Letter to Someone Who Wished to Become a Carmelite

Letter One

A Carmelite has a soul that has looked upon the crucified God. She has seen Him offering Himself to the Father as a Victim; and, reflecting upon this grand manifestation of the charity of Christ, she has realized His passionate love, and has willed to give herself with Him. She lives, as if in heaven, with God alone on the mountain of Carmel, in silence, in solitude, in endless prayer. He Who will one day be her beatitude and will satiate her with glory, has given Himself to her already; He never leaves her; He abides in her soul; the two are but one, so that she thirsts for silence that she may ever listen to Him and penetrate more and more deeply into His Infinitude. She is identified with Him she loves and finds Him everywhere. Is not that heaven on earth? You bear this heaven within you, for Jesus knows the Carmelite by what is within her, that is, by her soul. Never leave Him; do everything under His divine gaze, and rejoice in His peace and love.

Letter Two

Let us live in intimacy with our Beloved; let us be all His as He is all ours. You are deprived of receiving Him [in holy communion] as often as you wish, but remember that His love needs no sacrament to come to you; you can communicate all day, since He is living in your soul. Listen to what our Father Saint John of the Cross tells us:

"O thou soul, most beautiful of creatures, who so earnestly longest to know the place where thy Beloved is, that thou mayest seek Him and be united to Him? Thou art thyself that very tabernacle where He dwells, the secret chamber of His retreat where He is hidden. Rejoice, therefore, and exult, because all thy good and all thy hope is so near thee as to be within thee; yea, rather, rejoice that thou canst not be without it, for lo, 'the kingdom of God is within you'."[1]

This living in Him is the whole Carmelite life. Then all sacrifices, all self-denial, and all else become divine. Love silence and prayer, the essence of our life. Beg the Queen of Carmel, our Mother, to teach you to adore Jesus in His profound recollection. Pray to our holy mother Saint Teresa as well; she loved so deeply! . . . she died of love! Beg her to give you her passion for God and for souls, for the Carmelite must be zealous; all her prayers, all her sacrifices are for that.

Do you know Saint John of the Cross, who penetrated so deeply into the depths of the Divinity? I ought to have spoken first of Saint Elias, our first father. You see our Order is very ancient, since it dates back to the prophets. How I wish I could relate all its glories! Let us love it: there is none to be compared to it! As for the Rule, you will discover all its beauties some day. Live in the spirit of them now!

Appendix VII
Fragments of Letters

My Dear Madame,

Your little friend's heart longs to let you know how intensely she prays for you. Like Magdalen at the feet of my Master, I shall

[1] *Spiritual Canticle*, St. John of the Cross, stanza 1:8

Letters

intercede for you and tell Him: "He whom Thou lovest is sick."

Jesus gives His Cross to His true friends that He may draw nearer to them. I see a very deep love for you in His heart.

I unite myself to the angel you have lost, who is watching over you from heaven, so that I may touch the Heart of the good God.

I have just heard that God has offered you His Cross by asking of you the saddest of sacrifices, and I beg Him to be Himself your strength, your support, your Divine Comforter.

I share all your sorrow; you will read between these lines what my heart cannot utter. God alone can speak to us during such trials, for He is the supreme Consoler. The Divine Master, Whose Heart is so intensely compassionate, is near you; it is He Who received in heaven the soul we love so dearly, which will have a share in our prayers and sacrifices here every day. Dwell with it in that region which is so close to us. Let us lift the veil by faith and follow him who has vanished to where all is peace and light, where suffering is transformed into love.

I beseech God to be all that He has taken from you, and to wipe the tears from your eyes with His divine hand.

I know that you work with indefatigable zeal for the greater glory of God. That, under one form or another, ought to be the employment of our life, it is our "predestination", according to the words of Saint Paul. May this new year be a year of love, consecrated to the glory of God. How happy we should be at the last day if we could say with our adored Master, I have glorified Thee on the earth; I have finished the work which Thou gavest Me to do."[1] What a consolation to give God to souls, and souls

---

[1] St. John 17:4.

The Praise of Glory

to God! With such an aim, life becomes another thing. Shut in our cell, I follow you everywhere, and recommend to the Father of the household "those two" who labor so effectually for His harvest, while I am their little Moses on the mountain.

My Dear Madame—,
Your kind letter pained me, for I feel how profoundly sad you are. . . . I have prayed much for you, and communicated with the Word of Life, with Him Who came to bring solace for sorrows, and Who, on the eve of His Passion, in that discourse after the Last Supper in which He poured forth all His soul, said, in speaking of His own: "I come to Thee . . . that they may have My joy filled in themselves."[2] It is self-surrender, dear Madame which gives us to God. I am very young, yet it seems to me that I have suffered keenly at times. Oh! Then, when all was dark, when the present was so painful and the future seemed still more sombre, I closed my eyes, and put myself, like a child, into the arms of the Father Who is in heaven.

Dear Madame—, will you allow the little Carmelite who loves you so dearly to tell you something on the part of the Divine Master? It is what He said to Saint Catharine of Siena: "Think of Me and I will think of thee." We look at ourselves too much; we want to see and comprehend, and have not sufficient confidence in Him Who enfolds us in His charity. We must not stand before our cross to examine it, but, drawing back into the light of faith, we must rise above it, and consider it as the instrument used by divine love. "But one thing is necessary. Mary hath chosen the better part, which shall not be taken away from her."[3] This "better part", which seems my privilege in my loved solitude in Carmel, is offered by

[2] St. John 17:13
[3] St. Luke 10:42

Letters

God to every Christian soul. He offers it to you, dear Madame—, among all your cares and anxieties. You must believe that all He wishes is to lead you ever farther and farther into Himself. Yield yourself up to Him with all your troubles. . . . I have found my heaven on earth, since heaven is God, and God is in my soul. On the day that I understood that, I saw everything in a new light, and I want to tell all those I love of it, so that they, too, may adhere to God whatever happens, and Christ's prayer may be realized: "That they may be made perfect in one."[4]

Appendix VIII
Letter from M. L'Abbé D— to Mme. Catez

March 24, 1907

Madame,

It is easier to perceive the divine action in a soul, to witness its strength and sweetness, than to put into words, in our poor human speech, the impression left upon the memory. And yet it perhaps may be a duty to give testimony to sanctity when we have been happy enough to meet with it, though perhaps but for a short time, and to declare with Saint John: *"Nos vidimus et testamur"*. It is serviceable for the world and good, even for faithful Christians, not only to believe, but to know by tangible evidence that sanctity is always in existence, as a living and actual reality, and that the Church is never without saintly souls, those marvellous creations of grace.

The mother prioress, who day by day, step by step, accompanied the holy daughter you confided to her, and who guided her during her short religious life, has traced her portrait in

[4] St. John 17:23

The Praise of Glory

the pages addressed to her sisters. It is to be hoped that, for the pleasure and edification of a wider circle, she will tell them what she knows of her who was so fervent a "praise of glory" in this world, so that they may enjoy the fragrance of this flower of Carmel.

Although I saw her only for an instant, when administering Extreme Unction to her, and two or three times later on when I gave her holy communion, I look upon this providential meeting as one of the graces of my priestly life, and recall it as a thing precious and never to be forgotten, a deep and vivid impression, neither to be told nor to be described.

This, however, I can say, that if sometimes during the course of my ministry I have seen "the veil drawn back which hid from the dying the splendors of eternity", so that some glimpses were perceived by them; if I have sometimes seen a kind of transfiguration and aureole upon the face of those who were going to God—never has such an unearthly radiance been more visible to me than when I entered the cell of your dear Carmelite daughter to administer to her the last sacraments. With her hands clasped in prayer, she was so calm and almost smiling amid her agonizing sufferings; she answered the questions of the mother prioress with such lucidity; she received with such evident gratitude the graces that were brought her; her constancy, courage, surrender of self to God, and union with Christ were so evident from her expression—that I thought it needless to address to her the words that a priest owes to the sick upon such occasions.

With what deep faith she took part in the liturgical prayers! And while she received the holy unctions, she seemed to realize in all its meaning and with her whole will the consecration, the oblation of her body "as the holy, living, and pleasing sacrifice" to God, of which Saint Paul speaks.

Letters

It was a hard, a laborious sacrifice, only to be completed after long weeks of endurance, during which, as I was then saying Mass at the convent, I had on two or three occasions the happiness of bearing to her who was already called "the little saint", the living Bread which renewed her supernatural strength. I remember well the quick, decided movement with which she raised herself to approach the grille for holy communion. It seemed as if all her physical force returned to her that she might meet our Lord as He came to her.

Dear Madame Catez, I have ventured to write these few lines to you concerning a past which is both your joy and grief, a Calvary that you have mounted with Christian fortitude. But all these reminiscences ought to terminate in praise to God.

There is a thought that will fortify and console souls at all times—a sublime thought though overwhelming to our weakness, and religion alone has been capable of putting it before us: "Rejoice in the Lord always!" It is by this joy which is wholly spiritual, accompanied by resignation and hope, that you will best honor the blessed memory and will rejoice the heart of your saintly daughter as she watches over you. As for myself, I reckon upon the help which she promised me in the name of holy obedience, the efficacy of which I have already experienced more than once. Now that she is with God, she fulfils her vocation as a Carmelite by interceding for the clergy.

Appendix IX
A Second Retreat of Sister Elizabeth of the Trinity
Heaven on Earth

First Day

"Father, I will that where I am, they also whom Thou hast given Me be with Me; that they may see My glory which Thou hast given Me, because Thou hast loved Me before the creation of the world."[1] Such was Christ's last desire, His supreme prayer, before returning to the Father. He wishes that where He is, we too may be both in eternity and in the present time, which is eternity begun yet still progressing. Where, then, are we to be with Him, that His divine ideal may be realized? Saint John of the Cross tells us that the Son of God is hidden "in the bosom of the Father, which is the divine Essence, transcending all mortal vision, and hidden from all human understanding, as Isaias said, speaking to God: 'Verily, Thou art a hidden God!'"[2] Yet it is His will that we should abide permanently in Him; that we should dwell where He dwells in the unity of love. "Buried with Him by baptism", says Saint Paul.[3]

And again: "God hath raised us up together, and hath made us sit together in the heavenly places, through Jesus Christ: that He might show in the ages to come the abundant riches of His grace, in His bounty towards us in Christ Jesus."[4] He adds: "Now therefore you are no more strangers and foreigners, but you are fellow citizens with the saints, and

---
[1] St. John 17:24.
[2] Isa 45:1; *Spiritual Canticles*, Stanza 1. 2.
[3] Rom 6:4.
[4] Eph 2:6.

The Praise of Glory

domestics of God."⁵ The Blessed Trinity is our dwelling-place, our home, our Father's house, which we ought never to leave. The Divine Master said: "The servant abideth not in the house for ever; but the Son abideth for ever."⁶

Second Day

"Abide in Me."⁷ This command is given, this desire expressed by the Word of God. "Abide in Me": not for a few moments, a few passing hours, but abide permanently, habitually. Abide in Me, pray in Me, adore in Me, love in Me, suffer in Me, work in Me, act in Me. Abide in Me, whatever person or action you are concerned with, penetrating ever deeper into this abode. That is the true solitude into which God draws the soul that He may speak to it. But to grasp the meaning of this mysterious appeal we must do more than listen to it superficially; we must immerse ourselves deeply, and more deeply still, into the Divinity by means of recollection. "I follow after" exclaimed Saint Paul.⁸ So should we descend daily by this way into the abyss, which is God Himself. Let us glide into its depths with loving confidence. "It is there, sunk to its lowest depths, that the abyss of our nothingness will find itself face to face with the merciful, the infinite, the all-embracing God. There shall we find the strength to die to self, and, losing all self-interest, we shall be transformed into love."

"Blessed are they who die in the Lord."⁹

---

[5] mid., 2:9.
[6] St. John 8:35.
[7] *Ibid.*, 15:4.
[8] Phil 3:12.
[9] Apoc 14:13.

Heaven on Earth

Third Day

"The kingdom of God is within you."[10] God has just invited us to abide in Him, that our soul may live in the heritage of His glory; and He now reveals to us that we are not to go outside ourselves to find this inheritance, for the kingdom of God is within us. Saint John of the Cross says, that it is in the substance of the soul, which is inaccessible to the devil and the world, that God gives Himself to it. Then all the movements of the soul become divine, and though of God, still are the soul's, because God effects them within it, itself willing and assenting to them." The same saint also states that "the center of the soul is God. When the soul loves, comprehends, and enjoys Him with all its strength, it will have attained to its deepest and ultimate center in God."[11] When, however, the soul has not attained to this state, though it be in God, Who is the center of it, still, it is not in the deepest center, because there is still room for it to advance. Love unites the soul with God, and the greater its love the deeper does it enter God, and the more it is centered in Him. Thus, a soul which has but one degree of love is already in God, Who is its center; but when its love shall have attained the highest degree, it will have penetrated to its inmost depth or center, and will be transformed until it becomes most like God.[12] To such a soul, recollected in itself, may be addressed Pére Lacordaire's words to the Magdalen: *"Ne demandez plus le Maitre a personne sur la terre, à personne dans le ciel, car Lui c'est votre âme, et votre âme, c'est Lui."*[13]

---

[10] St. Luke 17:21.
[11] *The Living Flame,* Stanza 1:10, 11.
[12] *Ibid.* 1:1, 16.
[13] See note, p. 128.

The Praise of Glory

Fourth Day

"If any one love Me, he will keep My word, and My Father will love him, and We will come to him, and will make Our abode with him."[14]

Again the Master tells us that He desires to dwell within us. "If any one love Me!"[15] It is this which draws God to His creature; not an emotional love, but a love strong as death, which many waters cannot quench; which, because it loves the Father, does "always the things that please Him."[16] Thus spoke our blessed Master, and every soul that longs to keep close to Him should live by this word. Such a soul should make the divine will its food, its daily bread; it should allow itself to be immolated at the pleasure of the Father, as was the crucified Christ Whom it adores. Every occurrence, every event, each suffering and each joy is a sacrament which gives God to it, so that it is indifferent to them all, breaking through them and passing them by to rest in God Himself above all else. It is love's characteristic never to seek self; to reserve nothing but to give all to the beloved. Happy the soul that loves indeed; for love has made its Lord its Captive!

Fifth Day

"You are dead; and your life is hid with Christ in God."[17]

Saint Paul shows us the path that leads to the abyss. "You are dead." What does this mean but that the soul that aspires to dwell with God in the impregnable fortress of holy recollection must be separated, detached, and withdrawn from the

---

[14] St. John 14:23.
[15] Can 8:6, 7.
[16] St. John 8:29.
[17] Col 3:3.

Heaven on Earth

thought of all else? "*Quotidie morior.*"[18] "I die daily": I master and renounce self more every day so that Christ may increase and be exalted. *Quotidie morior.* I find my soul's joy (in will, not in emotion) in all that sacrifices, destroys, abases self, that I may give place to my Divine Master. "I live now; not I, but Christ liveth in me";[19] I desire to live my own life no longer, but to be transformed into Christ, so that my life may be rather divine than human, and that the Father, bending towards me, may recognize the image of His beloved Son, in Whom He has set all His pleasure.

Sixth Day

"Our God is a consuming fire."[20] "Our God", wrote Saint Paul, "is a consuming fire"—that is, a fire of love which destroys, which transforms into itself whatever it touches. The mystic death of which Saint Paul spoke yesterday becomes very simple and sweet to souls who yield themselves up to the action of its flames within the depths of their being. They think far less of the work of destruction and detachment left to them to accomplish than of plunging into the Furnace of Love burning within them, which is the Holy Ghost Himself—the love which in the Blessed Trinity is the bond between the Father and the Son. Such souls enter by a living faith, in simplicity and peace; they are raised by Him above all things, and above all sensible devotion, into the "sacred darkness" and transformed into the divine Image. They live "in fellowship"[21] with the Three adorable Persons Whose life they share.

[18] 1 Cor 15:31.
[19] Gal 2:20.
[20] Heb 12:29.
[21] 1 St. John 1:3.

The Praise of Glory

"I am come to cast fire on the earth, and what will I, but that it be kindled?"[22] The Master Himself here tells us of His longing to see the fire of love ignited. All our works and labors are as nothing in His sight: we can give Him nothing, nor can we satisfy His one desire of enhancing the dignity of our soul. Nothing so pleases Him as to see it increase, and nothing can so enhance it as its becoming, in some sort, equal with God. This is why He exacts the tribute of its love, the property of love being to put, as far as possible, the lover and the beloved upon a par. The soul which possesses such love appears upon a kind of equality with Jesus, because their mutual love makes them share all in common. "I have called you friends, because all things whatsoever I have heard of My Father, I have made known unto you."[23] But to attain to this love the soul must have first surrendered self entirely. The will must be sweetly lost in that of God, so that the inclinations and faculties may be moved in and by love alone. "I do all by love: I suffer all with love." Then it is filled, absorbed, and protected by love.

It has found the secret of growing in love wherever it may be. Even in its intercourse with the world and amid the cares of this life, it can truly affirm: "My sole occupation is love."

Seventh Day

"Without faith it is impossible to please God."[24] Faith is the substance of things to be hoped for, the evidence of things unseen."[25] That is to say, faith makes future blessings so certain and so present to us that they are evolved in our soul and sub-

[22] St. Luke 12:49.
[23] St. John 15:1.
[24] Heb 11:6.
[25] *Ibid.*, 11:1.

sist there before we actually enjoy them. Saint John of the Cross says that faith is the foot that journeys to God, and is possession itself in an obscure manner. Faith alone can enlighten us concerning Him we love, and should be chosen by our soul as the means by which to attain divine union. It fills us with spiritual gifts. Christ, when speaking to the Samaritan woman, alluded to faith when He promised to give those who should believe in Him "a fountain of water, springing up into life everlasting".[26] Thus, faith gives us God in this life, behind the veil, yet still God Himself. "When that which is perfect is come"—that is, say, the clear vision—"that which is imperfect", or, in other words, the knowledge given by faith, "shall be done away."[27]

"We have known, and have believed the charity which God hath to us."[28] This is our great act of faith, the means of rendering love for love to our God: "the mystery which hath been hidden"[29] in the heart of the Father, which at last we fathom and which thrills our soul. Henceforth we care little whether God sends us joy or suffering; we believe in His love. The more we are tried, the stronger is our faith, for it overleaps, as it were, all obstacles and finds its rest in the bosom of infinite love. The Master can repeat, in the secret depths of this soul vivified by faith, His words to the Magdalen: "Go in peace: thy faith hath saved thee."[30]

Eighth Day

"God hath predestinated us unto the adoption of children through Jesus Christ unto Himself; according to the purpose

---

[26] 1 St. John 4:14.
[27] 1 Cor 13:10.
[28] 1 St. John 4:16.
[29] Col 1:26.
[30] St. Luke 7:50.

The Praise of Glory

of His will: unto the praise of the glory of His grace, in which He hath graced us in His beloved Son. In Whom we have redemption in His blood, the remission of sins, according to the riches of His grace, which hath superabounded in us, in all wisdom and prudence."[31] Such a soul has truly become the child of God, because "whosoever are led by the Spirit of God, they are the sons of God." And again: "We have not received the spirit of bondage unto fear; but we have received the spirit of adoption of sons, whereby we cry: *Abba*! (Father!) For the Spirit Himself giveth testimony to our spirit that we are the sons of God. And if sons, heirs also; heirs indeed of God, and joint-heirs with Christ: yet so, if we suffer with Him, that we may also be glorified with Him."[32] It was that we might attain to this abyss of glory that God created us in His image and likeness.

"Behold", says Saint John, "what manner of charity the Father hath bestowed on us, that we should be called, and should be, the sons of God . . .we are now the sons of God; and it hath not yet appeared what we shall be. We know that, when He shall appear, we shall be like to Him because we shall see Him as He is. And every one that hath this hope in him, sanctifieth himself; as He also is holy."[33]

This is the measure of the sanctity of the children of God—to be holy as God is, to be holy with the holiness of God by living in contact with Him in the depths of the bottomless abyss: then the soul appears, to a certain extent, to resemble God, Who, though He takes delight in all things, yet never takes such delight as in Himself; because He possesses within Himself a supreme good in comparison with which all

---

[31] Eph 1:5-8.
[32] Rom 8:14,17.
[33] 1 St. Jn 3:1,3.

others are of no account. Thus, every joy which befalls the soul invites it to prefer the joy which it possesses within itself; with which no other can compare.

"Our Father, Who art in heaven."[34] We must seek Him, and above all, we must dwell in the little heaven He has made for Himself in the center of our soul. Christ told the Samaritan woman that the Father seeks adorers "who shall adore Him in spirit and in truth".[35] Let us be those fervent adorers and rejoice His heart. Let us adore Him in spirit, that is, with hearts and thoughts bent on Him, our spirits filled with the knowledge of Him imparted by the light of faith. Let us adore Him in truth by our actions, which make us true by our always doing what will please the Father, Whose children we are. In short, "let us adore in spirit and in truth". Then we shall be the children of God, and shall learn by experience the truth of what Isaias said: "You shall be carried at the breasts, and upon the knees shall they caress you."[36] In fact, God appears to occupy Himself solely with overwhelming the soul with caresses and marks of affection, like a mother who fondles her babe and feeds it with her milk. Let us listen to our Father's mysterious appeal "My son, give Me thy heart."[37]

Ninth Day

"*Si scires donum Dei*" ("Didst thou but know the gift of God"),[38] said Christ one evening to the Samaritan woman. What is this gift of God, but Himself? "He came unto His own, and His own received Him not,"[39] declares the beloved disciple.

[34] St. Matt 6:9;
[35] St. John 4:23.
[36] Isa 66:12.
[37] Prov 23:76.
[38] St. John 4:10.
[39] *Ibid.*, 1:11.

The Praise of Glory

To many a soul might Saint John the Baptist utter the reproach, "There stands One in the midst of you whom you know not."[40] "Didst thou but know the gift of God!" There is one created being who knew that gift of God, who lost no particle of it; a creature so pure and luminous that she seemed light itself. *Speculum justitiae*; a being whose life was so simple, so lost in God, that there is but little to say of her. *Virgo fidelis*, the faithful Virgin, "who kept all these words in her heart".[41] She was so lowly, so hidden within the secret of God's face, in the seclusion of the temple, that the Blessed Trinity took pleasure in her: "Because He hath regarded the humility of His handmaiden; for behold, from henceforth all generations shall call me blessed."[42] The Father, bending down to this creature, lovely, but so ignorant of her loveliness, chose her for the Mother, in time, of Him of Whom He had been Father for all eternity. Then the Holy Ghost, Who presides over all the works of God, overshadowed her; the blessed Virgin uttered her *fiat*: "Behold the handmaid of the Lord; be it done to me according to Thy Word"[43]: the greatest of all mysteries was accomplished, and by the descent of the Word into her bosom, Mary became God's own forever.

Our Lady seems to me to be, during the period between the Annunciation and the Nativity, the model of interior souls: those whom God has called to live within themselves, in the depths of the bottomless abyss. In what peace and recollection did she live and act! Her most trivial actions were sanctified by her, for amid all that was passing she adored the gift of God. Yet that did not prevent her spending herself for

---

[40] *Ibid.*, 1:26.
[41] St. Luke 2:51.
[42] St. Luke 1:48.
[43] *Ibid.*, 1:38.

Heaven on Earth

others when charity required it. The gospel tells us that "Mary, rising up, went into the hill country with haste" to her cousin Elizabeth.[44] The ineffable vision which she contemplated within herself did not lessen her charity to others, for "though contemplation is directed to the praise and eternity of its Lord, yet it owns, and will never loose, concord."

Tenth Day

"We have been predestinated according to the purpose of Him Who worketh all things according to the counsel of His will, that we may be unto the praise of His glory."[45] It is Saint Paul who speaks thus—Saint Paul, inspired by God Himself. How can we fulfil this great dream of the heart of our God, this immutable desire regarding our souls—in a word, how can we respond to our vocation and become a perfect "praise of the glory" of the most Blessed Trinity? In heaven, every soul is a praise of the glory of the Father, the Son, and the Holy Ghost, because each soul is grafted unchangeably in pure love, and lives no longer its own life, but the life of God. Then, as Saint Paul says, it knows Him as it is known by Him.

The "praise of glory" is a soul that dwells in God, with the pure, disinterested love which does not seek self in the sweetness of His love; a soul that loves Him above all His gifts, and would have loved Him as much had it received nothing; which wishes well to the object of its tenderness. But how can we wish well to God, except by accomplishing His will, since this will ordains all things for His greater glory? Such a soul should surrender itself fully, blindly, to this will, so that it cannot possibly wish otherwise than as God wishes.

---

[44] *Ibid.*, 1:39.
[45] Eph 1:12.

The Praise of Glory

The "praise of glory" is a silent soul, a lyre beneath the touch of the Holy Ghost from which He can draw sweet harmonies. Knowing that suffering is a chord which emits still more exquisite tones, this soul rejoices at giving it forth, that it may impress the heart of its God more pleasingly.

The "praise of glory" is a soul that contemplates God in faith and in simplicity; it reflects His whole being and is a fathomless abyss into which He can flow and outpour Himself; it is a crystal through which He can shine and view His own perfection, and splendor. A soul which thus permits the Divine Being to satisfy within it His craving to communicate all He is and has, is truly the "praise of glory" all His gifts.

Finally, the "praise of glory" is one who is always giving thanks; whose acts, movement, thoughts, aspirations, while more deeply establishing her in love, are like an echo of the eternal *Sanctus* in the heaven of glory. The blessed rest not day or night, saying, "Holy, holy, holy, Lord God Almighty . . . and falling down, adore Him that liveth for ever and ever."[46] The "praise of glory" begins now, within the heaven of her soul, the task that will be hers for all eternity. Her chant is uninterrupted; she acts beneath the influence of the Holy Ghost, although she may sometimes be unconscious of it, for human weakness prevents souls from keeping their attention fixed on God without distractions. She sings and adores perpetually, and has, so to speak, gone out from self and become absorbed in praise and love, in her passion for the glory of her God.

Let us, in the heaven of our soul, be a homage of glory to the Blessed Trinity. One day the veil will be withdrawn, and we shall be brought into the eternal courts: there we

---

[46] Apoc 4:8, 10.

shall sing in the bosom of Infinite Love, and God will give us "the new name" promised to him that overcometh. What will that name be? *Laudem Gloriæ.*